LETTERS

ON

LAY-BAPTISM,

BY

DANIEL WATERLAND, D.D.,
SOMETIME
MASTER OF MAGDALENE COLLEGE, CAMBRIDGE,
CANON OF WINDSOR,
AND ARCHDEACON OF MIDDLESEX.

REPRINTED FROM HIS "WORKS,"

WITH NOTES BY

F. NUTCOMBE OXENHAM, M.A.

AND A PREFACE BY THE

BISHOP OF ARGYLL AND THE ISLES.

WIPF & STOCK · Eugene, Oregon

Wipf and Stock Publishers
199 W 8th Ave, Suite 3
Eugene, OR 97401

Letters on Lay-Baptism
By Waterland, Daniel and Oxenham, F. Nutcombe
ISBN 13: 978-1-5326-4636-2
Publication date 12/29/2017
Previously published by J. Masters and Co., 1892

"The validity of such baptism (i.e. baptism by lay-persons) is a point which the Catholic Church, and the Church of England in particular, hath hitherto avoided to determine by any Synodical declaration."

(Resolution of the Lower House of Convocation of Canterbury, A.D. 1712, quoted in Lathbury's "History of Convocation," ad loc.)

"We have no proof that CHRIST ever promised to sanction Lay-baptism, or that He conferred the power of baptizing on any but the clergy, or that the Apostles ever imparted it to any other but clergy."

(Dean Hook. "Church Dictionary." Art. "Lay-baptism.") *Vide Note, p.* 13.

CONTENTS.

	PAGE
Preface by the Bishop of Argyll and the Isles	xv
Introductory Note by the Editor	xxix

DR. WATERLAND'S FIRST LETTER.

He once thought Lay-baptism to be valid, but saw reason to change his mind. Note on some books relating to the controversy . . 1—3
The cause depends on Scripture, Antiquity, and Reason . . 3

I.

As to Scripture—
  It is admitted
  i. That the commission to baptize, given to the Clergy, is clear and beyond dispute. Note on the expression that "Scripture confines the administration of Baptism to the Clergy."
  ii. That no Commission is recorded as given to any other persons.
  iii. That Scripture has nowhere even intimated that we may go beyond the recorded Commission. Note on "Lay-preaching and Praying" 3, 4
The maxim "*fieri non debuit factum valet,*" pleaded on behalf of Lay-baptism, but shown to be not applicable. Note on misleading use of maxims. The parallel of marriage misleading . . . 4, 5
The argument that Lay-baptism although sinful in the Minister is yet valid for the receiver shown to be unsound 6

II.

As to the Ancients—
  They "with one voice for above 300 years condemn Lay-baptism," all except perhaps Tertullian. Note on Waterland's meaning in the use of this phrase 7
  Heretical Baptism in some cases allowed; but this proves nothing in favour of Lay-baptism 8
  Did any of the Fathers before S. Augustine assert the validity of Lay-baptism excepting only Tertullian? Note on this question . . 9
As to "the Reformed Churches," if their Orders are good, their Baptisms are so too, and *vice versâ* 9

	PAGE
Doctrine of the invalidity of Lay-baptism objected to because "it condemns thousands." But so, in the same sense, do other Christian doctrines. Note on the danger of argument from "consequences"	9, 10
References to books by Mr. Lawrence and Dr. Brett	11

MR. KELSALL'S ANSWER.

He is surprised and unprepared for so formidable an adversary,—he would give up a "pleasing error," if convinced,—he is not swayed by "Great Names,"—he holds "every position in Divinity which is new, to be false,"—he believes history to be "the best decider" in religious controversy,—he agrees that this controversy depends upon the witness of Scripture, Antiquity, and Reason, but prefers to take Reason first. Notes on the abuse of "great Names," and on this beginning with Reason . . . . 12—14

I.

If the reason of the thing were considered alone, he would agree with Waterland's view 15

But the Church, "ever since S. Augustine," has in some cases allowed, and never annulled, Lay-baptism. Note on Kelsall's assertion that "most writers allow this" 15

The Roman Church allows not only *laymen*, but *women*, to baptize. Note on the formal teaching of Rome 16

On the supposed terrible consequences if Lay-baptism is invalid, especially in regard to the Clergy . . . . 17—20

On the argument, "a doctrine condemns thousands, therefore it is false" . 21

Waterland's doctrine said to raise fears and scruples, which it cannot allay, —to undermine the constitution of the Church,—to threaten a nullity to all ministrations of the Priesthood everywhere. Note on these assertions 21, 22

On the question whether one not validly baptized can be a true priest. Waterland says this "is well settled" in the affirmative . . 22

Kelsall denies this, and claims "antiquity," and "the greatest masters of reason," as being on his side. Note on "the main gist" of this question 22, 23

Baptism said to be "a qualification without which a man is incapable" of the ministerial commission. Note on this assumption . . 23, 24

The witness of Scripture and a dictum of S. Jerome. Note on this dictum, which states one of the strongest arguments on Waterland's side . 25

On the relation of Baptism to Ordination in the case of S. Paul and the other Apostles . . . . 25—28

On the supposed ministrations of uncircumcised Levites during the forty years in the wilderness. Note on Kelsall's statement that "GOD *may* dispense with His own institutions" . . . . 29—32

	PAGE
S. Paul in 1 Cor. xii. and Eph. iv. is "supposing" that all the Clergy are baptized	32
Kelsall thinks "the point not well settled"	33
He is not concerned with "the foreign Reformed Churches"	33, 34

II.

Dr. Waterland's assertion that Scripture "confines the administration of Baptism to the Clergy," which Kelsall denies	34, 35
What Calvin held	35
Kelsall thinks Waterland's view condemned, if only on account of its novelty. Note on a "novelty" which is at least sixteen centuries old	36
Note on the argument that laymen are at liberty to baptize, "because they are nowhere expressly forbidden" to do so	36
Kelsall's view of the baptismal commission, viz., that by it the Bishops are empowered not only to baptize themselves, but to commission any or all other persons to do the like. Note on this	37, 38
"This power the Bishops of the Primitive Church did put in practice." Note on the absence of any evidence to support this statement, and its inutility even if it were true	39
The supposed parallel of the Eucharist sent by lay hands. Note on this which is no parallel at all	40
Kelsall thinks "the question of Lay-baptism a question only of discipline, not of doctrine." Note on this	41
Is Lay-baptism "a going from the Institution?"	42
The case of Saul and of Uzza	43
Kelsall believes that the validity of Baptism by lay persons "depends altogether on the will of their ecclesiastical superiors." Note on this "startling assertion"	44
He only insists that it is "valid to the recipient." Note inquiring to whom else it could be valid	45
Of the maxim "*quod fieri*," &c., which Kelsall holds applicable. Note on Waterland's "private opinion"	46
Of the marriage of Quakers and other civil marriages. Note on the different senses of the word "valid"	47—49
Of the Apostolic commission, which "reaches to all acts of religion." Note on this argument	50
Four assertions which would be conclusive if they were true. Note that they are not true	50, 51
On the administration of circumcision by lay hands. Note that circumcision is not "a sacrament"	51—53
Some acts illegal, or even criminal, but not therefore void unless annulled. God not obliged "to annul" Lay-baptisms. Note that acts void *ab initio* do not need to be "annulled"	54, 55
Of "criminal reception" of Baptism, and of Infants who die unbaptized. Various theories about them	56, 57
Whether any Baptism which is "sinful in the administrator" can be yet "valid to the receiver." Note that these are distinct questions	58—60

III.

	PAGE
Of the judgment and practice of the Ancient Church.—Of Waterland's assertion that "the ancients do with one voice, for above 300 years, condemn Lay-baptism"	60, 61
Plea that rules laid down apply only to "ordinary cases." Note upon this plea	62
Of the Fathers who sometimes bear witness as to what is the received teaching of the Church, and sometimes give only their own opinion. Note upon this	63
The evidence of Tertullian	63—66
The evidence of S. Cyprian. How far he regarded heretical Baptism as Lay-baptism. The question of the indelibility of Orders. Note on the two-edged argument from silence. S. Basil's representation of Cyprian and Firmilian	67—72
Note on the contradictions to be found in extracts from the Fathers, and on one safe conclusion from these contradictions	72, 73
Of the Greek Church	74
Of the Council of Elvira, A.D. 305. Note on the statement that "nothing was more common" than Baptism by laymen in that age	75
The fable of a play-baptism by S. Athanasius. Note on what Ruffinus and Sozomen relate	76
The pseudo-Ambrosian Commentary on S. Paul	77
Optatus Milevitanus	78
S. Gregory Nazianzen	79
S. Jerome	80
S. Augustine, admitting that the Church had not determined, gives his own opinion	81
What Kelsall calls "positive evidence." Note on this	82
Dr. Smith's account of the practice of the Greek Church	83
A challenge and counter-challenge. Note on the insecurity of concluding that any doctrine was received, simply because it was not "expressly condemned." Note of the most prevalent view which has found expression in the saying, "once a priest always a priest"	84, 85
On Baptisms administered by degraded clergy	86, 87
On the practice of the Church of England. Kelsall's relation of what took place at the Hampton Court Conference. Note on the "bold misrepresentation" of this relation	87—91
Hooker's misleading analogy between "The Minister of the Word" and "The Minister of Baptism"	92
Of the change which Kelsall thinks has taken place in the attitude of Churchmen	93
Of the change made in the Rubrics at the Hampton Court Conference	94, 95
Of Bishop Jeremy Taylor, who "owns that the Church of England hath not determined this particular," but himself writes against the validity of Lay-baptism	96, 97
Of Archbishop Abbott, and Bishop Sparrow	97
Of Archbishop Bramhall and Dr. Fuller	98

Contents.

	PAGE
Of what was done during the Restoration Period	99, 100
A Summary of Principles. Note on these	101—103
Note on the Mischief of misleading comparisons	104

DR. WATERLAND'S SECOND LETTER.

The purpose of his "First Letter" 105
Desirable to have a distinct view of the exact point at issue, which is,
"Whether those that come to us from our Dissenters, having been
pretendedly baptized by men who never had Episcopal Orders, ought
to be baptized by us, or no" 106, 107
The controversy entangled by "many things which belong not to it."
Note on these "many things" 107
Needful to distinguish various kinds of Lay-baptism, which distinction has
not been made by sundry controversialists 108, 109
A vindication of Mr. Lawrence's method 110
An objection to Mr. Kelsall's method 111

I.

Waterland's reply to Kelsall's arguments from Scripture . . . 111
Kelsall asserts Lay-baptism to be sometimes lawful, and always valid. No
warrant from Scripture for this. Note on this absence of authority as
the primary objection to all Lay-baptisms 112
On Kelsall's view of the Apostolic commission to baptize—
   i. That it empowers the Bishops to appoint any persons, even laics to be
Ministers of Baptism. No warrant in Scripture or History for this.
No known means for Bishops to impart any ministerial commission
otherwise than by the imposition of hands . . . 114, 115
   ii. That it made the Bishops "the sole and supreme judges in case of
any irregular disputed baptism to annul it or receive it as valid."
Here too is there no warrant from Scripture, nor from Reason. No
such doctrine known to S. Cyprian or to Pope Stephen. Bishops
cannot make that to be Baptism which CHRIST has not made so,
nor vice versâ . . . . 116—118
On Kelsall's assertion that the permission given to a lay person to carry
the Eucharist to the sick is "as large a stretch of power, and as great
a variation from the primitive institution as the permission of Lay-
baptism." No parallel between these cases. The only parallel to
Lay-baptizing is not Lay-carrying but Lay-consecrating the Holy
Eucharist . . . . 119—121
If "necessity" is pleaded for Lay-baptism, why not also for Lay-Eucharists?
Note on reasons why this never allowed or attempted . . 122, 123
The story of Frumentius and the captive woman . . . 124
Of Corah, Uzziah, King Saul, and Uzza 125, 126
Notion of validity of Lay-ministration dangerous. Note on the argument
from uncertainty 127

PAGE

Reply to comments from the supposed analogy between baptism and marriage, which fails because (among other reasons) GOD is not necessarily "a party" to the covenant of marriage. He is necessarily "a party" to the covenant of Baptism . . . . . . 128—133

The supposed analogy of Circumcision to Baptism, which fails because (among other reasons) GOD "has appointed proper officers" for Baptism. He never appointed any proper officers for circumcision 134, 135

Waterland agrees with Kelsall on the falseness of novelties in Theology, and in the propriety of appeal to Scripture, Antiquity, and Reason 135

II.

Waterland explains what he means by saying that "the ancients condemn Lay-baptism." Note upon this . . . . 136—139

He replies to what has been said as to the witness of several of the Fathers.

(i.) Of Tertullian, A.D. 192.

Waterland admitted that Tertullian allowed Lay-baptism in cases of necessity, but held this to be only his private opinion. Kelsall replied that he gave the prevalent doctrine of the Church. Waterland gives reasons to show that this was not so . . 139—149

(ii.) S. Cyprian, A.D. 248.

Kelsall "has no positive evidence" from S. Cyprian in his favour. Waterland shows how there is much "positive evidence" the other way.

S. Cyprian rejected all unauthorized Baptisms . . . 150

He assumed that schismatics had "forfeited their Orders" (in which view the prevalent sense of the Church did not come to support him), therefore schismatical Baptism was, in his view, Lay-baptism 151, 152

S. Augustine's argument to show that Orders like Baptism are indelible . . . . 153—155

He thought that Baptism might be given "validly" though not "savingly." Note on the difficulty of this view . . 156

In what points S. Augustine agrees, and in what he disagrees with S. Cyprian 157

Kelsall mistakes S. Cyprian's meaning 158

Why some heretical Baptisms allowed, and not others . . 159

On S. Basil's report of the teaching of S. Cyprian and his adherents 160

(iii.) The Council of Elvira, A.D. 305.

Kelsall thought this Council "took for granted" the liberty of laymen to baptize, and desired to restrain that liberty . . 161

Waterland shows that no such liberty was "taken for granted," there being no evidence of the existence of such liberty. He points out the very strict conditions under which the Council permitted laymen to baptize . . . . . 161—164

(iv.) The Council of Arles, A.D. 314.

The famous canon of this Council relates to heretical Baptisms, and does not touch the question of Lay-baptism . . . 164

Contents.   xi

PAGE

(v.) The Council of Nice, A.D. 325.
 The eighth canon of this Council allows the Orders of the Novatian Clergy who return to the Church. S. Augustine refers to this as the Catholic decision on the indelibility of Holy Orders .   165
 Reasons to show that the story of the play-baptism of S. Athanasius is not worthy of credit 166, 167

(vi.) Hilary the Deacon, A.D. 355, more rigorous against Lay-baptism than S. Cyprian 167
 Yet he is thought to favour Lay-baptism by his appeal to the Baptism of Cornelius and his company—reasons to show the inutility of this appeal, i.e. (i.) the baptizers possibly were not "laymen," (ii.) certainly they were not "unauthorized" . . 168, 169
 Various statements in Hilary's commentary (if indeed it is Hilary's) are inaccurate and of uncertain import . . . 170, 171

(vii.) Pacian, A.D. 360.
 Some quotations from him to show his view—
  (i.) That the right to baptize belongs only to the Clergy.
  (ii.) That the validity of all Sacraments depends on the commission of the minister 171, 172

(viii.) Optatus of Milevis, A.D. 368.
 He says plainly that any one may baptize, and whatever his opinion is worth it is clearly in favour of Lay-baptism . . . 173, 174

(ix.) S. Basil, A.D. 370.
 He is a witness for the Greek Church. Kelsall represents him as holding
  (i.) That heretical and schismatical priests were mere laymen, and yet
  (ii.) That their baptisms were valid, which is a misconception of his meaning 175, 176

(x.) Gregory Nazianzen, A.D. 370.
 Kelsall quotes Gregory as saying that "all without any difference" have power to baptize: but it is clear from the whole passage that Gregory is speaking only of "all" the Clergy . . 177—180

(xi.) Apostolical Constitutions.
 Quotations therefrom which speak of all Lay-baptism as if it were both unlawful and invalid 181

(xii.) S. Jerome, A.D. 384.
 Both sides in this controversy have claimed S. Jerome. In his dialogue against the Luciferians he connects the validity of Baptism with that of Holy Orders, so that if the latter are valid the former must be also, and vice versâ . . . . 181—183
 The Donatists founded the validity of Baptism upon the right of the administrator, as Cyprian, Basil, and others had done before, as if it were a standing rule of the Church 184
 S. Jerome, in one place, suggests a theory, which would admit the validity of Lay-baptism, viz., that "what any one has received, that he may also give" 185

(xiii.) S. Augustine, A.D. 400.
 He deals with Lay-baptism in controversy with the Donatists, who urged that heretics and schismatics forfeited their Orders, and there-

	PAGE
fore could not validly baptize. S. Augustine, in reply, proves that Orders are indelible, which overthrows the argument of the Donatists; and then he adds "ex abundanti" some arguments to show that even if the Orders of any heretics had been forfeited, their Baptisms might still perhaps be received; he says, "I know not if any could rightly say that it (the Lay-baptism) ought to be repeated," this phrase he would not have used, if the point had been decided in the Church	187
S. Augustine wanders into many conjectures, and at length returns to a sound position	188
He urges that all Baptism is CHRIST'S Baptism, which is a petitio principii, that it does not depend on the personal qualification, or life or intention of the minister, which is true, but not to the point, since the only question at issue is, whether the commission of CHRIST be necessary or not	188, 189
S. Augustine was not ignorant of the practice of the Church in his day, therefore if the practice of Lay-baptism had received the approval of the Church, S. Augustine must have known it; but he evidently did not know of any such approval	190, 191
What the Advocates of Lay-baptism can show from antiquity. What they ought to show	191
Kelsall claims to have "positive evidence" from S. Augustine, which on examination proves to be mere hear-say	191—193
Summary of evidence from Antiquity—	
i. Authorized Lay-baptism, in cases of necessity, was allowed by one local council (Elvira) and by some of the Fathers, others being strongly against it, no "general sense of the Church" known and recognized by all.	
ii. Unauthorized Lay-baptism in ordinary cases (which is the sole point of the present controversy) not allowed to be valid by any council, nor by any Father, except Optatus, until S. Augustine, after whose time the opinion that such baptisms were valid, "crept gradually into the Western Church"	193, 194
Two probable presumptive proofs against Lay-baptism :—	
I. No general principle among ancients, on which validity of Lay-baptism can stand. Note on this presumptive proof . .	194
II. Some general principles which do by consequence overthrow it .	194
As to the first of these proofs :—	
None of the principles that have been cited as giving countenance to Lay-baptism were universally held.	
The plea of necessity, the priesthood of the Laity—all Baptism is CHRIST'S Baptism	195, 196
What is given is given—What a man has received he can impart—The permission of Elvira	196
Subsequent ratification supplies all deficiencies . . .	197
As to the second of these proofs :—	
Principles which virtually deny the validity of Lay-baptism and are universally received	198

Contents.

	PAGE
Lay-persons forbidden to intermeddle in sacred offices	198
Christian Clergy proper Priests: their ministries mystical and mediatory	199
The Eucharist could be consecrated by none but a Priest	200
Lay-ordination null and void	201

Two Inferences :—
  1. That certainly the general sense of the Primitive Church does not countenance Lay-baptism.
  2. That probably both the judgment and practice of antiquity were intended to condemn it 202

Kelsall asks what Lay-baptism "as such" means.
Waterland answers, it means "unauthorized Lay-baptism." For this no authority before S. Augustine except Tertullian . . . 203
Kelsall asks for a canon or Father "to confront" the council of Elvira. It is not reasonable to ask an express denial of all false theories: but in this case the Apostolical Constitutions, the Cyprianists and S. Basil do expressly deny the validity of Lay-baptism . . . 204
Kelsall asserts that the Church received the baptisms of some whose orders were declared void. This denied. Note on this point . . 205
Kelsall's four questions regarding the power of the Church to annul Holy Orders . . . . 206—209

III.

The Argument from Reason :—
It is not reason to account anything valid except upon some certain principle or some sufficient evidence 209, 210
Note giving Laurence's "five maxims" which go to prove that Lay-baptism is not valid 210, 211
"Difficulties" in both views 212
The analogy of Civil Commissions, which are null and void unless issuing from competent authority 212, 213
Question whether Lay-baptism is "safer" than no Baptism . 214, 215
That which is unlawfully done is not always invalid, but Lay-baptism is invalid because it is not really "done" at all . . . 216—218
Answer to Kelsall's argument from supposed "terrible consequences" 218—221
Notes on these "consequences" 219
Further discussion as to whether the lack of Baptism invalidates Orders 221—225
The wisdom of hypothetical Baptism in all cases of uncertainty. Note on this 226
Two Scripture instances of valid Orders apart from Baptism, (i.) S. Paul 227
(ii.) Israelite Priests not circumcised . . . 228—232
Of the Reformed Churches abroad 233

IV.

Of the theory and the practice of the Church of England.
  1. She has not expressly in terms determined either way.
  2. Common opinion and practice in favour of allowing Lay-baptism.
  3. Certain principles and positions laid down by the Church in her public acts, which by necessary consequence exclude Lay-baptism . 234

	PAGE
If this latter proposition is true, then it is vain to appeal to the private opinion of "eminent Divines," or to the prevalence at certain periods of sundry lax practices	235—239
A dilemma for Mr. Kelsall.	
Either the Church of England does not admit that Lay-baptism is valid, or she has been guilty of great neglect and cruelty in making (as it is allowed that she has made) no provision for such baptism in any case whatever	240
The notion of making anything valid *ex post facto* too romantic to need confutation	241
Mr. Bennet's wise and good conclusion	241
Mr. Kelsall's summary of his arguments in twenty-six propositions.	
Five very good, the rest either "not true" or "not accurate"	241, 242
Only two of these noticed which are inconsistent with each other	242
Conclusion	243, 244

PREFACE.

It is my privilege to write a few words by way of preface to this annotated reprint of Dr. Waterland's famous Letters on Lay-baptism. The question discussed, is one which no prudent or thoughtful Christian can afford to set aside, because it may seem to him uninteresting or tedious. Upon the decision arrived at, very grave practical consequences must depend. This will be evident to all who regard Holy Baptism as a solemn ordinance, instituted by CHRIST Himself for all time, as a Sacrament of the Gospel, and as one "generally necessary to Salvation." Only those who look upon Baptism as a matter of such small importance that it may be left to chance, can afford to dismiss what has been said on either side in this controversy, as unworthy of patient and prayerful consideration. And yet, strange to say, there are those who preach very strong doctrines about the grace of Holy Baptism, and who utter very terrible things as to the consequences involved by its neglect, who notwithstanding, have never seriously faced the question now before us. Such persons, as a rule, have adopted the popular current opinion, that though a duly ordained Minister is essential for a valid Eucharist, no such necessity exists with regard to the other great Sacrament of the Gospel. They have never seriously set themselves to ascertain whether this view has any sure foundation in what has been revealed to us by GOD in His written Word, or through the teaching of His Church. Or, if they have considered the question to any extent, they have probably been content to rely upon certain opinions expressed by individual writers, in various ages of the Church, without bringing these opinions to the test either of Holy Scripture or of Catholic tradition.

Three views present themselves for our acceptance with regard to Baptism administered by laymen, i.e., by those who have not been duly ordained to the Sacred Ministry—

I. Such Baptism may be unquestionably valid and sufficient.

II. It may be null and void, or,

III. It may be of doubtful validity.

Whichever of these three conclusions be adopted, the decision arrived at must, of necessity, involve very practical results, and must suggest a line of thought and of conduct, either with regard to ourselves or with regard to others, as to the importance of which there can be no dispute. If we find that Lay-baptism has been accepted by the Church of CHRIST as sufficient, all that the learned author of the following letters has brought forward to the contrary, either in his own words, or from the Fathers, must be reckoned vain, if not impious. But if, on the other hand, it appears to be either null and void, or of questionable validity, plain duty in the one case, and obvious Christian prudence in the other, demand that, through the administration of Baptism by a lawful minister, unconditionally or conditionally, what is either certainly wanting, or presumably wanting, should be supplied. And if the fear of sacrilegiously repeating the Sacrament should suggest itself, any such scruple may be set at rest by a due consideration of the force of the conditional formula distinctly enjoined by the Church, in all cases of doubt. The principle upon which this hypothetical administration of Baptism rests is one which must surely commend itself to all who would desire to exercise as much prudence with regard to spiritual matters, as they would do with regard to their temporal concerns. Few wise men would rest content with a questionable will, or with a title to an estate challenged by many, as invalid or defective. Wilfully to go on in such uncertainty, when the remedy is simple, would surely be the extreme of imprudence. Yet how often are the words of the Gospel fulfilled, "The children of this world are, in their generation, wiser than the children of light!"

It should, also, be borne in mind that the employment of the *conditional* formula does not commit us to the dogmatic assertion that Lay-baptism is certainly invalid. If we affirmed this dogmatically, we should, of course be bound to baptize all converts to the Church *unconditionally*. This, few, if any, would advocate. Conditional baptism leaves the matter an open question. It does not condemn Lay-baptism, but it goes upon the principle that its validity "is a point which the Catholic Church hath hitherto avoided to determine by any synodical declaration." The words of the late Bishop Christopher Wordsworth of Lincoln may also be quoted as expressing the matured opinion of a ripe scholar and theologian, and as illustrating both the theory and practice of Conditional Baptism. "The Church," he says, "has not *condemned* Baptism administered by laymen, but I have no hesitation in saying that if I had been baptized by a person whose commission to baptize was doubtful, I should desire to be

b

baptized with the hypothetical form by a duly ordained minister."[1]

With regard to Dr. Waterland himself, the author of the following letters, it may be well now to quote the words of Bishop Van Mildert who edited his works in 1823, and who thus writes in his Introductory Review—" Few names recorded in the annals of the Church of England stand so high in the estimation of its most sound and intelligent members as that of Dr. Waterland. During a period remarkable for literary and theological research, and fruitful in controversies upon subjects of primary importance, this distinguished author acquired by his labours in the cause of religious truth, an extensive and solid reputation. Nor did the reputation, thus acquired, die away with those controversies in which he bore so large a share. It has survived the occasions which gave them birth, and still preserves its lustre unimpaired. His writings still continue to be referred to by Divines of the highest character, and they carry with them a weight of authority, never attached but to names of pre-eminence in the learned world."

It should, however, be also remarked that Dr. Waterland lived at a period during which Sacramental belief was at a very low ebb amongst us, and that the prevalent teaching of the age in which he flourished,

[1] The same Bishop expressed himself willing to confirm over again, after conditional baptism, a person who had already received the rite of Confirmation while she had only as yet been baptized by a dissenting minister. See Elwin's "Minister of Baptism," page 322. In that "eminently candid and exhaustive work," (to quote the words of one of the most learned of the Bishops of our Communion) a storehouse of information will be found with regard to this important question.

may have, to some extent, influenced certain of his own writings. This is especially observable in his treatise on the Eucharist. But perhaps this very want of Sacramental fervour on the part of our author, may rather incline us to accept him as by so much the better fitted to form a calm and unprejudiced judgment upon a question such as the present. His conclusions also gain weight from the fact, that he once held an opinion favourable to the recognition of Lay-baptism, an opinion which, as will be seen from his letters, he was afterwards forced to abandon, though he confesses to a certain reluctance in having had to surrender "a pleasing error" in favour of the view which a further study of the question convinced him to be the true one.

I may now perhaps be permitted to add something as to my own Diocesan experience with regard to the question discussed in the following pages. For nearly five years I have felt it my duty to require conditional Baptism, in the case of all converts presented to me for Confirmation. I had not, however, made this an absolute rule when I addressed the following words to my clergy in our Diocesan Synod of 1886. Yet I think I may quote them in order to lay before the reader some considerations, which, though not immediately connected with Dr. Waterland's argument, certainly tend to strengthen the practical conclusion at which he arrives. What I said was as follows:

"Our old registers, especially those of the last century, which have been happily preserved, and notably, also, the recently published journals of Bishop Robert Forbes, bear witness to an interesting and important fact, viz., to the very frequent administration of Holy Baptism, at that time, in the case of those, who, from religious bodies external to our Church, were admitted into her communion.[1]

"That the conditional Baptism of new adherents is not now insisted on, as a general rule, is, I think, a cause for regret. Such Baptism does not at all involve any assertion as to the invalidity of lay or Presbyterian Baptism. The Church of Rome holds views, which, in the light of much that has come down to us from primitive antiquity (to say nothing of the opinions of many Anglican Divines), might be considered extreme, in favour of the validity of Lay-baptism. Yet for many years her general practice, in this country at any rate, and probably elsewhere, has been to give Baptism conditionally, to all converts to her communion. I mention this fact, not as a precedent for us, but in support of my statement that the conditional Baptism of converts does not involve any assertion as to the invalidity of the Baptism they may have previously received.

"What then is to be said in favour of baptizing conditionally? Much, I believe. For instance, if we carefully consider the essentials of Holy Baptism, as

---

[1] Bishop Robert Forbes, who died in 1775, in the course of a single Highland journey baptized about 277 persons out of 1521 to whom he administered Confirmation. In his journal there is the following interesting entry, made during his stay at Ballachulish, in July, 1770. "After Matins went to the Tent, Mr. Cameron not having quite finished in Gaelic. Then I preached, as formerly, upon Confirmation, from Acts viii. 14, &c., Mr. Cameron resuming in Gaelic. Then we adjourned to the Store House, where I confirmed 262, of whom 76 (were) baptized. This day's work bore hard upon me, insomuch that I was obliged to employ Mr. Cameron to baptize some of them. All glory be to GOD for all His mercies. Amen."—See "Bishop Forbes' Journals of Episcopal Visitations," Skeffington, 1886.

taught by the universal Church of CHRIST, and as restated in our Prayer Book,[1] I think we shall see that it is not always safe to assume that they have been complied with. I do not now lay stress on the assumption, in our rubric, that the child whose Baptism is to be accepted as valid, has been baptized by a 'Lawful Minister.' This, however, I might do,[2] if the expression quoted were read in the light of the Preface to the Ordinal, to which I would direct your attention. But here I only refer to the 'matter' and to the 'words.'

"As to the 'matter,' can we always be as sure as we ought to be? Baptism, for long, in communions external to our own Church, has been habitually administered from pulpits, and by aspersion. Surely this is rather a doubtful substitute, not only for the primitive practice of immersion, but even for the affusion, allowed as an alternative, by the rubric of our Book of Common Prayer. One drop is said to be sufficient for compliance with the LORD'S Institution. But can we always be reasonably sure, that in Baptisms administered as I have described, there is any contact at all, between the unbaptized child, and the sprinkled water?

---

[1] In this statement I was guilty of inaccuracy. The rubric referred to, which occurs at the end of the Office for the Private Baptism of children does not say that water and the appointed words are "the essentials of Baptism," though this is often carelessly asserted, as above. What is stated is that they are "essential parts of Baptism," and this makes all the difference. If "through fear or haste" either the water or the words were omitted, the Baptism would be essentially wanting in validity. But this does not necessarily imply that water and the words are the *only* essentials. In the Eucharist the elements and the words of institution are "essential parts." But something more is needed—a lawful Minister.

[2] See note at the end of this Preface.

"Then again as to the words—Not all who profess to administer Christian Baptism, do so according to the LORD's appointment: In the Name of the FATHER, and of the SON, and of the HOLY GHOST. There have been those who have gravely maintained (basing their error on a mistaken interpretation of Holy Scripture), that Baptism 'in the Name of CHRIST' is sufficient.[1] Moreover, if we remember of how little importance many persons consider *all* outward forms to be, we may well believe that, among the numerous sects of those who profess and call themselves Christians, strange departures from the essential words have been allowed to pass unrebuked.

"To my own mind, all this is sufficient to make conditional Baptism desirable, as a general rule, in the case of those who seek admission to our communion as adults. And I might also add another reason, viz.: that in many cases, no reliable evidence as to previous Baptism is obtainable, and that often it is utterly uncertain whether those who come to us have received any kind of Baptism at all. For by statistics it can be demonstrated that, both in Scotland and England, a very large proportion of the adult inhabitants of our large cities are certainly unbaptized.

"After what I have said, I need not tell you what my own practice is; and though I am not able in all cases[2] to exercise the cautions I should wish, in the case of those presented to me for Confirmation, I am, nevertheless, very clear in my own mind as to what, in this matter, is the more excellent way; and I would strongly recommend to my clergy a more general re-

---

[1] Compare sections 7 and 9 in "The Teaching of the Twelve Apostles."

[2] This was in 1886.

turn to the practice of the last century, in the case of all those who desire to be received as members of our communion. I might even suggest, as another reason for the practice I recommend, a charitable provision against those doubts and scruples which often arise in the minds of persons who, in after years, have reflected with anxiety as to their first admission into the Church. Again and again cases have arisen, to my knowledge, of persons who, long after Confirmation and admission to Holy Communion, have expressed doubts as to their Baptism in infancy. Surely such doubts are most detrimental to the spiritual life, even should they be groundless. In these cases, of course, there should be no hesitation in complying with the request, when made, for conditional Baptism. Yet how much better, if the possibility of all disquieting scruples had been provided against at the outset.

"We can well understand how, in the primitive Church, or in after ages, there may have been instances of reluctance or even of refusal to baptize *unconditionally* in cases of uncertainty. But, with the conditional form provided in our canons, and elsewhere, I think no such hesitation need hinder the private administration of hypothetical Baptism, before Confirmation, as a general rule, in all cases in which there is even a possibility of present or future misgivings.

"My own experience is, that when the matter is properly explained, and, above all, when judiciously carried out, not only no objections are raised, but, on the contrary, the conditional Baptism is thankfully accepted. Objections are certainly not likely to occur in the minds of those who are really in earnest in their desire to conform to Apostolic order and to submit themselves humbly to the discipline of the Church.

As to those who are not so minded, would it not be better that they should refrain from joining themselves to us?

"But what shall we say with regard to cases quite beyond our reach? Here, I think, we must specially exercise faith in the merciful loving-kindness of our LORD JESUS CHRIST. We must not, at any time, regard His supernatural gifts of grace in the same way as we should regard the operation of the ordinary laws of the natural world. In the working of these laws we see certain causes and certain effects linked together independently of any moral considerations. Not thus with the Sacraments. In them we have the outward signs, and they are also the ordinary channels of grace—but of grace, let us remember, freely given by our LORD JESUS CHRIST as the Sovereign Ruler of His People. So, though He has ordained His holy Sacraments as the appointed means through which He saves and blesses us, it is evident He cannot Himself be fettered by His own laws, with regard to their operation. Though we are bound, yet He is not.

"Let us then ever keep this in mind. We are bound. Therefore, let us bring to bear the utmost rigour, and the most scrupulous exactness in all our dealings as to the administration of the Holy Sacraments. CHRIST is not bound. Therefore, let us confidently hope in His mercy, should we ever fail in our efforts to remedy what is doubtful or irregular. We are bound. Therefore, for instance, in this present question of Baptism, let us follow what I have humbly submitted to be the more excellent way. CHRIST is not bound. Therefore in cases where we cannot interfere, let us rely on His sovereign mercy, and on His power to supply every needful gift out of the abundant treasures of His grace."

Soon after delivering the charge from which I have made the above extract, I felt it my duty to examine this question further, with regard to the administration of Lay-baptism, in order that I might more clearly ascertain the truth about this matter, as taught in Holy Scripture and by the voice of the Universal Church. The result was that I became convinced that the arguments in favour of the popular theory were unsatisfactory, or at any rate, that the opinion that the Church of CHRIST, as a whole, had acknowledged the validity of Lay-baptism, did not rest on any sufficient foundation—sufficient, that is, for the support of a view involving such momentous practical consequences. At the same time I could not see my way to following those Divines of ancient and modern times, who have dogmatically asserted that Lay-baptism is certainly null and void. The position, in short, to which I found myself driven was that expressed in the often quoted pronouncement on this subject in the Lower House of the Convocation of Canterbury, in 1712. So while unable to regard Lay-baptism as certainly invalid, and while still honestly hoping that it might be valid, I dared not accept it as satisfactory.

As a consequence of this, I felt myself in a position of considerable difficulty with regard to the administration of Confirmation. To me, (though others may not be able to share or understand my scruples,) it seemed no longer right, whatever my hopes might be, to say, officially before GOD and man, over candidates about whose previous Baptism I had a serious doubt, the solemn prayer in which it is asserted that they have been regenerated "by water and the HOLY GHOST." I felt therefore that I must either cease to exercise my office, or else make the conditional Baptism of such persons an invariable rule. With much anxiety I decided to follow the latter course. The result confirms me in the belief that I was rightly guided in so doing, for during the four years that have been completed since the new rule came into operation, there have been many more persons confirmed by me in the Diocese, than during the four previous years. Had it been otherwise however, the theological argument would not have been affected, and I could not have acted differently. Many, perhaps, may be inclined to condemn the course which I have felt it my duty to pursue, but it is some consolation to me to reflect that my practice (whatever may be said as to the theories on which it is founded) is in harmony, in this respect, at any rate, with the practice of the overwhelming majority of the Bishops of CHRIST's Church throughout the world. For outside the limits of our Communion, into which, on this particular point, much unauthorized laxity has been allowed to creep, I know of no Bishops who would, without conditional Baptism, admit to Confirmation or to Communion, persons who have been baptized by Ministers, in Orders that they disallowed, or by lay persons, not in communion with the Church, according to their definition of that expression.

Before concluding, I feel bound to apologize to the reader and also to my friend the Editor of this book, for the length of this Preface, and for having said so much in it about myself, and about my dealings with the poor and scattered remnant in this wide Diocese, amongst whom I have been called to minister. I hope I fully recognize my insignificance among the Bishops of CHRIST's Flock, and realize the small importance which must attach to my views and conclusions, so far as they are my own. But I have ventured to lay before my brethren in the Sacred Ministry, and before others, the results of a practical and somewhat varied pastoral experience during the last twenty-five years, and in humble submission to all that the Catholic Church has taught.

That we must all come to wrong conclusions, if left to follow the guidance of private judgment and of our own intellects, darkened as they have been by the Fall, cannot be doubted. But He Who ordained that Holy Sacrament, which is the subject of the following letters, has said to us, Ask and ye shall receive, and has added this most gracious assurance, If ye, being evil, know how to give good gifts unto your children; how much more shall your Heavenly FATHER give the HOLY SPIRIT to them that ask Him. May that Blessed SPIRIT, Whom JESUS has sent unto us from the FATHER, and by Whom the whole body of His Church is governed, sanctified, and guided into all the truth, so direct our hearts and minds, according to that truth, that in this and in all things, we may have a right judgment, and having peace through believing, may evermore rejoice in His holy comfort!

J. R. ALEX. CHINNERY-HALDANE,
Bishop of Argyll and the Isles.

NOTE AS TO THE RUBRICS IN THE BAPTISMAL OFFICE.

Nothing can be gathered in favour of the validity of Lay-baptism, as conferring spiritual grace, from the rubrics of the Book of Common Prayer. As a matter of fact these only deal with Baptisms performed by a "Lawful Minister"—either the "Minister of the Parish, or, in his absence, any other *lawful* Minister." And it should be observed that immediately before the prescribed questions as to the circumstances and details relating to a Baptism privately performed, in a time of extremity, there is a rubric which sanctions such questions *only* in the case of children who have been baptized by a *lawful* Minister—"If the child were baptized by any other *lawful* Minister, then the Minister of the Parish shall examine," &c. And, should it be asked why the Minister of the Parish is thus to inquire as to the due administration of Baptism by one of his own brethren, the answer is ready to hand in the wording of these questions themselves—"*Because* some things essential[1] to the Sacrament may happen to be omitted, *through fear or haste in such times of extremity*, therefore I demand further of you," &c.

For the meaning of the expression "lawful," as relating to the Minister of a Sacrament, reference should be made to the Preface to the Ordinal. There it is stated that no man shall be accounted or taken to be a *lawful* Bishop, Priest, or Deacon in the Church of England, or suffered to execute any of the said functions, except he be called, tried, and admitted thereto, according to the form hereafter following, or hath had previously Episcopal Consecration or Ordination.

In the Ordinal itself, the Baptism of infants "in the absence of the Priest" is specified as one of the functions that may be performed by a Deacon. But nowhere does the Book of Common Prayer hint at any other possible Minister of Baptism, who is neither Bishop, Priest, nor Deacon, or in other words, who has not received authority for administering this Sacrament from CHRIST and His Church.

---

[1] Compare this expression "*some things* essential" with the other—"which are essential parts of Baptism."

INTRODUCTORY NOTE.

THE following Letters of the learned theologian, Doctor Waterland, are re-published with notes, in the hope that they may serve to spread and to strengthen a belief as to the character and value of Lay-baptism, which rests for its foundation on the witness and authority of holy Scripture—which has been widely held and taught throughout the Catholic Church from the earliest times—which is so consonant with the whole body of Catholic Truth that its denial would seem to be plainly inconsistent with that body of Truth, in more than one point—which is so consonant with right reason, that its contradictory is wholly unreasonable, unless we are prepared to contradict some other beliefs, which all Christian people agree to hold.

Waterland's belief as to Lay-baptism is briefly stated in his own words, that "since there is no Divine law or rule to found its validity upon, it can no more be valid than it can be lawful. For nothing is plainer to me than that what has no foundation for its validity, has no validity at all; or that nothing can be valid, which has no sufficient authority to make it so."

It may be well that the reader should be reminded here, *in limine*, what is the exact subject under discussion in the following "Letters," because many side-issues have during the controversy of Lay-baptism been raised, attention has been distracted by attempts to prove what no one denies, and to disprove what no one asserts, so that the ordinary reader gets confused, the real question in dispute is lost sight of, and one party, or the other, in the controversy is thought to have proved his case, when in point of fact what he has proved, or disproved, is something quite different from the real question at issue.

That question, the subject of Waterland's Letters, is this:—

Is there any sufficient ground for asserting the validity, i.e., the spiritual efficacy, of baptism administered otherwise than as Christ Himself ordained, administered not by Apostles, or their successors, and the inheritors of their divine commission, but by other persons, who have (so far as we know) no such commission, who undertake to act in GOD's Name, and to dispense GOD's gifts, without having (so far as we know) any divine authority so to act, or any power to impart these divine gifts.

Let it be observed that there is no question whatever as to what GOD *can* do. No one thinks of denying that GOD can give spiritual efficacy to external actions however irregular, or even presumptuous, they may be. The only question is, whether we have any sure ground for asserting and teaching that GOD *always will* give this efficacy to certain external actions, even when they are done without His commission and contrary to His ordinance, or whether such an assertion is not rash and groundless, and such teaching perilous, and pernicious to all who may be led thereby to trust in an uncertain outward rite, when they might have a true "Sacrament of the Gospel," if they were not held back by the false assurance of this dangerous teaching.

Further it should be noted that there is here no question as to whether the Bishops, who hold the commission of the Apostles, or any one of them, might not impart that commission to a layman so as to authorize and empower him to baptize. This question might perhaps very fairly be raised; but here it is not raised. Here the sole question is about the validity of the (so-called) baptisms of those to whom no commission, or authority has ever been given. And it is certainly remarkable, that if Bishops have the power thus to authorize laymen to baptize, no Bishop has ever been known to authorize any layman to baptize in any age or country since Christianity began. But whether Bishops have this power or not, the question of unauthorized Lay-baptism is not thereby affected at all; and that is the only question here at issue.

It will be useful also here to call attention to one fertile source of confusion, which continually perplexes the reader in this controversy, and it perplexes the thoughts of readers because it has first confused the thoughts of the writers. I mean this, that no definition has been given of the word "valid," and consequently that word is used in a variety of different senses, without any recognition that these various senses are different. The result is, that arguments, e.g. to show that marriages, under certain conditions, are not "valid" in the sense of being *legal*, are produced, as if they were equally conclusive to prove that baptisms under the same conditions are not "valid" in a totally different sense, i.e. in the sense of not *conveying grace*. (Vide Kelsall's "Answer," p. 100 (44) et seq.) And *vice versâ* arguments to prove that Lay-baptism is "valid," in a certain sense, (which perhaps no one would care to deny) are used as if they also proved that such baptism is "valid" in quite another sense, which cannot at all be granted, e.g. the authority and the arguments of S. Augustine to prove that Lay-baptism is "valid," in a somewhat vague sense, which he does not define, but of which he says that he takes such baptism to be valid, so far that the "outward rite" need not be repeated, but not valid in the sense of conveying grace or any spiritual benefits. These arguments are constantly reproduced, and the authority of S. Augustine claimed in support of the theory that Lay-baptism is "valid" in the sense of conveying all the grace which true Baptism conveys, a theory which he expressly disclaims. (Vide S. Aug. "De Baptismo," Lib. i. cap. 18, and lib. vii. cap. 53.) Bingham notices this limited sense of validity. (Schol. Hist. of Lay-bapt. cap. i. sec. 21.) So does Kelsall in his "answer to Waterland," p. 122, (81.) And yet S. Augustine and the whole body of Fathers and Councils, to which he refers in support of his own theory are boldly claimed as supporting a totally different theory of "the validity" of Lay-baptism, according to which it is held that "any baptism is equally valid, whether the administrator be a priest or a layman, a man or a woman, a Christian or a heathen," and that "the special grace of Baptism" is conveyed equally surely in any one of these cases. No theory could be, more than this theory is, directly contradicted by the teaching of S. Augustine, and wholly unsupported by any single Father or Council in the ancient Church.

DR. WATERLAND'S
FIRST LETTER ON LAY-BAPTISM.

To the Rev. Mr. P(yle), Rector of L(ynn.)

M. C. October 29, 1713.

REVEREND SIR,

I HUMBLY thank you for your very obliging letter, wherein you do me too much honour to suppose me either equal to so large and difficult a subject, or able to hold the argument, however just and good, against the ingenious and learned Mr. Kelsall.

Nevertheless I should think myself very happy could my affairs permit me to accept of your kind invitation, because I am sure the conversation of two such worthy persons could not but be both agreeable and edifying; and if I should lose my cause, I should still be a gainer. However, till opportunity favours me with what I much wish for, be pleased to take a few thoughts in writing, as they occur to me amidst a crowd of other business, and to excuse either the inaccuracy of style and method, or any hasty slips of a running pen.

I am not at all surprised at Mr. Kelsall's judgment on the case. It is not very long since I was myself of the same opinion, being led to it, as I suppose he may be, partly by the good-nature of it, and partly by the authority of great names, as the Bishops of Sarum and Oxford, &c., besides some passages of antiquity not well understood; and I was pleased, I confess, to see all, as I thought, confirmed by Mr. Bingham's Scholastical History of Lay-baptism.[1] But second thoughts and further views have given a turn to my judgment, and robbed me of a pleasing error, as I must now call it, which I was much inclined to embrace for a truth, and could yet wish that it were so.

The arguments or scruples mentioned in your letter have all, besides many more, been considered, canvassed, answered, carefully, solidly, and, in my humble opinion, fully and completely. If Mr. Kelsall had seen Mr. Lawrence's Answer to Mr. Bingham, I hardly think he could despise that gentleman's learning or judgment. But I must have a care of being too positive, lest I should seem too far to trust *my own*, or to pay too little deference to *his*, which I have a great value and veneration for.

I have sent what papers I had by me relating to the controversy. And some I had lent out, otherwise you would have had all.

It were needless for me to say anything in the cause, after what hath been said infinitely better: only to give

---

[1] Bingham's "History of Lay-baptism" was written in reply to Lawrence's "Lay-baptism invalid." Lawrence answered in the Second Part of "Lay-baptism invalid," and Bingham again replied in the Second Part of his "History." Bishop Talbot, of Oxford, and Dean Hickes (besides others of less note) had also discussed this question on either side. Waterland had all the evidence of these writers before him when he wrote his "Letters," here reprinted, and he concludes against the validity of Lay-baptism after hearing all that could be then urged in its favour.

you a little present ease, till you can have leisure to peruse the whole controversy, I shall venture to offer a few things about it.

The cause depends upon Scripture, antiquity, and reason.

I.

As to Scripture, it is confessed that it confines the administration of Baptism to the Clergy,[1] as much as it does any other of the *sacerdotal powers*. The commission is plain and clear, and certainly leaves no more room for Lay-baptism than for Lay-ordination, Lay-absolution, Lay-consecration of the Eucharist, Lay-preaching, and praying.[2] If therefore we take the

---

[1] This is one of those expressions which have been strangely—one is tempted to say perversely—misunderstood by the advocates of Lay-baptism (vide Kelsall's "Answer," p. 94). Waterland's meaning is plain enough. Scripture "confines the administration of Baptism to the clergy," in this sense, that it records a commission given to the clergy to baptize, and it does not record any such commission given to any others. No one thinks of saying that Scripture "expressly forbids" all men, except the clergy, to baptize. When a sovereign gives a definite commission to any particular person, or persons, does he ever "expressly forbid" all other persons to execute that commission? Who would ever suppose such a prohibition necessary? All other persons, except those to whom the commission is given, are simply left without any power or authority in the matter, and any attempt on their part to execute a commission, which had not been intrusted to them, would be evidently unwarrantable and presumptuous: nor could the king, in whose name they thus presumptuously assumed to act, be expected to ratify their actions. This is exactly the case of Lay-baptizers.

[2] Waterland seems to be mistaken here in speaking of these last two points, as if they were on a par with the first four;

liberty of going from the institution in one case, we may as reasonably do it in all, supposing the like necessity. And yet Scripture hath no where intimated that we may do it in any; but has rather taught us by some severe examples, as in the case of Saul and Uzza, that positive ministrations, confined by the institution of them to certain rules or persons, must rather be left unperformed, than performed irregularly.

This perhaps you will grant, but still will insist upon it, that they are valid to the *recipients*, though against rules and orders: and here the maxim, *quod fieri non debuit factum valet*, is brought in to confirm it, and the instance in the case of marriage is also thought to be pertinently alleged, as if the case were parallel. But to all this it is answered:

1. That the maxim mentioned is true only of *errors in circumstantials*, not of *errors in essentials*.[1] Sup-

but he explains further on what he means by "Lay-preaching and praying." (Vide p. 150.)

[1] No arguments are more misleading than those which are grounded on maxims, or other common sayings, wrongly applied, e.g., "Bis dat qui cito dat," therefore you will do double good if you give "quickly" to a beggar without stopping to inquire whether he is deserving, or not; or, "De minimis non curat lex," therefore, because "not" is a very small word, the law does not care whether you are entitled to "do" something, or "not to do" it. So with the maxim, "Fieri non debet, factum valet:" it is liable to be very misleading unless we will take the trouble to consider whether it is rightly applicable to the case before us, or not. Very little consideration will show that it is not applicable to the case of Lay-baptism. The most obvious reason why this maxim is not rightly applicable to the case of Lay-baptism is that the very attempt to apply it begs the whole question at issue, viz.: the question *whether there is any "factum"* of the kind sup-

pose a man to marry his sister, or a second wife while the first is living; here is an error in *essentials*, and the fact is null and void, notwithstanding the maxim, *quod fieri*, &c.

2. It is asserted, that though the minister be not essential to marriage, yet to Baptism he is. In marriage it is *decent* that it be done by a Priest or Deacon, in Baptism it is *necessary*. Marriage is a covenant between the two parties: its essence is their mutual contract, the minister is a circumstance only. Baptism implies a covenant between GOD and man; its essence is their mutual contract in such manner and form as is appointed. The administrator acts for GOD, and in GOD'S name, which none can do without commission from Him. Such commission therefore is *essential;* and without it the whole is void, as much as if I should pretend to act in the queen's name without order or warrant, to levy soldiers, naturalize strangers, or anything of like nature. All would be null and void, and the maxim of *quod fieri*, &c., would here be false and impertinent.

posed? As to the "factum" of the external act in Lay-baptism there is no dispute; there it is, whatever it may be worth, that is evident. But as to the supposed "factum" of the conveyance of "the special grace of Baptism," which is essential to its validity as a Christian Sacrament, this is the very point in question. Of course if there is this "factum," if "the special grace of Baptism" has as a matter of fact, been imparted to the receiver of Lay-baptism, then obviously "factum valet;" but this whole controversy turns on the question whether there is any such "factum," or not; and it is not settled by simply begging the question, and then saying, "factum valet." Vide "Lay-baptism. An Inquiry into the Spiritual Value and Validity of that Ceremony." 2nd ed. p. 75 et seq. (J. Masters, London, 1888.)

3. To this I add, that from your own concession, that a "layman is guilty of a sin in the very act of baptizing," it seems to follow that the *act* is *void*. I never could well digest that assertion, that it is *sinful* in the *administrator*, and yet *valid* to the *receiver*. It is a hard saying, that one may be *damned* for doing that, without which the other could not have been *saved*. I suspect some fallacy in this, though where it lies I cannot perhaps tell you. Were I a layman, and thought that the salvation of any one or more depended upon my baptizing them, I would certainly do it; but then, I could not think it a sin, but a duty, as one of the highest acts of charity, to do it. How will you get off this, but by saying, that if it is a sin in the administrator, it is likewise ineffectual to the receiver? If the salvation of another depends upon it, it is certainly no sin: therefore, say I, if it be a sin, it can be so only in such cases as where nothing depends upon it, that is, wherever such Baptism is sinful in the whole act, or ought not to have been given, it is *void*. I will not be positive in this argument, being sensible it wants many distinctions and cautions to make it go down, which I have not room to consider. But I am persuaded it is right in the main, and well deserves some further consideration.

Having seen then that Scripture gives no commission to any but the *Clergy* to baptize, that therefore Lay-baptisms are unauthorized and sinful, and therefore, as I have endeavoured to prove, *invalid*, notwithstanding the exceptions brought to the contrary; I now proceed to a distinct argument drawn from the judgment and practice of the ancients.

II.

The ancients do with one voice, for above three hundred years, condemn Lay-baptism,[1] not so much as putting in any exception for cases of necessity. Tertullian indeed within that time does speak in favour of it; but it is only his own private opinion, and founded upon a very weak reason. Him I except. All the rest are for us, or not against us. But Mr. Kelsall thinks, that though the ancients did condemn Lay-baptism as not fit to be, yet if it was given, they thought it valid, and never to be repeated. This I very much want to see proved, or so much as probably inferred, from anything that occurs in the ancientest writings.

I know that heretical Baptisms were allowed to be *valid* both before and after S. Cyprian's time, (though he himself and some other Bishops differed in their judgment and practice in that point from other churches, and appealed to ancient custom in defence of themselves;) and I scruple not to own, that within a while it became a constant rule in most churches, that such heretical or schismatical Baptisms should stand good,

---

[1] Here Waterland uses a phrase, which might easily be misinterpreted, as Kelsall in fact does misinterpret it, expressing "astonishment" (vide p. 109). Waterland explains further on (p. 159) that in saying that "the ancients do with one voice condemn Lay-baptism," he does not mean that every one of them expressly mentions Lay-baptism and condemns it: but he means that all the ancient Fathers held certain general principles, which "condemn" Lay-baptism; while no one of them maintains any general principle upon which Lay-baptism could be defended, (vide p. 200.) He excepts only Tertullian, whose witness is not very clear, nor always consistent. (Vide pp. 161 et seq.)

provided they were administered in the Name of the Trinity. If this be what Mr. Kelsall attempts to prove by "the many and great authorities" you speak of, it is readily granted, nor will any one dispute so clear a point with him. But then it is insisted upon, that this proves nothing for Lay-baptism. Those heretical and schismatical Baptisms were not Lay-baptisms; or if they were, those very churches that allowed them to be valid would have annulled them. They were administered by men of a *sacerdotal character*, and on that account were reputed *valid*. It was thought that neither schism nor heresy, nor any censures of the Church, could deprive them of the *indelible character;* so that at any time, if they returned into the Church, they were received in without being *reordained*. Upon this ground their Baptisms were esteemed *valid*, and so were not reiterated; or those churches, who for a time did rebaptize, did it because they thought heresy and schism nulled the orders of heretical and schismatical priests, and consequently their Baptisms, and every other ministerial performance of theirs. The question in those times was not, *whether Lay-baptisms were null*, both sides supposing that as an undoubted principle: but whether *heresy and schism nulled Orders, and reduced heretical priests to mere laymen*. It was at length determined in the negative. And therefore the Baptisms of heretical or schismatical priests or deacons, if administered in the Name of the Trinity, were received as *valid*, having all the essentials of Baptism, *water, commission,* and *form*.

If I am mistaken in this, upon which the whole controversy in great measure depends, I shall be glad to be set right; and I shall be further thankful to Mr. Kelsall, if he will give me but one plain authority, except Tertullian, for the validity of Lay-baptism, as such, before S. Austin.¹

If I have thus got over "the many and great authorities," the other smaller objections will be easily dealt with.

You say, we hereby unchurch the reformed churches abroad.

We answer, that this principle of the invalidity of Lay-baptism, which several of them hold as well as we, does not unchurch them, if their want of episcopal ordination doth not, which is a distinct question. If their Orders are good, their Baptisms are so too. If you deny them *that*, they will not thank you for the *other*.

As to our own Church, we hope the consequences² drawn from this principle are not so black and tragical as is imagined, and many reasons might be given to show that they are not. But this were needless and tedious. Suppose the worst: the argument is weak

---

¹ This is a challenge, which neither Kelsall, nor any other advocate of Lay-baptism, has ventured to take up. The "authorities" frequently cited in favour of the validity of heretical or schismatical Baptism do not, as Waterland points out, touch the question of Lay-baptism, as such.

² The argument from supposed "consequences," either for, or against any doctrine is very dangerous—and quite as dangerous one way as the other—there are some false doctrines, which appear to involve happy and consoling "consequences," as e.g., the Calvinist doctrine of the Indefectibility of grace; there are also some true doctrines, which appear to involve sad and painful "consequences," as e.g., the Catholic doctrine of the necessity of true repentance. Such "consequences" may serve to raise an apparent *primâ facie* probability for, or against some doctrine; but the Christian faith does not depend upon apparent *primâ facie* probabilities.

and inconclusive. *A doctrine condemns thousands*, therefore it is false. Apply this to the *doctrine of the necessity of holiness*, which condemns more: apply it to the doctrines we hold against the Church of Rome, which condemns more than all the Protestants perhaps put together: apply it to the *doctrine of salvation by Christ alone*, which condemns millions, or may be five parts in six of the whole world. Are the doctrines therefore false? No surely. To what purpose then is it to allege the multitudes concerned in the consequences of them? The argument, if it proves anything, proves this only, that the age has been either very ignorant, or very corrupt, to reject sound doctrine, and that it wants to be reformed, and to be instructed better. And I hope this may be a sufficient answer to what you hint of the act of toleration, and French Refugees; though it may be said further, that a man's want of *valid Baptism*, if he is episcopally ordained, does not void his ministerial performances. A man may have orders and authority to make others what he is not himself; as one, that is not himself free, may by commission make others so.[1] This you will see en-

---

[1] The opinion (never decided one way, or the other by the Church,) that one who has been ordained a priest, but has not been baptized, may validly administer Baptism, and perform validly all other ministerial acts, rests upon the generally admitted truth, that the validity of Sacraments depends not on the personal character, or spiritual condition of the minister, but on the virtue of the Divine commission, which he has received. If therefore any man, baptized, or unbaptized, has received this Divine commission, all the actions, for which that commission empowers him, are thereby rendered valid. Vide further discussion of this point, pp. 86 et seq. and pp. 217 et seq.

larged upon very handsomely by Mr. Lawrence and Dr. Brett. And if this point be well settled, as I think it is, it takes off very much from the force of your objection of the many and unavoidable ill consequences of our doctrine of the invalidity of Lay-baptism. But why should I be further tedious? You have the books from whence I have taken my hints, and what I have here written is little more than an extract from them. Be pleased to peruse the whole controversy, and give me your thoughts as frankly as I have given mine. If yourself, or Mr. Kelsall will be so kind, as either to clear my apprehension on any points which are yet to me obscure, or to set me right where I am wrong, the favour will be accepted with all possible thankfulness and respect by,

Good Sir,
Your most affectionate humble Servant,
D. W.

P.S. I ventured to show this letter to a very learned and considerable man here, who came occasionally to see me; and he was pleased to give me his approbation.

REV. E. KELSALL'S ANSWER
TO DR. WATERLAND'S FIRST LETTER,

Addressed to the same Gentleman to whom the foregoing Letter was written.

May 12, 1714.

REVEREND SIR,

I WAS much surprised upon the receipt of your letter with Mr. W.'s enclosed; being very sensible that the discourse I had with you at our last meeting did not deserve the notice you have taken of it; and no less concerned to find that the occasion of your giving yourself so much trouble.

I ought and would sooner have paid you my respects upon this occasion, but that (besides many interruptions) those books lately written upon the subject of our discourse, which I had seen, were got out of my hands; and it required some time and trouble to recover a sight of them again; (for they were not my own;) without which, I would not go about to answer the very fine letter which you sent me.

Indeed I must complain of you for thus setting a gentleman upon me, whom I am so little able to encounter; who has, in few words, spoken so very well for his own opinion, that I find cause enough to wish you had not cut out such work for me, unless I had had more skill and capacity to manage it with success.

The very large and undeserved compliments he makes me, I must attribute wholly to the honour I have of being in the number of your acquaintance. Mr. W. can have no other excuse for misplacing them upon a stranger. Sir, I shall not at present offer any return to that part of his letter, but to congratulate him with a very sincere respect upon the eminent station which his merit has lately placed him in.

Had I the honour to be known likewise to him, there would be no need to assure him, that I can with ease forsake the most *pleasing error*, when convinced that it is an error. The *good-nature*, or pretended charity there is in a false opinion, cannot make it near so welcome as the most ill-natured truth, if truth can deserve such an epithet. And as for *great names*,[1] if any such have influenced my judgment, they are the Whitgifts, the Bancrofts, the Hookers, the ancient

---

[1] "Great names" unfortunately in this, as in many other controversies, are unsafe guides, at least when they are used with so little scruple as in this present case. The wholly unwarrantable use which Mr. Kelsall has made of the "great name" of Whitgift I have shown in Note 1, page 126. Another "great name," nearer our own day, has been so audaciously dealt with that any opportunity of exposing the imposture must be welcome to all honest controversialists. The late Dean Hook in his "Church Dictionary" wrote an article on Lay-baptism, enumerating certain historical and other facts, which he considered of importance, and concluding, as his own judgment, that Lay-baptism, because it has no warrant from Holy Scripture and no sufficient authority from the Church, is unlawful and invalid. Since the death of the venerable Dean, a new edition of his "Church Dictionary" has been published, in which some of the articles, as the Preface informs

Rubrics, and even present practice of our Reformed Church of England, together with the Councils and Fathers of the primitive ages. Sir, I believe every position in Divinity which is new, to be false; and that in all questions relating to religion, discipline, or government, *reason* ought to submit to *Scripture*, and Scripture be interpreted by the sense and practice of *antiquity;* and consequently that *history* is the best and shortest decider of this and of every controversy in religion.

Mr. W. very well observes, that the cause depends upon these three. Having considered what offers itself, 1st, from Scripture, 2ndly, from antiquity, he gives you, in the last place, his thoughts upon that which reason has to allege against his opinion. I crave leave, Sir, to communicate to you my thoughts upon this last article first, which will let us into a full view of the importance of this question, and of the consequences which the doctrine of the absolute invalidity of Lay-baptism is attended with.[1]

us, have been re-written; among these is the article on Lay-baptism, which has been re-written in a sense diametrically opposite to that of the original article, ignoring important facts which Hook adduces, and asserting a conclusion the direct contradictory of that at which Hook arrived. Nevertheless this is the article on Lay-baptism now presented to the innocent reader in Hook's "Church Dictionary!"

[1] On this beginning with reason Waterland well observes that it seems "something wrong:" and on this plain ground, "because there is no reasoning to any good purpose on this question, till some foundation be laid in Scripture or antiquity, or both, to reason upon." (Vide p. 142.)

We neither do know, nor can know anything at all about the validity of Baptism except from what it has pleased GOD to reveal in His Word, or by His Church. Therefore, to begin an inquiry into what GOD has revealed, by setting out a

I.

1. And here I make no scruple to confess, that were the reason of the thing to be considered alone, had there been no intimation from Scripture, especially no authorities of our own, nor precedents of the primitive Church to influence this dispute, I should have still been (as some years since I was) strongly prejudiced in favour of Mr. W.'s opinion.

2. In the mean while, if it shall appear, as I apprehend it will, that in some cases Baptism by lay-hands hath been permitted by the Church, and in no case (if administered with water in the Name of the blessed Trinity) altogether disannulled, so as that the receiver should be baptized anew, what must we do? I think Mr. W., I am sure most writers on both sides of the question allow this to have been the case ever since S. Austin, at least in the Western Church.[1] And

number of supposed inconvenient "consequences" which would follow from this, or that revelation, if such had been given, or not given, is merely an attempt to prejudice the question and to obscure the truth. This attempt is the more remarkable here because the writer had, just above, very truly said that on such a question as this "history is the best and shortest decider," and, just below, he admits that "were the reason of the thing to be considered alone" he should agree with Waterland's view.

[1] If we are to "allow this" we must be careful to see what Kelsall means by these two statements. That "in some cases Baptism by lay-hands hath been permitted by the Church," is of course true, if it is meant that many Bishops and Doctors in the Church have permitted, in the sense of allowing the validity of such Baptisms; but if it is meant that "the Church" as a whole, either in any general council, or by any universally accepted practice, has permitted such Baptisms, then this cannot be allowed at all, since it is not true. And when Kelsall

if we derive our sacraments, as we do the succession of our priesthood, through the corrupted channels of the Church of Rome, then I am very much afraid, that an invalidity proved in the first, will inevitably infer an invalidity in the latter too.

3. The Church of Rome, ever since S. Austin,[1] hath allowed not only *laymen*, but even *women* in cases of necessity to baptize; and we can produce canons of that

---

says that "in no case" has Baptism, ("if administered with water in the Name of the Blessed Trinity") been "altogether disannulled, so as that the receiver should be baptized anew," here too we must "allow," or disallow this just as with the former clause. The whole Church has never decreed Lay-baptisms to be null and void; but many great councils (though no "general" one) and many great Bishops and Doctors have so taught: and many "receivers" of Lay-baptism have been "baptized anew." So that we can only "allow" these sweeping assertions in a very limited sense, and this a sense in which they will be of no service to the advocates of Lay-baptism, and no difficulty to us.

[1] Would it not be more true to say "ever since the Council of Trent," where for the first time this doctrine was decreed? But it should be remembered that even the modern Roman Church has guarded her acceptance of Lay-baptism by one express provision, (which Kelsall here, and the advocates of Lay-baptism generally, leave unnoticed.) The Council of Trent decrees that the baptizer must act "with the intention of doing what the Church does." (De Bap. c. iv.) And the *Catechismus ad Parochos* insists further on this same proviso. Whatever this proviso may mean, it would seem evident that if an "intention to do what the Church does" is a condition for valid Baptism, then the absence of any such "intention" would render Baptism invalid. The primary "intention" of the Church in Baptism is, beyond question, to administer "the sacrament of regeneration." Is this the "intention" of any large number of Protestant baptizers, (whether lay or clerical?)

Church[a] requiring the curates to instruct their people in the form of baptizing, that, where necessity should require, they might know how to do it aright. Which practice was so exceeding frequent among them, that it was morally impossible, but that many of their Clergy must be such as had in their infancy been so baptized.

4. Now to suppose such Baptisms are altogether null and void, must needs have a terrible influence upon the state, not of the Church of England alone, but of all the churches of Europe. For if the Baptism of such Clergymen as we now speak of was invalid, so was their Ordination too: they were laymen still, and of the lowest class, laymen unbaptized. They could not have the keys of the Church delivered to them before they were members of it. Such men, acting as Priests, could not baptize; acting as Bishops, could not ordain. And yet they did pretend to do both, as apprehending no cause to doubt the competency of their own authority. The effect whereof must needs be an endless propagation of nullities in respect both of Baptism and Ordination. So that here is a dreadful

---

Would not such an "intention" be by most of them repudiated? If so, we must pause before we claim, or admit the claim made for the Church of Rome as a supporter of the validity of Lay-baptism by anybody. Whether the doctrine of intention, as taught in the Roman Church, is a true doctrine, or an erroneous one, is a question which need not be here discussed; but, whether true, or untrue, it is beyond dispute a Roman doctrine, and it is impossible fairly to estimate the teaching of the Church of Rome if this doctrine is left out of sight.

---

[a] Concil. Salisb. A.D. 1420. Rubr. de Baptismo, apud Binium, tom. vii. p. 2. Item Concil. Ravenn. A.D. 1311, R. 11, et Concil. Ravenn. A.D. 1314, R. 14, ibid. Can. 2, Concil. Arelat. A.D. 1260, ap. L. E. Du Pin. Eccles. Hist. tom. xi.

blow given to the episcopal succession at once through the whole Western Church. Nay, through the Eastern too, if our accounts of that part of Christendom may be depended upon : which tell us that the Grecian churches, as well as the Roman, have for many ages permitted laymen, in cases of necessity, to baptize. I do not say
84 that the succession of the priesthood is hereby totally destroyed; but the marks and evidences of it are so obscured, and indeed made so entirely invisible to mortal eyes, that upon this hypothesis we can have no assurance without a revelation from heaven, that we ourselves are in the Church, and consequently in a state of salvation, or that there is a Bishop, a Sacrament, or a Christian, in the whole Christian world.

5. You see the consequences drawn from *this principle* (viz. the utter invalidity of Lay-baptism) are altogether as *black and tragical* as can be *imagined*. And they affect the Church of England the more in this respect, that whilst she was reforming from the errors, corruptions, and heresies of the Church of Rome, she made no alteration in the matter of Lay-baptism; but on the contrary *confirmed* the opinion then received,[b] that Baptism administered by lay-hands in the Name of the blessed Trinity ought not to be repeated : as we shall see in the sequel of this letter.

6. I know not whether I need to add, that many of our Clergy, ordained since the accursed rebellion of forty-one, when royalty and episcopacy both were trampled under foot, are and have been such as were baptized in those times by laymen, *by vile wicked laymen, usurpers of the priesthood, acting in defiance of the episcopal authority.*

---

[b] See the Rubric in the Office of Private Baptism, in King Edward VI. and Queen Eliz. their Liturgies.

7. Now to pronounce a nullity upon all the ministrations of Clergymen so baptized, is what neither the interests of our own, nor those of the Church Catholic will permit. Which nullity nevertheless is a consequence, that I see not how the advocates of the aforesaid principle can avoid. But let us hear what they say to this.

8. First therefore some of that side make short work of it, and roundly tell us, they will not answer for consequences; and that if their opinion be true, no consequences can make it otherwise.

9. But with submission, I cannot but think an objection grounded upon consequences so very important requires and deserves a better answer than this. Give me leave to add, that I can by no means believe any position in Divinity to be true, which inevitably draws along with it consequences so exceedingly grievous, absurd, and intolerable.

10. Indeed should this answer come from a Cartwright, from an enemy of our Church, from a fanatic, or any one tinctured with that leaven, I should not wonder at it. Any doctrine attended with consequences destructive to the episcopal succession will be grateful to such a palate. And in this case it will be our concern, more than his, to look after consequences.

11. But my business is not with such. I speak to gentlemen who are true and zealous lovers of the Church of England particularly, as well as of the Catholic Church in general, and abhor consequences prejudicial to either. If it be true (what I think we are all agreed upon) that the indefectibility of the Church, promised by her LORD and Spouse, cannot otherwise subsist, than with the joint subsistence of the episcopal succession; then I desire it may be observed, that

they who content themselves with this answer, give up for an opinion, (conceived by many learned men to be altogether new,) the very *being* of the Church of England, and of the Catholic Church too; give up even their own *character of Christians*, at least make all these things very doubtful, till a revelation from heaven shall determine who among us are *validly* baptized, ordained, &c. and who are not.

12. And Mr. W. is desired (if it be possible) to find out some way to cure the just suspicions, and remove the endless scruples, which his hypothesis will naturally suggest to the minds of thinking men concerning the validity of their Baptism, and the reality of their being within the covenant of grace, and in a state of salvation.

13. For in this case it is not sufficient that a Clergyman, or a reputed Clergyman, was his, or your, or my immediate baptizer, unless we be well assured that *he* was baptized by one in holy orders too, and the same of *this other* baptizer also, and so upwards to the very infancy of Christianity. An error in any part of the succession from the Apostles' time to ours, though never so remote, will in this case have as fatal a tendency, as if it were never so near us. Nay, the older it is, the more mischievous, because propagated through many hands, and length of time so far, that the original and extent of it are not to be discovered at this distance of time, and the effects of it are consequently not capable of redress.

14. In the mean time I must ask this gentleman's pardon, if I cannot think he states the objection fairly; when (in that paragraph of his letter, where he speaks of the influence this doctrine is thought to have upon the state of the Church of England) he represents our

sense of it barely thus ; "a doctrine condemns thousands, therefore it is false." I agree with him, that such "an argument is as weak and inconclusive" as he can wish ; and am therefore the less obliged to take notice of the parallel which on this occasion he makes between this and other doctrines, viz. " of the necessity of holiness, of salvation by CHRIST alone," and "those doctrines wherein we differ from the Church of Rome ;" all which, to be sure, are not the less true, because multitudes are thereby condemned. But by the way, I cannot but observe that his parallel is defective, because these last named doctrines do indeed *condemn thousands*, but upon a quite different ground, namely, a voluntary culpable defect in the persons so condemned ; whereas the doctrine of the invalidity of Lay-baptism condemns many more thousands, not for any culpable defect residing within themselves, or occasioned through any negligence of their own, but for a misfortune altogether inevitable, as being derived to them through a train of errors and nullities from those who have lived long before them ; and the more inevitable as well as irremediable, because it is impossible to discover the fountain-head where it began, and consequently to trace the succession of it, or find out who are affected by it, and who not.

15. You see the objection, as I have stated it here, implies no less, than that this doctrine does, by its consequences, 1st, raise fears and scruples of the last importance in the consciences of the best and most innocent Christians living, for which it provides no satisfaction : 2dly, it undermines the very foundations of our ecclesiastical constitution, by darkening all the evidences we have of the episcopal succession ; and thereby, 3dly, threatens a nullity to all the ministrations

(nay to the very being) of the priesthood through the whole Christian world.[1]

16. But in answer to this, Mr. W. tells us, that "a man's want of valid Baptism, if he is episcopally ordained, does not void his ministerial performances," &c. I agree with him, "that this point well settled takes off much from the force of our objection of the many and unavoidable ill consequences," &c., for it takes off all that I think worth insisting upon. But when he tells us, he thinks this point *is well settled*, I must crave leave as yet to dissent from him. For after the best inquiry I can yet make, I do not find that this doctrine hath any countenance either from antiquity, reason, or Scripture.

17. That this opinion hath no encouragement from ecclesiastical *antiquity*, I must take for granted, till I see antiquity alleged in favour of it, which no advocate hath yet pretended, as despairing, I suppose, to find anything of it there. It is a notion altogether new, not heard of till after this dispute about Lay-baptism arose, and now advanced merely to serve a turn, to set aside an objection, which is too hard for any other answer. It was news to S. Jerome to hear, that a man (no Christian) could make a Christian, that is, baptize:

[1] It can be hardly necessary to remind the reader that neither Waterland nor any other theologian taking his side in the controversy, would admit the truth of either one of these supposed "consequences" except the first, and that is only half true. It is true that the doctrine of the invalidity of Lay-baptism does, and ought to, "raise fears and scruples of the last importance in the consciences" of those who have received nothing better than "Lay-baptism." But it is untrue that "it provides no satisfaction for such fears and scruples." The satisfaction for them is plain and close at hand: let them receive a baptism, the validity of which cannot be questioned.

so far was he from imagining, that one in those circumstances could consecrate, ordain, &c. "Novam rem asseris, ut Christianus quisquam factus sit ab eo qui non fuit Christianus." Hier. Dial. adv. Lucif. cap. 5. In the mean time, as was said before, the novelty of any doctrine is a sufficient ground to believe it false, and the very *silence* of antiquity an effectual condemnation.

18. And I dare appeal to the greatest masters of *reason* and good sense to judge, whether one that is no Christian can be a Christian Priest,[c] one that is not of CHRIST's family be a steward of it, one that has no right to partake of the Body of our LORD be a sufficient dispenser thereof, one that is not a member of the Church be a governing member.[1] For I take all the rightful spiritual governors of this holy society to be members, even the most illustrious members of it, considered as a society purely spiritual. 1 Cor. xii. Ephes. iv.

19. I know no person that affirms a man's Baptism to be a *part*,[d] much less an *essential*[e] *part of his ministerial commission*. But I take it to be a qualification, without which a man is incapable of such a commission.[2] And though what Mr. W. offers be true, that

---

[1] This sounds plausible: but see Waterland's reply, (pp. 217 et seq.) the main gist of which lies in the fact "that it is not a man's Baptism, but his commission, that empowers him to act as GOD's minister."

[2] This is an assumption which cannot be admitted without proof; and, as bearing on the present controversy, it appears highly improbable; for it is not supposed that any bishop

---

[c] Dr. Hickes's Letter to the Author of Lay-baptism Invalid.
[d] Dr. Brett's Inquiry into the Judgment and Practice of the Primitive Church, Appendix, page 111.
[e] Lay-baptism Invalid, part i. Append. p. 135.

"one, who is not himself free, may by [an extraordinary] commission make others so;" yet, I presume, no laws of any kingdom will suffer an alien to be a standing officer in the government, as Bishops, Priests, and Deacons are in the Church. And now we are considering the force of commissions, I will suppose a prince, through ignorance, grants a commission to one that is dead, or become an idiot, or fallen under some other natural incapacity. You will hardly say, such a commission is valid.[1] Suppose then the spiritual governors of the Church grant, through mistake, a spiritual commission, in order to transact spiritual matters, to one that is spiritually dead, that is, unbaptized; why should the latter be thought valid, the former not?

20. Indeed had the Fountain and Giver of all spiritual gifts said it should be valid, then we had had nothing to do, but to acquiesce. But nothing like this is to be met

ever ordained any man whom he knew to be unbaptized. On the contrary it has been invariably assumed as a matter of course, if not in every case proved, that every candidate for Holy Orders has been baptized, to such persons the Bishop imparts the ministerial commission, as he is authorized and commanded to impart it, with every circumstance known, or believed to be necessary. Is it reasonable to assume that GOD will decline to ratify such a commission, because of the unintentional and unconscious omission of a preliminary "qualification," which He has nowhere Himself demanded, but which has ever been felt to be due and proper, and which was here fully intended and thought to have been fulfilled? "I dare appeal to the greatest masters of reason and good sense to judge."

[1] Surely! "such a commission is valid." It is an absolute impossibility that the person to whom it is addressed should execute it, that is the only difficulty; the commission is valid enough.

with in the *Holy Scriptures*, wherein He has revealed to us what is His will and pleasure. Upon which account Mr. W.'s *point*, which he thinks *well settled*, is at the best but precarious, or rather evidently false, having neither *Scripture, reason*, nor *antiquity* to support it. It is the rule of the Church of England, as well as of S. Jerome, *Quicquid de scripturis sacris auctoritatem non habet, eadem facilitate contemnitur qua probatur*.[1]

21. Dr. Brett indeed alleges S. Paul for an instance to countenance this opinion,[f] whom he affirms to have been "validly ordained, before he was baptized, by CHRIST Himself, Who called him by a voice from heaven:" and that this was "the only ordination he received." But then he grants that that Apostle "did not execute his commission till after he was baptized." So that, whatever date the commission might bear, it is plain he could not use it till he was baptized, this being a fundamental qualification for it. Which observation, I think, destroys the inference he would make from this example, or rather turns it against him.

22. So our blessed LORD invested His Apostles with their commission[g] before His ascension. Which commission nevertheless was not to take place till they were "endued with power from on high,"[h] that is,

---

[1] The whole of this clause, word for word, is precisely the fundamental argument against belief in the validity of "Lay-baptism!" And the words quoted from S. Jerome, as expressing "the rule of the Church of England," express also the rule by which those who object to Lay-baptism desire to guide themselves.

---

[f] App. in Answer to Lord Bishop of Oxford, p. 111, &c.

[g] S. John xx. 21, 22, 23.
[h] S. Luke xxiv. 49.

"were baptized with the HOLY GHOST and with fire,"[i] as S. John the Baptist expresses it, and thereby qualified for the effectual discharge of their apostolical office.

23. And after all, that which this learned and reverend author takes for S. Paul's *only ordination*, I cannot conceive to be any ordination at all, or other than a declaration of the meaning and design of that miraculous light which he saw, and of our LORD's will and purpose concerning him, in answer to those questions of his, "Who art Thou, LORD?" and, "What wilt Thou have me to do?" To me it seems plain, that his solemn consecration to the apostolical function came afterwards, and is recorded Acts xiii. 2, 3. And if so, S. Paul is again so far from furnishing *a demonstrative argument* in favour of the cause which he is alleged for, that he is a noble instance against it.

24. As for the Doctor's objection, that in this case, "he would have been an Apostle by man, though not of man," contrary to the style he uses Gal. i. 1, I think S. Luke has effectually cleared that, 1st, by the history of his conversion, where we plainly see that his designation to the office was not *by man;* was not owing to any human or deputed authority, but to CHRIST Himself, Who declared it to him by a voice from heaven; and, 2dly, by the account he gives us of his consecration to that office by imposition of hands, which was also performed, not upon any human consultation or resolution concerning him, but by the immediate command of the HOLY GHOST;[k] so that upon these grounds he might well assert to himself the magnificent titles which he uses in the inscription of his

---

[i] S. Luke iii. 16. Acts ii. 3, 4.   [k] Acts xiii. 2.

Epistle to the Galatians, although he did receive imposition of hands from those who were his seniors in that office.

25. If it be replied, that he preached before he was thus consecrated by imposition of hands, I might answer from Dr. Brett,[1] that it was *an extraordinary case*, like divers others recorded in the New Testament, occurring in that age of miraculous and extraordinary dispensations, from which no conclusion can be drawn to affect us now, when the Church is settled, and we tied down to forms and methods of Divine appointment, handed to us through the several ages of Christianity.

26. But I rather choose to make use of Dr. Hammond's answer upon another occasion. The Socinians (his adversaries in that discourse[m]) asserted a right in the laity to exercise the sacerdotal function, especially in cases of necessity, and to prove it, pretended, "that those who were dispersed after the death of S. Stephen, were not ordained by any, and yet preached the doctrine of CHRIST." Dr. Hammond having refuted and exposed this last assertion of theirs, adds in the close, that supposing it true, that some of those who were then dispersed were not ordained, and yet nevertheless preached the Gospel, "yet of them these two things must be observed; 1st, that they were in a remarkable manner filled all with the HOLY GHOST, Acts iv. 31, which was certainly done to fit them for some extraordinary work, such as there follows, the speaking of the word of GOD with boldness. And for this they were as fully qualified by the descent of the HOLY GHOST

---

[1] App. in Answer to Lord Bishop of Oxford, p. 112.
[m] Discourse of the Imposition of Hands, &c. in his Letter of Resolution to Six Queries, sect. xciv.

upon them, and the effects thereof, speaking with tongues, or prophesying, or gifts of healing, as any are by imposition of the Apostles' hands pretended to be. And yet, 2dly, all that we find assumed by them is, divulging the Gospel wheresoever they came, chap. viii. 4, and xi. 19. And that liberty, where the Gospel is not yet known, we shall not deny to any." These are his words.

27. Now this was exactly S. Paul's case. He received the Holy Ghost at the same time with his Baptism, by the ministry of Ananias, Acts ix. 17. After this we find him preaching the Gospel, ver. 20. But we hear not of anything else that he did till after his consecration, recorded chap. xiii. 3. Then indeed he ordained elders, chap. xiv. 23, confirmed the disciples, chap. xix. 6, dispensed the sacraments, chap. xx. 7, and did everything that the other Apostles had power to do.

28. I have done at present with Dr. Brett. I am next to consider what the author of Lay-baptism Invalid offers out of the Old Testament in favour of this opinion.[n] He urges the similitude of circumstances betwixt a person uncircumcised and one unbaptized; and pretends, that as the want of circumcision during the forty years' abode of the Jewish Church in the wilderness, did not vacate the ministry of those priests and Levites who were born in that time; so neither can the want of Baptism now vacate the ministrations of one that is consecrated to the Christian priesthood by episcopal hands.

29. I answer, 1st, it is well known that the Levitical priesthood was hereditary, that the posterity of Aaron

---

[n] App. to the first part of Lay-baptism Invalid, p. 137.

and the tribe of Levi were born with a right to the several branches and degrees of it, and therefore might in a large sense be called priests before their actual consecration, or even their circumcision, being from their birth designed for the priesthood. Now, admitting it true, that some of these had, even before they were circumcised, been allowed by GOD to exercise their sacerdotal function, it will prove nothing more than this, that GOD, Who hath formerly ratified the ministrations of an uncircumcised Levite, (designed for, though as yet not initiated in, the priesthood,) may still dispense with His own institutions when He pleases, (though we must not,) and ratify things transacted in His Name by persons unbaptized, who (continuing such) are incapable of an ordinary call to the priesthood. But that He actually does so, it is presumption in us to imagine, without a Divine warrant signifying His will and pleasure.¹

30. But, 2dly, this suggestion of Mr. L.'s supposes for truth, what I take to be evidently false, viz., that some who by birth were entitled to the priesthood in the Jewish Church, acted in that capacity before they were circumcised. For what need was there of this? There were priests enough to do it without *them;* persons regularly circumcised and consecrated to the

---

¹ Well may Waterland wonder (vide p. 222) at this argument from one who is pleading for the certain validity of Lay-baptisms. "GOD *may* dispense with His own institutions when He pleases (*though we must not*,") He *may* "ratify things transacted in His Name by persons" unauthorized so to do . . . "But that He actually does so, it is presumption in us to imagine, without a Divine warrant signifying His will and pleasure." Most true, but what becomes of the "imagination" that GOD will "ratify" Lay-baptism?

office. For the proof whereof, I desire three things may be considered:

31. 1st, That Aaron himself died but a few days before they entered into the land of Canaan, Num. xxxiii. 38, who had to assist him, Eleazar, Phinehas, Ithamar, &c.

32. 2dly, That not only Eleazar, Phinehas, Ithamar, &c., but (for aught that appears to the contrary) such in general of the tribe of Levi as came out of Egypt, and were afterwards consecrated to the priesthood, lived to come into the land of Canaan. I expect here to be told, that they all perished in the wilderness, by the sentence passed upon them, Num. xiv. 23. But Joshua v. 4, 6, tells us, they were only the *men of war* who so perished. And the sentence itself, as it is repeated and explained, Num. xiv. 29, affects those only who had been numbered from *twenty years old* and upwards, plainly referring to the account taken, chap. i. where the tribe of Levi is left out, nor so much as mentioned till ver. 47, where we are told that the Levites were not numbered among them. And accordingly Dr. Hammond, in his paraphrase on Ps. xc. 10, mentions those men of war, who were condemned to die in the wilderness, under the exact number of 603,550, which is the sum total recited, Num. i. 46, without including the tribe of Levi. The numbers of the Levites are taken afterwards by themselves, from *one month* old upwards, Num. iii. 15. So that to me it seems very plain, that the sentence declared chap. xiv. 29, does not include the tribe of Levi; and consequently that the Jewish Church might, at their arrival in the land of Canaan, have many priests among them, who were not born during their abode in the wilderness. Since my writing this, I find myself confirmed in this

conjecture by two eminent commentators, besides Dr. Hammond, viz., Corn. à Lapide in Numbers xiv. 29, and Masius in Josh. xxiv. 4.

33. I am aware, in the mean while, that in the twenty-sixth chapter, after the recital, not only of the twelve tribes, (who are there again numbered from twenty years old and upwards, ver. 2,) but of the Levites too, (who likewise, as before, are again numbered from one month old and upward, ver. 62,) it is expressly said, ver. 64, 65, "Among these there was not a man of them whom Moses and Aaron the priest numbered, when they numbered the children of Israel in the wilderness of Sinai. For the LORD had said of them, They shall surely die in the wilderness. And there was not left a man of them, save Caleb, the son of Jephunneh, and Joshua the son of Nun."

34. But that this remark of the sacred historian must relate only to the twelve tribes, and not to that of Levi, is still plain, (I will not say from Moses himself being still alive, who was of this tribe, and makes this remark, but) from Eleazar's living some years after the Israelites were settled in Palestine, who was born long before their departure out of Egypt, being then at man's estate, and consecrated to the priesthood at the same time that his father Aaron himself was, Exodus xxviii. 1, Lev. viii. and chap. x. 6. And the same answer I give to any objection that may seem to offer itself from Num. xxxii. 11.

35. 3dly, Suppose our evidence of the tribe of Levi's exemption from the general sentence passed upon the Israelites were less than it is, yet it is certain from Num. xiv. 29, that none of any tribe under twenty years were concerned in it. Which space of time affords room enough for a sufficient number of priests

of the tribe of Levi, who had been born and circumcised in Egypt, being grown up, to supply the places of those who died in the wilderness; and consequently takes away all pretence of a necessity for Levites *uncircumcised* to minister in that office.

36. It appears therefore, that Mr. L.'s scripture argument for the validity of holy orders conferred upon an unbaptized person, is grounded upon a case altogether fictitious and imaginary, and therefore proves nothing but a great want of better arguments. And in truth, it seems at first sight a wild imagination to fancy, that, when GOD would not permit any of the sons of Aaron, who had a blemish upon his body, to officiate or come nigh to the altar, Lev. xxi. 23, (whom nevertheless He suffered to eat the holy bread, ver. 22,) He should yet suffer any to exercise the office of Priest who was uncircumcised, and consequently under an incapacity of so much as eating the passover, Exodus xii. 48.

37. And now I shall leave this argument with one observation of my own from Scripture relating to this matter, viz. that S. Paul in his discourses 1 Cor. xii. and Ephes. iv. pressing the duty of peace, unity, and charity, so speaks in both places of the Christian Clergy, as supposing them of course to be members of the Church or Body of CHRIST, (which no unbaptized person is,) this seeming a fundamental qualification for the character they were adorned with. He arms the laity against all suggestions of envy, repining, or discontent, upon account of preference or superiority of one above another, with this consideration, that they, as well as their Bishops and other ministers, are members of the same body, partakers of one and the same spirit, candidates of the same hope of their calling, initiated by

the same sacrament of Baptism, &c. This is enough, considering that no instance of an unbaptized priest is recorded to have happened, much less to have been approved or ratified by the Church in all the ages of Christianity; I say, this is enough to inform us what qualifications the Church, the Apostle, and especially the HOLY GHOST, Who guided his pen, did expect and require in a minister of the Gospel.

38. So that, upon the whole, I am still of opinion, that this *point* of the validity of holy orders, conferred upon an unbaptized receiver, is not *well settled*, and am strongly inclined to despair that it ever will. And till it be, I cannot see how the modern invalidators of Lay-baptism can avoid the consequences before recited, so destructive to the succession of the Christian priesthood, and consequently to the very being of the Church and of the sacraments, supposing at present, what by-and-by will be but too easily proved, that Baptism by lay-hands hath so far been allowed and owned as sufficient for the ends of Baptism, as not to need repeating, in the primitive as well as modern ages of Christianity.

39. You see, Sir, I do not concern myself with the case of the foreign Reformed, of whom we are told the Calvinists and Zuinglians have espoused the principle [94] of the invalidity of Lay-baptism, going herein further than Calvin probably intended, and directly contrary to Zuinglius. What they will *thank us* for granting, I matter not, nor does it concern the question. The Church of England seems to have determined their case, allowing their Baptism to be valid, their Orders not. For she receives them to Lay-communion without rebaptization, but not into her priesthood without reordination. All my request concerning them is, that

(after her example) seeing, by command from our ecclesiastical superiors, we have often prayed for them by the title of the Reformed Churches, we would allow them as good a right to that appellation, as (in the defect of other administrations) a valid Christian Baptism can confer upon them. Which though administered by lay-hands, Mr. L. himself seems now and then to admit in cases of extreme necessity, when not done in defiance of the episcopal divine authority. Such among them is the case of all persons, especially of inferior quality, who are forced so to receive that sacrament, or not to have it at all.

40. I know not what Mr. W. intends by his mentioning the *act of toleration* and the *French Refugees*. I presume it is no advantage to his cause, that the Church of England at this day receives all those Refugees, who conform to her doctrine, into her communion, and some of them to holy orders too, without insisting upon a rebaptization. But her judgment of this matter we shall have further occasion to speak of by-and-by.

II.

1. As to Scripture, Mr. W. tells us, "it is confessed, that it confines the administration of Baptism to the Clergy." I suppose the scripture he intends is the commission to baptize, recorded S. Matt. xxviii. 19, 20. "Go ye," &c. And if he means, that Apostles and their successors alone are the ordinary regular dispensers of it, I agree with him. But if his meaning be, that the effects of Baptism are by the words of the commission made to depend in all cases upon the administrator's being in holy orders, I know not who those are that *confess* this, unless Mr. Lawrence and

his followers.[1] I believe it will appear, that the ancients, (such of them as speak to the point,) Optatus Milevitanus, S. Gregory Nazianzen, and others, are of a different opinion.

2. Calvin indeed, in his letter to the Protestants of Mompelgard, argues in this manner; "Quibus enim, obsecro, dictum est, Ite, baptizate, nisi his quibus data jam erat docendi potestas et munus commissum?" And from him the English Puritans (who were his great admirers in the days of Queen Elizabeth) imbibed their notion of the invalidity of Lay-baptism, as they did their other beloved notion of the non-necessity of that sacrament.

3. And yet Calvin was not absolutely for rebaptizing all that had been baptized by lay-hands. In one of his letters (dated Nov. 13th, 1561) he has indeed these words; "Adulterinum Baptismum censemus, qui administratus est a privato homine." But in the same letter he adds, that in respect of the particular state of religion at that time among them to whom he writes, "Non tantum errori danda est venia, sed ferendus est qualiscunque Baptismus." The error he speaks of relates to the Lay-administration of that sacrament. He concludes with condemning, and advising them absolutely to condemn, all Baptisms administered by women, for which he quotes the Council of Carthage. "Deinde," says he, "quia veteri Decreto Concilii Carthaginensis prohibitæ sunt fœminæ ab officio baptizandi, neminem offendet novitas, quæ metuenda ooooct in viris." It seems, in his opinion, Baptism administered by *laymen* had the countenance of antiquity, so far as to be reputed valid; for which reason he cautions them against

---

[1] Vide note 1, p. 3, on Waterland's meaning, p. 76.

the scandal that would attend the repeating of it, which he thought the world could not but look upon as an innovation. Upon the whole, it is very plain that Calvin did not look upon the minister to be of the *essence* of the sacrament; for whatsoever is that, must not be dispensed with upon any considerations whatsoever.

4. So that, for aught I perceive, Mr. W., Mr. L., and their friends, are the first that have so rigidly expounded the commission, as to make the *ye*, the persons to whom it was delivered, *essential* to everything transacted by it. Now the *novelty* of their interpretation is alone a just objection against it.[1] But it is well, if it does not hurt their own cause, as much as it

---

[1] It is perhaps a little bold to speak of "the novelty" of an "interpretation" (i.e., that of Waterland and Lawrence: not Kelsall's travesty of it,) which, whether it be right, or wrong is at least as old as S. Cyprian, and which he speaks of as being the accepted tradition of the Church in past ages.

"We put forth our opinion," he says, "not as a new one, but we join with you in equal agreement in an opinion long since decreed by our predecessors, and observed by us—judging, namely, and holding it for certain that no one can be baptized abroad, outside the Church, since there is one Baptism appointed in the Holy Church." (Epistle 70, ad Januarium, cap. 1.)

"This Baptism (i.e., the baptism of heretics) we cannot consider as valid, or legitimate, since it is manifestly unlawful." (Epistle 72, ad Julianum, cap. 1.)

Moreover it may be noted that this favourite argument of the supporters of Lay-baptism, if it were worth anything, would dispose of the necessity of the appointed "matter and form" just as easily as it is thought to dispose of the necessity of the appointed minister. "True," they say, "the commission to baptize was given only to the Apostles and their successors: but no other persons were expressly forbidden to baptize. Therefore all other persons are at liberty to baptize

will ours. It ought to have been considered that the words, "Go ye," &c. were spoken to *Apostles* only, and their *successors*, viz., the *Bishops* of the Church. And if the minister be *essential*, then none but such, none but Apostles and Bishops, neither Deacon, Priest, nor laic, must baptize. Thus, though the primitive Church did not make the minister *essential*, yet they thought the office so firmly tied to the episcopal chair, that no man could regularly baptize without leave from thence; and accordingly would not ordinarily suffer either a Presbyter or a Deacon to administer this sacrament in the presence of a Bishop; even by the same rule, as all succeeding ages have forbidden laics to do it, when a lawful minister can be had. It is true, in the New Testament we hear of Deacons baptizing, but that was when no Apostle or Bishop was present; and only furnishes us with a precedent, that upon some emergencies others may *validly* baptize, besides those to whom the commission so to do was first given.

5. Sir, with submission to better judgments, I rather take the commission to be a conveyance of power to the Apostles and Bishops, the spiritual governors of the Church, not only to receive the converted world into the Church, by baptizing them with water in the Name of the Trinity, but also to appoint the ministers of that rite, not only Presbyters and Deacons, but

96

just as well as the Apostles, or their successors." If so, then we may argue with equal justice that we are indeed commissioned to baptize with water in the Name of the Holy Trinity; but we are nowhere "expressly forbidden" to use any other "matter, or form." Therefore we are at liberty to use any other "matter, or form" just as well as water and the Holy Name. If the argument holds in one case, it holds just as well in the other.

(where these cannot be had) even laics too,[1] and moreover to be the sole and supreme judges in case of any irregular or disputed Baptism, to annul it, or to receive it as valid, and all this under no other restraint or limitation, but what the analogy of faith, the needs of the Church, and their own discretion shall impose upon them. And this, with a promise from our LORD to ratify what they shall jointly decree in matters of that nature; "Lo, I am with you," &c., and, "Whatsoever ye shall bind on earth shall be bound in heaven; and whatsoever ye shall loose on earth shall be loosed in heaven."

6. This, I think, Mr. Bingham has in the main proved for me, in the second and third sections of the first part of his Scholastical History of Lay-baptism. To this account may be referred those passages quoted by our adversaries from S. Ignatius and others who wrote in the infancy of the Church, in which the dispensing of the sacraments, and other branches of the ecclesiastical power, are lodged solely in the Bishop. And in the same sense we may well understand S. Chrysostom, when he affirms, that "these things are administered only by those sacred hands, the hands he means of the Bishop,"[o] whom he calls ἱερεὺς, as the

---

[1] There is not the least hint in Scripture that "the commission" did mean this, nor that any one of the Apostles so understood it. But supposing this commission did empower "Apostles and Bishops" to "appoint" any persons, "even laics," to be "the ministers" of Baptism, this will not prove the validity of baptisms ministered by persons whom no Apostle, or Bishop ever did "appoint," who even deny the value, and openly reject the need of any such appointment. Vide pp. 144, 145.

---

[o] Τῶν τοῦ ἱερέως λέγω. Vide infra.

Latins called him *sacerdos*. And to the same purpose Tertullian, Jerome, Isidore of Seville, and others speak, as we shall see by-and-by; of whom howsoever they might lodge the right of administration originally in the Bishop, yet not one made the minister (as some moderns have done) *essential* to the sacrament.

7. This power the Bishops of the primitive Church did put in practice. The same power the Bishops of the Reformed Church of England did ever claim, have ever used,[1] not finding themselves confined or abridged in the use of it by any general Council: sometimes allowing laymen to baptize in case of necessity; at other times obliging their people to call in a lawful minister on those occasions; never declaring Lay-baptism null, but (in conformity to the practice of the primitive Church) taking always more care of the matter and form, than of the minister of the sacrament.

8. This, Sir, at present is my opinion. And I do

---

[1] We must pause at this. "This power," of which Kelsall has just spoken, is the power to appoint laics to be ministers of Baptism. But when, or where, either in "the Primitive Church," or "the Reformed Church of England," did any Bishop ever thus "appoint" any laic to baptize? And if no Bishop, in any age, or any country, ever did attempt to do this, (in spite of the obvious convenience very often of such an arrangement) it seems only reasonable to conclude (exactly reversing what Mr. Kelsall here asserts) that the Bishops did never claim, and have never used this power, for the simple reason that they never supposed themselves to possess such a power.

That many Bishops not in "the Primitive Church," but after the time of S. Augustine, and many English Bishops have admitted the validity, more or less, of Lay-baptism is a well known fact; but they have done so not on the ground that they had "appointed" this, or that laic to baptize, but on the ground that no such appointment was required.

not yet see, that I hereby carry the power of the Church or of her Prelates *higher* in this than it ever was in the dispensation of the other sacrament, which was never yet (and, I hope, will not now begin to be) thought a grievance by the true sons of the Church, so long as there was no mutilation, nor any error committed in *essentials*. I mean no more than what Dr. Cave gives an account of in his Primitive Christian. part i. chap. 11, where he says, the Eucharist was wont to be sent home to those, who could not be present at the public service, by the hands of a Deacon, or, in cases of necessity, by any other person. He instances in the story of Serapion, to whom the Priest, who kept it ready consecrated by him, being himself sick, and unable to visit him, sent it by the hands of a little boy, (the historian Eusebius calls him παιδάριον,) who, as he had been instructed by the priest, put it into the old man's mouth a little before he expired. The story is in Euseb. Hist. Eccles. lib. vi. cap. 44. This was certainly as large a stretch of power, and as great a variation from the primitive institution, as the permission of Lay-baptism can well be imagined, and yet not unusual in that age.[1]

[1] To this curious misconception it is obvious to reply that the parallel to Lay-baptism, in "the other sacrament" is Lay-consecration of the Holy Eucharist, and if the "stretch of power" has been "as large," and only as large, in regard to each one of the two great Sacraments, then we must hear of the Church appointing a layman to celebrate the Holy Eucharist, before any parity of reasoning can be alleged in support of Lay-baptism. Indeed, if the position taken by the modern advocates of Lay-baptism is to be sustained, we must have the Church recognizing the validity of "Eucharists" celebrated by any person whatsoever, whether he, or she has been in any

9. I add, that if the account here offered (of the commission, "Go ye," &c.,) be true, it seems to me extremely to alter the whole nature of our dispute;[1] and to make the question of Lay-baptism a question only of discipline, not of doctrine. And then our superiors may admit a Baptism irregularly administered by a lay-usurper as *valid*, if they please, at the same time that they censure his presumption in so acting; or, if [98] they think fit, they may refuse to ratify such Baptisms, and order a readministration, without censuring what former ages or other churches have done, and consequently without bringing themselves or the Church under those inconvenient and indeed ruinous consequences, which have been shown to be inevitable, and to lie very heavy on Mr. W.'s side of the question, whilst it is looked upon as matter of doctrine. For doctrines are sullen things, and admit no alteration or abatement for the sake of any inconveniences, how great soever. But discipline is variable, and has been changed, and may be so again, as the circumstances and necessities of the Church shall require.

10. But let us hear what Mr. W.'s judgment of the

way appointed, or not, provided only that he, or she, uses bread and wine and the proper words of consecration! Yet one almost shrinks from putting such an idea into words. Waterland has replied at length to this parallel, p. 148.

[1] No doubt it does so: and the attempt (however unsuccessful) to "make the question of Lay-baptism a question only of discipline, not of doctrine," seems to betray a consciousness that if it be clearly seen that the question is "one of doctrine," then it will be a hard matter to defend Lay-baptism: and yet what could be more distinctly doctrinal than the question, What is essential to the due administration of a sacrament?

commission is. He says, "It leaves no more room for Lay-baptism, than for Lay-ordination, Lay-absolution, Lay-consecration of the Eucharist, Lay-preaching and praying;" and adds, that "If we go from the institution in one case, we may as reasonably do it in all, supposing the like necessity." But I deny, that admitting the Baptism of a layman, under the qualifications foregoing, as "valid, is going from the institution." Besides, the like necessity cannot be supposed in the instances he alleges. For neither ordination, nor absolution, nor the Eucharist, are so universally nor so absolutely necessary to salvation, as Baptism is declared to be.[p] What he means by "Lay-preaching and praying" in this place, I do not well know. I presume he will not forbid lay Christians to pray together in public in those countries, (supposing there be such,) where there are no Clergy, nor any possibility of procuring a Clergy to do it for them: and where there are, there is not *the like necessity*. And so for *Lay-preaching*. Shall a lay Christian, in a savage infidel nation, think it unlawful for him to publish the Gospel among such people? Who ever blamed the captive maid of Iberia for attempting the conversion of that nation, which she happily effected by her divulging the Gospel, and by the miracles which GOD enabled her to work on that occasion? Who ever found fault with Frumentius, a Christian layman, for the like attempt in the Indies? Both these did indeed take care by their counsels and endeavours to have in due time a regular Clergy settled in those countries. But till that could be done, necessity, which has no law, justified what they did.

11. With submission, I think he (as well as the

---

[p] S. John iii. 5.

author of Lay-baptism Invalid) mistakes the case of Saul and Uzza, whom he produces as instances of GOD's displeasure for meddling with the priesthood, although in extraordinary emergencies. It does not appear to me that Saul usurped the sacerdotal office. For the sacrifices he offered were done indeed *by his order*, and in that sense he may be said to be the doer of them: but they were done by the ministry of the priests, who were there present, say the learned, being by their office (a competent number of them) constant attendants upon the army. Num. x. 9; Deut. xx. 2; 1 Sam. xiv. 18, 19, 36. But his crime was his impatience and distrust of the Divine Providence, which prevailed with him to violate the orders given him to wait till Samuel came, 1 Sam. x. 8, who, had he been there, was not qualified with his own hands to have offered sacrifice, being himself no priest, but a Levite, 1 Chron. vi. 33; Psalm xcix. 6; on which account, whenever we hear of Samuel's offering sacrifices, we must understand no more than that he, being a prophet, a judge, and eminent magistrate in the government, caused or ordered it to be done by the proper minister, and was the chief person present at the solemnity.

12. Neither do I think Uzza to have been an usurper of the priesthood. He was a Levite, and probably a Cohathite. Which order was appointed to *carry* the ark of GOD themselves, not (like Philistines) to put it into a cart. So that, whatever danger the ark might seem to be in, it was a danger occasioned through their neglect and omission of their duty. But the same law which required them to carry it themselves, required them so to carry it *upon staves* as not to touch it, Num. iv. 15, death being the penalty threatened in case they did. Which penalty accordingly Uzza suf-

fered for his *rashness,* rather than *usurpation* or *ambition* of an office that did not belong to him.

13. In the mean time, the question among us is not whether lay persons may lawfully baptize, much less exercise other parts of the sacerdotal office. So far am I from affirming any such thing, that I believe, whatever pretence they may have, so much as to baptize even in cases of utmost necessity, depends altogether upon the will of their ecclesiastical superiors,[1] who may allow or disallow it, as they see cause, being a matter wherein the discipline rather than doctrine of the Church is concerned, as I said before. But to presume to do it in ordinary cases, in defiance of the Christian priesthood, as our schismatical Lay-preachers do, is what we all readily agree, there is no more ground for in Scripture, than there is for *Lay-ordination, Lay-absolution,* &c. Concerning such usurpers, Mr. W. and we are all of the same opinion: and, were there room or leisure for it, or were it pertinent to my design, I should willingly join with him in treating such acts of sacrilegious impiety and presumption with all the

---

[1] This is a startling assertion, and certainly if it be true, Lay-baptism differs from Christian Baptism in one vital particular. The power and authority of a priest to baptize, or to minister any other Christian Sacrament, depends altogether on the institution of CHRIST. But the "pretence" of laymen to baptize "depends altogether" so we are here told, "upon the will of their ecclesiastical superiors!" A weighty difference surely: one a true Sacrament of the Gospel, "ordained by CHRIST Himself:" the other a ceremony which "ecclesiastical superiors" are supposed to have authorized! And yet this is a difference pointed out by a writer, who wishes us to admit that one sort of Baptism is, for all its high and mysterious ends, as good as the other.

severity of language he can desire. All that we insist upon is, (as he very truly observes,) that a Baptism administered (though by a lay Christian,) with water in the Name of the blessed Trinity is *valid to the recipient*,[1] howsoever criminal it may be in the administrator. To which purpose some have (not amiss) applied the maxim, *quod fieri non debuit factum valet*. Others, I perceive, allege the case of a marriage solemnized by a person not ordained, as parallel to this, and apply

---

[1] It is difficult to see what Mr. Kelsall, (and others who use the same phrase) mean by speaking of Lay-baptism as "*valid to the recipient*," as if baptism of any sort could ever be "valid" to any one else except "the recipient!" This, he says, is "all that we insist upon," as if this were not the kernel of the whole matter! It would seem, from much that has been written on this subject, that the validity of baptism is treated as if it were some technical matter, which, if not quite correctly done at the time, could be set right afterwards. But in truth the question whether any baptism is "valid" or not, is tantamount to the question whether the person, so baptized, did, or did not, then and there receive "remission of sins" and "a new birth unto righteousness." These are definite spiritual acts, which were either done, or not done, then and there, and nothing which occurs subsequently can possibly alter the fact one way, or the other. In the natural world it would be evidently unmeaning to speak of "making" a child's birth "valid" some time after it was, or was supposed to have been born. The child either was born, or it was not born; and if, as a matter of fact it was not born, nothing done afterwards by other persons could conceivably "remedy" or "set right" that primary defect. In the spiritual world is it any the less unreasonable, and really unmeaning to speak of "remedying" or "setting right" a "defective" baptism? It would seem only possible to speak thus when we have forgotten what Baptism really is. (Vide Bingham's "Scholastic History of Lay-baptism." Part I., Chap. i. sec. 21.)

the maxim alike to both cases. Whether the parallel be in every respect just or not, I shall not take upon me to determine; only shall offer you my reasons why Mr. W.'s account of this matter gives me no satisfaction.

14. He begins with telling you, that "the maxim is true only of errors in circumstantials, not of errors in essentials." His distinction is very good, and touches the cases home, which he there puts, of polygamy and an incestuous marriage. But it will do him no service in the case before us, till it be proved, first, that the minister is *essential* in Baptism; secondly, that he is not equally so in marriage too. He does indeed affirm, that he is essential in the first, and but circumstantial in the other; that in the case of marriage it is *decent* that it be done by a Priest or a Deacon, that in Baptism it is *necessary*. But he barely *says* this: he tells us, in the case of Baptism, that "the commission is plain and clear, and leaves no more room for Lay-baptism, than for Lay-ordination," &c., and in the case of marriage, that "it is no more than a covenant between the two parties, that its essence is their mutual contract, and that the minister is a circumstance only." All this he *affirms*. But till some proof be offered for it besides his own affirmation, he will not take it amiss to be answered, as Tertullian, S. Austin, and others of great name have lately been answered, that "all this is only his own private opinion."[1]

---

[1] But is it true that "all this is *only* his private opinion?" or rather, does not this "all" include (1) some facts, plain and incontrovertible, e.g., that the commission to baptize was given to the Apostles, and was not given to any one else, and (2) some theories generally accepted by the learned, e.g., that the essence of the marriage rite consists in "the mutual contract" of the man and the woman?

15. In the mean time, if this be so, if marriage be no more than "a covenant between the two parties, if its essence be their mutual contract, and the minister but a circumstance;" then I cannot see, but the pretended marriages of the Quakers are as *valid* as ours, though not so *decent* and regular. They have the essence, the covenant, and mutual contract between the two parties. And their want of the minister is only an *error in circumstantials*, which, howsoever it may affect the *decency* and regularity of the thing, cannot render it *invalid* or *null*. And then, why does not our Church receive and own such a marriage? What need the civil legislature, whenever they have occasion in any act of parliament to speak of such pretended marriages, always to subjoin a proviso, that nothing in that act shall extend or be construed so as to declare them good? And what need the Quakers, more than others, be so careful not to die intestate, but that they know, without a will the law will not suffer their children to inherit, as looking upon them to be illegitimate?[1]

16. And those, who, under Cromwell's usurpation, being not content with having been joined together in a pretended marriage by the civil magistrate, were desirous to have a minister do that work for them again, desired this, I am inclined to think, not merely upon secular considerations, to rescue their children from

[1] In this passage Kelsall confounds what is "valid" with what is "legal." A marriage may be "valid" morally, i.e., it may be a binding contract, which justifies the man and the woman in living together as man and wife, and it may have all the sanction which the rites of the Church can give to it; and yet it may be—as in Italy at the present time it would be—not "legal;" and the offspring of such a marriage would be illegitimate.

the disgrace and inconveniences attending an illegitimate issue, (which they had cause enough to fear, in case the royal family should ever come to be restored,) but especially to satisfy their own consciences that they were really married, and consequently that their cohabitation as man and wife was lawful.

17. I ever thought, that in every vow or promissory oath which we make to one another, GOD had become a party as well as we, being called in, not only as a witness, but as a judge too, a revenger if we violate our vow: and consequently, that in marriage, (an act of religion of Divine institution, and a most solemn vow,) there had been, besides *the two parties contracting*, a third party also, even the author of marriage, the GOD Who calls Himself Love, Who appears there by His minister, His representative, proxy, and commissioner, to ratify and complete the whole transaction, as well as to give His blessing to it. This to me appears very plain from the institution itself, from GOD's owning it to be *His* act, Mal. ii. 15, from the nature of religious actions in general, and from our own rubrics and form of matrimony prescribed in our most excellent Liturgy. In this sense, I presume, it is GOD Who receives the woman at the hands of her father or other friend, and disposes of her where she is designed, in allusion to Prov. xix. 14. And more plainly, when the man and the woman have performed their share of the solemnity, GOD, by the hands and mouth of His Priest who represents Him, completes the whole action by joining their hands together, proclaiming it to be His own act, ("Those whom GOD hath joined together," says the Priest who acts in His name, "let no man put asunder,") and then declaring them to be "man and wife together." Which declaration the Priest makes

The parallel of Marriage.   49

"in the Name of the FATHER, and of the SON, and of the HOLY GHOST." And here it is that the conjugal relation begins: now they commence man and wife, and from henceforward in the remaining part of the office they are so styled, which they were not before, all the former part being only preparatory to this. So that to me the essence of the marriage seems to consist in this last act of the Priest's joining both together, and declaring them to be man and wife in the Name of the blessed Trinity: unless you would rather have it consist in the joint concurrence of all the three parties acting in it, which I shall not dispute with you.

18. It is plain, through the whole solemnity the minister acts "for GOD and in GOD's Name, which," Mr. W. says, "none can do without commission from Him." From which account of marriage, I flatter myself that I have gained the point I aimed at, and proved, that the Priest is at least as *necessary* in marriage, as he is in Baptism; or that, if he is but *circumstantial* in that, he is not *essential* in this; and consequently, that in respect of a layman's acting instead of the Priest, the maxim, *quod fieri non debuit*, &c., will hold as well in Baptism, as it will in marriage. For in both GOD is alike represented by him that ministers; and if, when a layman usurps the office in one, even Mr. W. being judge, the act shall nevertheless be *valid*, I see no reason at all why it should not in the other too.

19. The only thing that can be alleged here is,[1] that there is an express commission ("Go ye," &c.) granted

---

[1] If the matter in hand were not grave, there would be something comical in the simplicity of this admission, which in reality entirely upsets Kelsall's argument at one touch. "*The only thing* that can be alleged" to prove the difference

50   "*All acts of Religion*" *not alike.*

only to the Apostles and their successors to baptize, which cannot be said of marriage.

20. But not to repeat what has been said already concerning this matter, I think this objection will still admit of a twofold answer.

21. 1st, That the *general* commission given to the Apostles and their successors, (viz. to the whole Christian priesthood,) to represent Almighty GOD, and to act in His Name in His several transactions with mankind, reaches to *all* acts of religion, and consequently to the solemnization of marriage too, and thereby makes marriage and Baptism equal, in respect of the pretended necessity of a lawful minister to the validity of the action.[1]

22. 2ndly. That so to interpret the baptismal com-

between these two cases being "that there is an express commission" from GOD Himself in one case, and not in the other! As if anything more were necessary to prove the difference!

[1] But if this argument were sound, then not only "marriage and Baptism" but also "all acts of religion" would be "equal in respect of the pretended necessity of a lawful minister." There would be no difference between celebrating the Holy Eucharist, and saying one's own private prayers, no difference between ordaining priests, and teaching in a Sunday school; all are equally "acts of religion;" all equally would require the hand of "a lawful minister."

But who does not see the error of Kelsall's assertion that the "commission, given to the Apostles," "reaches to all acts of religion?" There are innumerable "acts of religion" which do not require any commission; and the whole dispute about Lay-baptism turns on the question whether Baptism is one of those "acts of religion" for which such a divine commission is required, or not. Simply to assume that "all acts of religion" are "equal" in this respect is to beg the question at issue; and moreover it is manifestly contrary to the fundamental principles of the Catholic Church.

mission as to make the minister *essential* to true Baptism, is to teach a doctrine which is altogether new, is countenanced by none of the ancient Fathers, is contradicted by some, is disclaimed by the known practice of the primitive Church, and ought therefore to be rejected by us.[1]

23. This ought not to be said without proof, which is to appear by-and-by. In the mean time, Holy Scripture suggests something further in relation to this matter, from the parallel case of circumcision, a parallel more just and nearer akin to the subject of our dispute than that of marriage was.

24. If the administration of the sacrament of circumcision[2] was *not restrained* by the institution to the priesthood, as Mr. L. suggests, (Lay-baptism Invalid, part i. p. 104,) but left in common to such of the Jewish laymen as had skill and dexterity enough to perform it, as is the general opinion ; then we have an instance from

---

[1] If the four historical assertions contained in this brief paragraph were true, then obviously there could be no reasonable dispute about Lay-baptism : but every one of these assertions, except perhaps the third, is false, and has been proved to be false again and again in the course of this controversy.

[2] Why Kelsall calls circumcision a "sacrament" it would be hard to say, unless it be for the purpose (in which he may often have been successful) of confusing his readers in their consideration of this supposed parallel between circumcision and Baptism. The essence of a Sacrament is that it has "an inward and spiritual grace," as well as "an outward and visible sign." Circumcision (so far as we are informed by Holy Scripture) had no "inward and spiritual grace ;" therefore it was not a "sacrament," and the dispute whether it could, or could not be rightly performed by a lay person, has no bearing on a similar question with regard to Baptism.

Scripture of a sacrament esteemed even in *ordinary* cases to be *regularly* administered by lay-hands. And seeing the Christian sacrament of Baptism is, if not more, certainly not less necessary to salvation than circumcision was, John iii. 5, seeing Baptism and circumcision have both the very same spiritual intendment and mystical signification, and are in a manner the same in substance, conveying the same grace, sealing the same covenant, Rom. iv. 11, and Col. ii. 11, and differing only in the rite of administration; we want a reason why Baptism may not in like manner be *validly* at least administered by the laity in cases *extraordinary*, where a lawful dispenser of the sacrament cannot be had. Sir, I shall (till better evidence appear) presume to affirm, that there is no appearance of any ground for this difference between the one and the other in the reason and nature of the two ceremonies; nor any real foundation for it in Scripture interpreted, as it ought to be, by the judgment and practice of antiquity, and of the Catholic Church in all ages.

25. But if the dispensing of that Jewish sacrament *was confined to the priesthood*, it is nevertheless plain, from the instance of Zipporah circumcising her own child, Exod. iv. 24, 25, 26, that cases of necessity were excepted. It is pleasant here to observe, how Mr. L. in considering this case, gives up all his principles at once. He says, upon supposition, that "circumcision was to be performed by the master, as he was the priest of his family; yet it does not follow that Zipporah did anything more than what she had a right to do; because her *husband's authority* was devolved upon her in his sickness, when he was unable to do it himself;—that he might *order* his wife to do it in his stead, and consequently it was interpretatively done by himself, be-

cause by his authority," &c. These are very remarkable words; and I hope he will not hereafter blame us, although we should say, that in cases of extreme necessity, when the Priest is absent, or (if present) under a natural incapacity, his power may *devolve* upon a *woman;* that in such cases he (much more the Church) may *order* those (even *women*) to dispense a sacrament, who have no authority so to do by the institution; and that, what such substitutes do in pursuance of those orders, is *by interpretation his* act, or rather the act of the Church from whom they received their deputation. I think, all this follows plainly from Mr. L.'s own concessions.

26. But the Calvinist writers have treated Zipporah very coarsely,[q] and passed hard censures upon her on this account. They have styled her, *stulta et iracunda mulier*, and fear not to deny that GOD approved what she did. Calvin, and our countryman Cartwright,[r] labour to aggravate her pretended crime as much as possible; and will not allow the event to be a sufficient declaration that the act pleased GOD. Zanchy observes, that the angel was appeased,[s] "because the child was circumcised, not because it was she that did it." In which words he gives us all that we need to insist upon in the question: "For seeing our adversaries," to use Mr. Hooker's words on this occasion, "are not able to deny, but circumcision, being in that very manner performed, was to the innocent child which received it true circumcision; why should that defect, whereby

---

[q] Calv. Inst. lib. iv. cap. 15, sect. 22. Jun. et Trem. in locum. H. Zanch. Expl. cap. v. Ep. ad Eph. loc. de Bapt. cap. 4, 11, 17. Wendelin. Christ. Theol. lib. i. cap. 22, thes. 8.

[r] Quoted by Hooker, Eccles. Pol. book v. note 62.

[s] Placatus fuit angelus: verum quod fuerit circumcisus puer, non quod illa circumciderit. *Zanch. in loco supra citato.*

circumcision was so little weakened, be to Baptism a deadly wound?"

27. And here it will not be unseasonable to add the observation of a learned writer well versed in the Jewish customs.[t] He says, that a Christian, being himself uncircumcised, is therefore not admitted among the Jews to circumcise an infant: but adds, that, if such a thing should nevertheless at any time happen, they do not esteem a circumcision so administered to be invalid, but reckon such a child truly circumcised, and justify themselves by a proverbial maxim, *quod factum factum*, exactly answerable to ours, *quod fieri non debet, factum valet*.

28. As I am writing this part of my letter, another instance of a *female* administration of this rite occurs to me, which I should have placed a little before, had I thought of it, and am not content yet to pass it by. It is in 1 Maccab. i. 63, in the original thus, Καὶ τὰς γυναῖκας τὰς περιτετμηκυίας τὰ τέκνα αὐτῶν ἐθανάτωσαν κατὰ τὸ πρόσταγμα.

29. I have done with the case of circumcision. But before I enter upon the third part of my design, there remain yet one or two particulars in this part of Mr. W.'s letter to be considered.

30. He argues from the nullity of subjects acting in the civil government without a competent authority, viz. "levying soldiers, naturalizing strangers," doing other things in the queen's name without order and warrant. I know not in what sense the levying of soldiers without authority can be said to be *null* and *void*. *Illegal* indeed it is, *criminal*, and penal in the highest degree. But concerning such actions in general, does the consequence hold from things secular

---

[t] J. Buxtorf. Synag. Jud. cap. iv.

and civil to sacred? Are the reasons the same in both? Because all grants, deputations, commissions, &c. from earthly princes to their subjects, and in general all human transactions, whereby we bind ourselves to each other, ought to appear genuine and voluntary, and must therefore pass under forms of law, to ascertain the rights of all parties concerned, and prevent the mischiefs which must otherwise accrue through fraud or forgery, will it follow, that we must not trust GOD Himself also without the like securities? GOD is not under the like necessity in the administration of Baptism, that mortal princes are in the administration of their earthly governments, to annul that which is done in His Name by an usurper of His authority.[1] I say, He is under no *necessity* to do this: much less to do it to

---

[1] Here again, as at p. 3, (76) there is a curiously perverse misconception of the position of those who are unable to believe the validity of Lay-baptism. No one ever said, or supposed that GOD was under any "necessity to annul" unauthorized baptism. An act which is *per se* and *ab initio* null and void does not require to be annulled: it is null already and never was anything else. What Lay-baptism wants is, not to be annulled, but to be made valid: and because GOD is "under no necessity" to make valid an act which He has never promised to make valid, therefore it is that we hold it a dangerous presumption to assume that GOD will do what He has not promised to do. Of course no reasonable believer would doubt that GOD can, if He chooses, give the inward grace of true Baptism together with the outward form of pseudo-baptism. So can He equally, if He chooses, give that inward grace without any outward form at all: but it would be a strange conclusion to infer from this that it is just the same thing whether a man is baptized, or unbaptized, because in either case equally GOD *can* give such a man any inward grace that He chooses to give.

106 the prejudice of an innocent person, a person incapable by his age of refusing or choosing the baptism of a schismatical usurper. Nay, where the receiver, by choosing or knowingly accepting a baptism so irregularly given, makes himself equally criminal with the giver, no man can prove, that he has not even in this case received the sacrament, that is, the outward part of it, which the Church never yet thought fit to be repeated, although he be still destitute of the grace of the sacrament by reason of the schismatical state and indisposition he lies under, rendering him at present incapable of it. Which incapacity his sincere repentance, absolution, and reconciliation to the communion of the Church will effectually remove, and perfect that which before was defective. But this can be the case only of adults, who are bound not only to demand the sacrament of Baptism as soon as they are qualified for it, but to demand it too of the proper minister, and in a regular manner. If an infant be baptized by improper hands, the guilt and all the consequences of it lie at their doors who were actors in it. The infant, having received the whole substance (the matter and form) of the sacrament, is as sure of the grace attending it, as all the promises of the New Testament can make him. Nor is it to be imagined, that he can miss the blessing purely for a defect that cannot be justly charged upon him, who was only passive in the administration.

31. I speak here more especially of such graces, blessings, and privileges attending this sacrament, as the infant is at present capable of possessing and reaping benefit from, during the state of infancy. In which state if he dies, I can by no means think it is all one to his future condition, whether he were baptized or not,

Infants dying after Baptism. 57

as some notions lately advanced would incline us to believe. We have been told, that the practice of Lay-baptism in cases of necessity was at first grounded upon an opinion, that that sacrament is of absolute necessity to the receiver. And what do they say to this? the Calvinists, and of late others, have been pleased to condemn this opinion, and brand it as superstitious, (though it prevailed almost universally in the Church in all former ages,) and have put a new, a loose, and uncertain construction upon those decretory words of our LORD, John iii. 5, that they might with the better grace object to the practice said to be grounded thereupon.

32. Now concerning the state of baptized persons dying in infancy, the Church affirms, with good authority, that they are undoubtedly saved: concerning others, the Church of England chooses to affirm nothing, rather than affirm without warrant, only excludes them from her office of Christian burial. S. Austin, that *hard Father* styled by some, affirms children, dying without Baptism, to be "in damnatione omnium mitissima,"[u] by which perhaps he might mean the punishment of loss rather than pain. But admitting that he meant the latter, that the good Father's zeal against the Pelagians carried him too far in this, and that infants dying without Baptism do not suffer any torments in the next world: does it necessarily follow from hence, that they are not losers by having gone unbaptized out of this? What if Mr. Dodwell's notion of the *immortalizing Spirit* conferred in Baptism be true? then every soul that departs without Baptism, not under the stain of actual sin, is (not miserable indeed, but) lost to all

---

[u] August. de Pecc. Meritis, lib. i. et passim alibi.

eternity. What if S. Gregory Nazianzen's opinion[x] should prove to be right; that children dying unbaptized shall be free from pain, but shall not be received to glory? For innocence alone, (as that Father observes in the place cited,) though it exempts from punishment, will not entitle to reward. Nay, do but suppose there are different degrees of glory and happiness in that world, and that the very lowest place there is prepared for the infants of heathens, and of others who suffer their children to go out of this life under all the disadvantages of being unbaptized. Methinks if this, if any of these suppositions be true, if it be but probable, or even possible, that infants, by being baptized, as they are distinguished in this world from the children of infidels, may also be preferred above them in the next; we have sufficient inducements (as our predecessors in former times did) still to affirm, that Baptism is necessary, *absolutely* necessary, for infants, for adults, for all; and consequently, if this were the original ground of Lay-baptism, it and the practice built upon it will continue as truly justifiable, as they were anciently believed.

33. But Mr. W. is at a loss to understand, how that which is *sinful* in the *administrator*[1] is yet *valid* to the *receiver*. If, instead of *valid*, he had used the word *efficacious*, and by *receiver* had meant an *adult*, who

---

[1] How far Lay-baptism is "sinful in the administrator" is a question quite distinct from that of the validity of such Baptisms. The administrator may truly and honestly believe that he is doing what he ought to do; in which case the action is not "sinful" in him. But it does not follow that his act is valid, because it is innocent. A. may give B. a forged bank note, fully believing it to be a good one, but that does not

[x] Greg. Naz. Orat. xl.

chooses and prefers such a *sinful administration* before that which is regular and agreeable to the order which [108] GOD hath established in His Church, he might well be at a loss to understand it; because such an indisposition of mind hinders the effect, till it be removed by repentance, absolution, &c., as we observed before.

34. In the mean time, the Church, especially the lay part of it, were in an evil case, if every sinful circumstance in the administration should make the administration itself void and null to a receiver duly qualified to receive benefit by it. This were to make the efficacy, nay, the very *being* of the sacraments, depend, not upon GOD, but man. What think you of all schismatical and heretical administrations in former ages? were not they sinful? Yet that they were altogether *null*, Mr. W. himself will not say, being performed, as he observes, by "men of sacerdotal character; which being indelible, neither schism, nor heresy, nor any censures of the Church could deprive them of; men, who, if they returned to the Church, were received in without being reordained."

35. Further, he thinks it "a hard saying, that one may be damned for doing that, without which the other could not have been saved." Sir, it is not a new assertion, that GOD so husbands the sinful actions of men, as thereby to serve the ends of His providence, the needs of His Church, and the necessities of His servants. Judas, and Pilate, and the Jews, who con-

---

make it a good one. The question whether the note is a good one, or not, does not depend the least upon whether A. was innocent, or guilty when he passed it. No more does the question whether Lay-baptism is valid or not, depend at all upon whether the administrator was "sinful," or not in his action.

spired against and killed the LORD of life, (such of them as did not afterwards repent and believe in Him,) are in hell for having done what they did; and yet without it mankind could not have been saved. And this answer I take to be sufficient with respect to all baptisms administered in defiance and opposition to the Christian priesthood, by those lay usurpers, counterfeit ministers of the Gospel, who officiate in fanatical congregations, and act without episcopal ordination. And as for other laymen, who, without any design to affront or invade the priesthood, or disturb the peace and settled order of the Church, acting upon inducements truly Christian and good, shall venture, when a lawful minister cannot be procured, to baptize a dying infant themselves, or do the like to an adult not baptized before, dying, and afraid to die without this "seal of the servants of GOD upon his forehead,"[y] and earnestly desirous to receive it; I say, as for such, even supposing the principle they act upon to be a mistake, yet I can by no means think they are in any danger of being severely handled by a kind, an equitable, and most merciful Judge, for such their pious and charitable intentions. I do not say, that a good intention will justify an action that is plainly evil. But surely it will go far to excuse an action that is at worst but doubtful, and recommends itself too with so fair an appearance of charity to a soul in danger. And supposing the principle, which in this case they act upon, to be no mistake, then there is neither sin nor danger in what they do.

III.

1. The third thing to be considered in this dispute, is the judgment and practice of the ancient Church.

---

[y] Rev. vii. 3.

This I shall pursue no further than from the apostolical age down to S. Austin.

2. Sir, I cannot without astonishment find Mr. W. assuring us, that "the ancients do with one voice, for above three hundred years, condemn Lay-baptism, not so much as putting in any exception for cases of necessity;" (only Tertullian he excepts;) when I recollect, that, in all that period of time, there are only two writers that make any mention of Lay-baptism; of whom Tertullian (the elder of the two) affirms it to be valid; and the other is an impostor, the forger, I mean, of the Apostolical Constitutions, who, as he is quoted by Mr. Bingham, does no more than forbid the use of it in ordinary cases, but pronounces nothing concerning the validity or invalidity of it even then.[1]

3. I deny not, but it is easy to collect (what, I suppose, Mr. W. means) many passages out of S. Ignatius and others of the *ancientest* writers, wherein the right of administering in religious matters is asserted to the *priesthood*, as proper *only* to them, and the people forbidden to meddle or do anything in holy things without the concurrence and approbation of the Bishop. To the same effect S. Chrysostom, (who flourished in the beginning of the fifth century,) discoursing of the dignity of the Christian Priesthood, and thereupon mentioning the two sacraments of the Church, the Power of the Keys, &c., says, "All these things are administered by no other, but only by those sacred hands, those, I say, of the Priest."[2] By observing the original words in the margin, which I have transcribed from S. Chry-

---

[1] See Note (p. 7,) on p. 78.

[2] Πάντα δὲ ταῦτα δι' ἑτέρου μὲν οὐδενὸς, μόνον δὲ διὰ τῶν ἁγίων ἐκείνων ἐπιτελεῖται χειρῶν, τῶν τοῦ ἱερέως λέγω. *De Sacerd.* lib. iii. cap. 5.

sostom, you will see Mr. L., by his translation of them,[a] has favoured his own cause more than he could in strict justice do. But no matter. In these and the like sayings, to be met with in ancient authors, no more is intended, but to set forth the dignity and pre-eminence of the Priesthood, especially of the episcopal order, and to deter laics from despising or invading those offices which belong to men of the episcopal or sacerdotal character. To which end it was highly proper to allege the settled order and general rules appointed in *ordinary cases*:[1] and it would have been highly improper to descend to *particular circumstances*, to *cases excepted* out of the general rule, *cases extraordinary*, and for which extraordinary provision must be made. I know no reason why any Divine of the Church of England may not freely do the like, (as without question most of us have done,) join in such speeches with S. Ignatius, S. Chrysostom, &c. and assert the just rights of the Christian Clergy, without thinking himself thereby obliged to say that Lay-baptism is invalid; which is the construction that our adversaries put upon these expressions of the great men before cited. For a further answer to what is alleged from S. Chrysostom, I refer you to Mr. Bingham's Scholastical History of Lay-baptism, part i. sect. 5 and 15.

[1] It should be observed that in the passages here referred to, nothing whatever is said to limit their application to "ordinary cases," nothing whatever about "particular circumstances" which might justify the disregard of the principles laid down. There is no law, human or divine, which might not be evaded on the plea that it is "only a general rule," to which we may make exceptions when we please.

---

[a] Lay-bapt. Inval. part i. Prel. Disc. p. 16, 17, he translates thus; "All these are things which *can be* administered by no other man *living*, but by those sacred hands alone, the hands, I say, of the Priest."

Of the private opinions of the Fathers. 63

4. Mr. W. is content to give up Tertullian, having first used the modish sovereign charm to take off, at least to discredit his evidence. He lived and wrote his treatise of Baptism about the end of the second century, and is the *oldest writer* extant who mentions the practice of Lay-baptism, and yet (which is strange!) is not allowed to be a competent witness upon the case. It is said, he spoke not the practice of the Church, but *only his own private opinion*, and that too *founded upon a very weak reason*. A nimble and easy way this, of taking off an evidence that we do not like! So S. Austin, so the Council of Eliberis, so S. Jerome, Optatus Milevitanus, and others, *spoke only their own private opinions*, in what they delivered relating to this dispute. And we on the other side, with as much right, may say the same of any ancient writer, who shall be quoted (if any can fairly be quoted) for the opposite side of the question, and cry out, such or such a Father spoke only his own private opinion. By which means among us we shall have found out a most compendious way to stifle and set aside all the authority of the primitive Church, (except what relates to those few articles of faith and discipline which have been established by general councils,) and make for the future all convictions from antiquity impracticable and impossible.[1]

5. Let Tertullian's *reason*, upon which he is said to *found* his opinion, be never so weak, we have at present

---

[1] Vide pp. 161, 2, where Waterland points out the need of carefully distinguishing between what the Fathers give as their own opinions only, and what they assert to be the teaching of the Church. To make this distinction is not "a nimble and easy way" of "taking off an evidence that we do not like;" but a reasonable method of discerning what the evidence before us actually is, whether we like it or not.

nothing to do with that. A man may be very well acquainted with the customs and usages of the Church, without always knowing the true ground and reason of them. And admit, that a mistake is committed in the latter, that ought not to prejudice the account he gives of the other. Our business then is to learn from him (if we can) whether the Church in his days did in any case permit laymen to baptize, or did receive persons so baptized to the Eucharist, without insisting upon their being baptized by a Bishop, a Priest, or a Deacon. To this purpose Mr. Bingham very well observes, that it would be strange, if Tertullian, describing just before the practice of the Church in permitting Presbyters and Deacons to baptize by the *Bishop's* authority, should invert his discourse immediately in the very next words, and not mean the practice of the Church, when he comes to speak of laymen. Scholast. Hist. of Lay-baptism, part i. chap. i. sect. 8. Mr. Dodwell, who was the first that thought so, had reason to acknowledge that conjecture of his to be a paradox.

6. I cannot see that Tertullian's own words[b] give any ground for it, which I paraphrase thus; "The Bishop hath the (original) right to give Baptism. Next under him the Presbyters and Deacons, but not without permission from and dependence upon the Bishop, for order's sake and decency in the Church of GOD, which is necessary for the preservation of peace." (It is plain he speaks here of the ordinary administrations performed in public.) "Else" (i.e. abating for the necessity of preserving peace, order, and decency, as

---

[b] Tertull. L. de Bapt. cap. 17. Dandi quidem habet jus summus sacerdos qui est Episcopus. Dehinc Presbyteri et Diaconi, non tamen sine Episcopi auctoritate, propter Ecclesiæ honorem. Quo salvo, salva pax est. Alioquin etiam laicis jus est. Quod enim ex æquo accipitur, ex æquo dari potest, &c.

before) "there is nothing in the nature of the sacrament itself, but what laymen may administer too; for what is received in common may be given in common." In the following words he seems to reprove the forward presumption of some laics, who took upon themselves to baptize, even when there was no great necessity for it, admonishing them to be more modest and cautious in the use of this power, seeing even their superiors in the Church, the Presbyters and Deacons, have it in subordination to the Bishop, and must not usurp the episcopal office, and therefore that they much more should content themselves to use it in private, not in public, and that too but in cases of extreme necessity, and when the ordinary administrator cannot be had.

7. This testimony from Tertullian will receive further light and strength from another passage in the same author. In his exhortation to chastity he inveighs violently against second marriages; and among other arguments which he brings against them, he alleges this for one,[c] that, considering the necessity a layman may sometime lie under (in the absence of a Priest) to baptize, and do things which ordinarily belong only to the sacerdotal order, he ought to observe the sacerdotal discipline too; and that it would be a great absurdity for a man twice married to do these things, because a second marriage, according to the discipline of those times, unqualified a man for being ever admitted to holy orders. You see, Sir, he insists upon the same qualification in any layman, who in case of necessity should baptize, which the Council of Elvira did some

---

[c] Tertull. Exh. ad Cast. cap. vii. Igitur si habes jus sacerdotis in temetipso ubi necesse est, habeas oportet etiam disciplinam sacerdotis, ubi necesse sit habere jus sacerdotis. Digamus tinguis, Digamus offers &c., edit. Pamel.

time after in their thirty-eighth canon, wherein they give leave to those laymen only, whose own Baptism was entire, and who had not been twice married, to baptize a catechumen in case of necessity. Both Tertullian and the Council desiring to have that office done, if not by a clergyman, at least by a layman not unqualified to be a clergyman; and both the one and the other agreeing, that, in such cases of extremity, a layman might do it consistently enough with the discipline then in use.

8. And to prevent any objection from the layman's *offering* being here spoken of, as well as his baptizing, it is sufficient to remember what Dr. Cave tells us relating to this matter,[d] viz. "That in those early times nothing was more common than for Christians to carry, or to have sent to them, some parts of the Eucharist, which they kept in some decent place in their houses against all emergent occasions." Their religious use whereof upon such occasions is doubtless what Tertullian here means by *offering*.

9. It is true, Tertullian was a Montanist when he wrote this. But what then? Sure he could not be so forsaken of his understanding, or of his integrity either, as to argue upon premises which he knew to be false. Certainly no man of common sense would wilfully make himself so ridiculous, as to pretend to persuade men against second marriages, upon the topic of supposing them to be thereby unqualified to baptize, &c., in cases of necessity, if Baptism by laymen (howsoever qua-

---

[d] Prim. Christ. part i. chap. 11. This custom continued long in the Western Church. See can. lviii. of the Sixth Council in Trullo, and Balsamon's note upon it: Οἱ μέντοι Λατίνοι ἄζυμα διηνεκῶς ἐγκόλπια φέροντες, καὶ λαϊκοὶ ὄντες, οὐ μόνον ἑαυτοῖς τούτων μεταδιδόασιν ὡς ἁγιασμάτων, ἀλλὰ καὶ ἑτέροις. Latini autem azyma assidue in sinu ferentes, etiamsi sint laici, ea non solum sibi, ut sacramenta, impertiunt, sed etiam aliis. *Apud Bevereg. Pand.* tom. i. p. 225.

lified) had at that time been never practised, or, if practised, rejected as null and void. In a word, he supposes no more concerning Lay-baptism in this, than what he had affirmed before in his treatise of Baptism, which he wrote whilst he was a Catholic, and wrote particularly against the Montanists. And from both places together we may fairly conclude, that Lay-baptism was used in that age in extraordinary cases both among Catholics and others, who by schism or heresy were fallen from the communion of the Church.

10. Having done with Tertullian, we come next to him who loved to call Tertullian his master, viz., S. Cyprian, from whom, I confess, I have no positive evidence. But I am apt to think his very silence upon this subject, when he had such an inviting occasion to speak of it, will afford us a fair presumptive argument, that Baptism administered by a layman with water, in the Name of the Blessed Trinity, was not (at least not generally) thought invalid in his time, and particularly that it was not so in his own opinion of it. As Pamelius[e] has made it evident beyond contradiction, that Tertullian was of S. Cyprian's mind in the question of rebaptizing heretics; so it seems extremely probable that S. Cyprian had the same sentiments with Tertullian in the affair of Lay-baptism. Else how comes it to pass, that S. Cyprian, among all his arguments for the nullity of heretical baptism, should never urge the probable danger there was of its being administered among them by the laity? If he had thought a lay-administration a fundamental defect in this sacrament, how was it possible for him to pass over in silence

---

[e] Pamel. in Tertull. Parad. xii. et passim in Annot. in S. Cypriani Opera.

an objection of so great importance, and which had so very probable a foundation?[1]

11. It is not sufficient here for Mr. W. to tell us, as he does, that the Baptisms administered among heretics were "administered by men of sacerdotal character." I grant those heretics had (generally) episcopal orders and government among them; the validity whereof I refer you to Mr. Bingham for an account of, especially in the second part of his Scholastical History. But what I insist upon is, that, considering the many enormities and uncanonical practices usual in heretical congregations, S. Cyprian had reason enough to believe, that *laics* did among them presume to baptize, even where no necessity could be pretended. Tertullian will justify this suggestion by the account he gives of the heretics in those times, Lib. de Præscrip. adv. Hæret. cap. 41. "Ipsæ mulieres hæreticæ quam procaces, quæ audeant docere, contendere, exorcismos agere, curationes repromittere, forsitan et tingere." And by-and-by, "Nusquam facilius proficitur quam in castris rebellium, ubi ipsum esse illic, promereri est. Itaque alius hodie Episcopus est, cras alius; hodie Diaconus, qui cras lector; hodie Presbyter, qui cras laicus. Nam et laicis sacerdotalia munera injungunt." And S. Augustin in his tract of heresies tells us,[f] that the Pepuzians and Quintillians (cotemporaries with Tertullian and S. Cyprian) dignified even the women

---

[1] But see how this argument tells the other way. If it had been the accepted doctrine of the Church, that Baptism was valid (if in due form and matter) whoever administered it, why did not Cyprian's opponents refer to this fact, and the controversy would have been closed?

---

[f] Tantum dantes mulieribus principatum, ut sacerdotio quoque apud eos honorentur. *Aug. Lib. de Hæres.* c. xxvii.

with the honour of the priesthood. There are other evidences in being that will prove this, which I cannot come at for want of books; Epiphanius particularly, from whom S. Augustin makes his short collection, and quotes him in that very chapter. And if the case was thus, especially if these things were done (as all things [*in castris rebellium*] among schismatics and heretics are done) in defiance of all power and order established in the Church; then certainly it is not possible to imagine, that the Cyprianists (among their other arguments) should not make use of this, the most plausible of them all, if Lay-baptism had in that age been generally thought null and invalid.

12. Thus we might fairly presume. But it seems S. Basil is in our way, who was born about seventy years after S. Cyprian's martyrdom. He tells us,[g] that S. Cyprian and his own predecessor Firmilian had affirmed concerning the Cathari, the Encratites, the Hydroparastatæ, and the Apotactitæ, that by their heresies they had forfeited the grace of the HOLY SPIRIT, that their clergy thereby were become laics, and had lost the power of baptizing, ordaining, &c., and therefore ordered, that those who had been baptized by them should, if they returned to the Church, be again cleansed with the true Baptism of the Church, as having before been baptized only by laymen.

13. But it ought to be observed, that S. Basil does

---

[g] S. Basil. ad Amphil. can. i. ap. Bever. Pand. tom. ii. Πλὴν ἀλλ' ἔδοξε τοῖς ἀρχαίοις, τοῖς περὶ Κυπριανὸν λέγω καὶ Φιρμιλιανὸν τὸν ἡμέτερον, τούτους πάντας μιᾷ ψήφῳ ὑποβαλεῖν, Καθαροὺς, Ἐγκρατίτας, καὶ Ὑδροπαραστάτας, καὶ Ἀποτακτίτας· δι' ὃ ἡ μὲν ἀρχὴ τοῦ χωρισμοῦ διὰ σχίσματος γέγονεν· οἱ δὲ τῆς ἐκκλησίας ἀποστάντες, οὐκέτι ἔσχον τὴν χάριν τοῦ ἁγίου Πνεύματος ἐφ' ἑαυτοῖς. ἐπέλιπε γὰρ ἡ μετάδοσις τῷ διακοπῆναι τὴν ἀκολουθίαν.——οἱ δὲ ἀπορραγέντες, λαϊκοὶ γενόμενοι, οὔτε τοῦ βαπτίζειν, οὔτε τοῦ χειροτονεῖν εἶχον τὴν ἐξουσίαν, οὐκέτι δυνάμενοι χάριν Πνεύματος ἁγίου ἑτέροις παρέχειν, ἧς αὐτοὶ ἐκπεπτώκασι. δι' ὃ, ὡς παρὰ λαϊκῶν βαπτιζομένους τοὺς παρ' αὐτῶν, ἐκέλευσαν ἐρχομένους ἐπὶ τὴν ἐκκλησίαν, τῷ ἀληθινῷ βαπτίσματι τῷ τῆς ἐκκλησίας ἀνακαθαίρεσθαι.

not give us the words either of S. Cyprian or Firmilian; at most, he only says, they were of that opinion, and that they gave order so and so. And though it is not improbable, but S. Basil might see some writings of theirs which are not extant now; yet, considering that there is no such thing to be met with at this day in all S. Cyprian's writings, nor in Firmilian's letter to him preserved among S. Cyprian's works, there is room to think, first, that S. Basil might forget and mistake his authors, or mistake their meaning, and the true ground upon which they built their arguments. Dr. Brett's suggestion, that S. Cyprian used the foregoing argument in his letter to Firmilian, which is now lost, and which he supposes S. Basil might see in the archives of Cæsarea, is wholly precarious, as easily denied as affirmed; and the less likely to be true, because there is no mention of any such thing in Firmilian's answer. I add, that it is hard to think he would make use of an argument in one single letter to Firmilian, which in all his other writings upon the same subject he never thought fit to mention.

14. There is room to conjecture, that S. Basil, by his τοῖς ΠΕΡΙ Κυπριανὸν καὶ Φιρμιλιανὸν, might mean, not the *persons* of Cyprian and Firmilian, but the disciples and followers of their party: who, though they sided with these great men in the dispute, might mistake the principles upon which they acted, or might act upon different principles of their own. For instance, Tertullian was for rebaptization, but not upon the same grounds that our adversaries tell us S. Cyprian was. I see not at present how this conjecture can be disproved; and if it be allowed, it easily reconciles the difference between Firmilian's and S. Cyprian's own account of the principles they went upon, and this account of S. Basil.

15. But suppose in the mean time, what cannot be proved, that S. Cyprian himself had argued in that manner as is pretended; then, as on the one hand Mr. W. must upon his own principle confess, that S. Cyprian spoke therein not the doctrine of the Church, but "his own private opinion;" (for Mr. W. owns, that "that question, whether heresy and schism nulled orders, and reduced heretical priests to mere laymen, was determined by the Church in the negative;") so, on the other hand, I cannot see how Mr. W. can prove, that the nullity of Lay-baptism (if it was his opinion) was other than *his own private opinion* too. He says indeed of the Cyprianists and their adversaries, that "both sides supposed the nullity of Lay-baptisms as an undoubted principle;" and that the main dispute was "whether heresy and schism nulled orders." He says this, but upon what authority, we are left to seek. And certainly he gives us a very wrong account of the state of that controversy. For, were it true, what he affirms, that the nullity of Lay-baptisms was received by both sides as an undoubted principle, it would be next to miraculous, that no one word of this should be met with in the many letters and treatises that were written upon that dispute, not the least mention made of such a principle, when there was so fair an occasion for it, neither by Pope Stephen and his party on the one side, nor by Firmilian, S. Cyprian, or any of their adherents on the other; nay, that the direct contrary to this, the validity of Lay-baptism, should be affirmed, and taken for granted too (as if he expected no contradiction in it) by Tertullian, who was a stout and learned champion of the latter party, and indeed senior to Cyprian and Firmilian in that dispute, and doubtless understood the grounds of it as well as they. So far

is it from being certain that Cyprian, Firmilian, or their adherents, who asserted the rebaptization of heretics, (much less their opposers,) "supposed the nullity of Lay-baptisms as an undoubted principle!" whilst, on the other hand, it is demonstratively certain, that Tertullian, who asserted the same thing, did it upon principles altogether different.

16. I have offered all I had to offer concerning S. Cyprian, and persuade myself that Mr. W. and his friends cannot easily wrest him away from us: but if they could, still I am of opinion that they must give us S. Basil in exchange.[h1] For after this Father had laid before us the Cyprianic notion, that heresy extinguished the sacerdotal character, insomuch that a Bap-

---

[1] Waterland, in his reply, has dealt at some length with these citations from S. Basil and others of the old Fathers: but it should be remembered that it is very unsafe to draw conclusions as to the opinions of any one of the Fathers on the strength of a few quotations, cited apart from their context. It would be quite possible to make two sets of extracts from some of the more voluminous writers, one set in support of some disputed doctrine, and the other set against it. Nothing but a close acquaintance with the whole original writings would enable us to judge with certainty which set of extracts truly represented, and which misrepresented the real opinion of the writer. Moreover the Fathers were not always very distinct, and not always quite consistent with themselves, so that it has been quite possible for two learned and

---

[h] Ἐπειδὰν δὲ ὅλως ἔδοξέ τισι τῶν κατὰ τὴν Ἀσίαν, οἰκονομίας ἕνεκα τῶν πολλῶν, δεχθῆναι αὐτῶν τὸ βάπτισμα, ἔστω δεκτόν. S. Basil. ibid. It is to be observed, that he makes the same concession also in favour of the Encratites, who by their irregular Baptisms defied, and particularly studied to prevent the Baptism of the Church. For speaking in the next words of Baptisms administered by those heretics, he inclines in his own private opinion to have them repeated: but immediately adds, Ἐὰν μέντοι μέλλῃ τῇ καθόλου οἰκονομίᾳ ἐμπόδιον ἔσεσθαι τοῦτο, πάλιν τῷ ἤθει χρηστέον, &c., and gives a reason for it grounded upon prudential considerations.

tism administered by an heretical priest ought to be so esteemed, as if administered by a mere layman, although (as Mr. L. truly observes, Second Part of Lay-Baptism Inval. p. 178,) S. Basil himself espoused the same notion, (and perhaps the whole Catholic Church with him,) reckoning persons in such circumstances to be reduced to laymen; yet he concludes, nevertheless, that a person so baptized may be received into the communion of the Church with confirmation alone, without being rebaptized, if such be the custom of that particular church where the case happens: and

honest men, such as Waterland on one side, and Bingham on the other, each to claim the same Father as being on his side; and the ordinary reader, who has no access to the originals, is at a loss to decide which claim is well founded. But there is one conclusion bearing upon the present controversy, which the ordinary reader may feel secure in drawing from the long array of these varying and disputable extracts from the Fathers—I mean this, that there was, during the first four centuries in which these Fathers lived, no one accepted Catholic doctrine on the subject of Lay-baptism. On whichever side the truth lay, during all those ages, the question was an open one, otherwise there could not have been that variety of assertion and of opinion, which undoubtedly there was. It is sufficiently evident that this conclusion is a very important one. If the validity of Lay-baptism was not a Catholic doctrine during the first four centuries, it is not a Catholic doctrine now. If it was a matter of uncertainty then, it is a matter of uncertainty now. And this is the main point, for which Waterland and all others who have taken his side in the controversy have constantly contended. The practical outcome of this conclusion is also sufficiently evident; namely, that if the validity of Lay-baptism is uncertain, then the man who values his own soul and the souls of his brethren will seek himself, and help others to seek, for a Baptism, the validity of which is not uncertain.

he justifies this concession with reasons drawn from ecclesiastical policy. All which sure he would not have done, had he thought Lay-baptism to be so far null and void, that it is not even in the power of the Church to receive or ratify it in any case. It is plain S. Basil thought this a point of discipline rather than of doctrine, and consequently subject to the rules and customs of particular churches, and to be governed as the interests of religion should require. And if what Dr. Brett suggests[1] be true, that "when we cite a canonical epistle of S. Basil, we do not produce the authority of a single Father, but of the whole Greek Church;" then we have the authority of "the whole Greek Church" asserting, that the Church may, if she pleases, receive and ratify a Baptism administered by a mere layman. For in S. Basil's judgment, (not to mention now S. Cyprian and Firmilian,) an heretical priest is no more.

17. Mr. L. says, that the Baptisms here allowed of by S. Basil were only schismatical, not Lay-baptisms. It may be so. But our question concerning them is not what they really were, nor what opinion the Asiatic churches had of them, but what S. Basil's opinion of them was. And that both appears plainly from S. Basil's own words, and is also granted by Mr. L., viz., that the ministers of those Baptisms were by their schisms and heresies become mere laymen. I say, Mr. L. grants this to have been S. Basil's opinion. And yet even such Baptisms S. Basil consents to allow upon prudential motives, for the sake of peace, and a due regard to those Asiatic churches who did receive them, and particularly οἰκονομίας ἕνεκα τῶν πολλῶν, for the sake of those *great multitudes* who were concerned

---

[1] Mr. B.'s Scholastical History Considered, part i. sect. 15, p. 59.

therein. I wish the same considerations might have an equal regard now.

18. I have been forced to join S. Cyprian and S. Basil together, though considerably distant in time. But the next evidence in order of time, after Tertullian and S. Cyprian, are the Fathers of the Spanish Council of Elvira, or Eliberis, held in the year 305; who in the thirty-eighth canon[k] do not so much assert, as suppose and take for granted the liberty of laymen to baptize in cases of necessity, nothing being more common in that age;[1] but restrain the use of that liberty to such alone of the laity as had not unqualified themselves for holy orders. This we observed before, in examining the evidence from Tertullian.

19. I cannot imagine to what end we are here reminded by Mr. L. and Dr. Brett, that this Council was not general; seeing we inquire only into fact. And it is to be hoped, that the Bishops of so great a nation as Spain, being assembled together in council, may afford as considerable an evidence of the doctrine and discipline of the Western Church, as a letter from one single Bishop to another (S. Basil[l] to Amphilochius) can of the Eastern. It is not at all likely, that such an assembly of Catholic Bishops would decree anything

---

[1] This is an assertion, which, *if true*, would be of great weight in this controversy: but, as Waterland well asks, "whence could Mr. Kelsall learn this?" There is not a particle of historical evidence to support this statement. (Vide Waterland's reply, p. 176.)

---

[k] Peregre navigantes, aut si Ecclesia in proximo non fuerit, posse fidelem, (qui lavacrum suum integrum habet, nec sit bigamus,) baptizare in necessitate infirmitatis positum catechumenum, ita ut si supervixerit ad episcopum eum perducat, ut per manus impositionem perfici posset. *Concil. Illiberit.* can. xxxviii. *apud Barth. Carranzam.*

[l] Dr. Brett, part i. sect. 5, of Mr. B.'s Schol. Hist. Considered.

(especially in matters of such importance as are the Christian sacraments) contrary to the received doctrine and discipline of the Church; and less likely yet, that they could do such a thing without being censured for it, either by the writings of private Fathers, or by some public act of some other council. This, I say, is not at all likely; if we consider how great a flame had been raised in the Church upon the question of heretical Baptisms not many years before, which was a question not of greater importance than this.

20. Whether the story of S. Athanasius's baptizing his playfellows, when a boy, be true or false, yet it ought to be observed, that Ruffinus and Sozomen, who relate, seem to applaud the decree[1] made upon it, at least censure it not: which surely they must have done, or must have incurred censure themselves, had Lay-baptism been invalidated by the discipline of the Catholic Church in those times. Ruffinus would have been sure to have S. Jerome upon his back, who, living as he did in Palestine, so near Alexandria, where this thing is said to be done, could neither be ignorant of the discipline used in that part of the world, nor want opportu-

---

[1] It is hard to see how Mr. Kelsall could have felt himself justified in saying that Ruffinus and Sozomen "seem to applaud the decree." Ruffinus does not express the faintest approbation or disapprobation of what Bishop Alexander is supposed to have done. He simply records a story, ("Historia Eccles." Book I., chap. 14,) which Sozomen repeats; and therefore he was not likely to have incurred any other "censure," than that which he did incur of being a very untrustworthy writer, credulous, and prone to propagate fables. (Vide Waterland's reference to Cave's Historia Litteraria, p. 181.) Dean Hook, in his Life of S. Athanasius, says of this story that it "is now rejected as unworthy of credit by all judicious critics."

nity of detecting the falsity of the story, and would have been forward (had there been room for it) to expose Ruffinus on that account, for whose reputation it is well known he had no extraordinary tenderness or regard.

21. The author (whether Hilary the Deacon, or whosoever he was) of the commentary upon S. Paul's Epistles, extant under the name of S. Ambrose,[m] wrote under the Pontificate of Damasus, that is, somewhat after the middle of the fourth century, in a learned age, and not very distant from the apostolical, when it is not easy to think, either that the nature and extent of the baptismal commission was not well understood, or that the practice of the apostolical age was entirely forgotten. He (contrary to the sense of Calvin and other moderns) supposes the offices of baptizing and preaching *separable*,[n] though they are both joined together in the commission. And elsewhere[n] he tells us,[120] that at first, for the swifter propagation of the Gospel, leave was given to all promiscuously to teach, baptize, and explain the Scriptures, nay, to do these things *in Ecclesia*, whereof he gives an instance in the circumstances of Cornelius's Baptism, Acts x., which, he says, S. Peter, having at that time no deacons with him, did

---

[m] V. Pseud-Ambros. Comment. in 1 Tim. iii. 15.
[n] Non omnis qui baptizat idoneus est et evangelizare. *Pseud-Ambros. in* 1 *Cor.* i. 17, idem in Gal. iv. Neque Petrus Diaconos habuit aut diem quæsivit, quando Cornelium cum omni domo ejus baptizavit, nec ipse, sed jussit fratribus qui cum illo ierant ad Cornelium ab Joppe. Adhuc enim præter septem Diaconos nullus fuerat ordinatus. Ut ergo cresceret plebs et multiplicaretur, omnibus inter initia concessum est et evangelizare, et baptizare, et Scripturas in Ecclesia explanare. At ubi autem omnia loca circumplexa est Ecclesia, conventicula constituta sunt, et rectores et cætera officia in ecclesiis sunt ordinata, ut nullus de clero auderet qui ordinatus non esset præsumere officium, quod sciret non sibi creditum vel concessum, et cœpit alio ordine et providentia gubernari Ecclesia, quia si omnes eadem possent, irrationabile esset, et vulgaris res vilissima videretur. Hinc est unde nunc neque diaconi in populo prædicant, neque clerici vel laici baptizant.
What he says of S. Peter in this place, he had affirmed before in 1 Cor. i. 17, viz., Apostolus Petrus credentem Cornelium cum suis *jussit baptizari*, nec dignatus est, ministris adstantibus, hoc opus facere. See *Dissenters' Baptism null and void*, sect. 17.

not administer himself, but commanded it to be done by those that were present.

22. He does indeed, a little after, say, that this large commission was withdrawn, when the circumstances of the Church made it no longer necessary, "Hinc ergo est," says he, "unde nunc neque diaconi in populo prædicant, neque clerici vel laici baptizant." Which words imply, not that the one or the other were under a total prohibition in all cases, as Mr. L. seems to understand it,[o] but only that they did not do these things *in populo*, in their public assemblies for religious worship, not in ordinary cases, or when there was no necessity for it. Much less do these words imply, that, if they did it, it was not valid. For that would have been a contradiction to what he had been saying but just before.

23. Optatus Milevitanus wrote about the same time, who, it is plain, never thought the minister was of the essence of Baptism. In his fifth book against the Donatists, (p. 135, of M. Casaubon's edition at London, 1631,) he says, that of the three things concurring in Baptism, viz. the Name of the Trinity, the faith of the receiver, and the person who administers, the last is not of equal authority or importance with the two former. "Duæ priores permanent semper immutabiles et immotæ: Trinitas enim semper ipsa est: fides in singulis una est; vim suam semper retinent ambæ. Persona vero operantis intelligitur duabus prioribus speciebus par esse non posse, ideo quod sola esse videatur mutabilis." And p. 145, speaking of our LORD's commission to His Apostles, he delivers his sentiments thus: "In quo baptizarentur gentes, a Salvatore mandatum est: per quem baptizentur, nulla exceptione decretum est.

---

[o] Second Part of Lay-baptism Invalid, chap. ii. sect. 2.

Non dixit Apostolis, Vos facite, alii non faciant. Quisquis in nomine Patris et Filii et Spiritus Sancti baptizaverit, Apostolorum opus implevit." He prosecutes this notion there for several pages together.

24. S. Gregory Nazianzen lived and wrote about the same time. I have only a Latin version of his works, where in Orat. xl. which is an exhortation to Baptism, I read these words: "Omnes *citra ullum discrimen* vim perficiendæ animæ habere existima, qui modo eadem fide sint informati." A little before he had said, "Tu vero neminem non satis dignum atque idoneum ad Baptistæ munus obeundum existima; qui modo inter pios censeatur, ac non aperte condemnatus sit, atque ab Ecclesia alienus." He gives such advice, as any of us would give to an adult in the like case, if any emergency should drive him to desire Baptism at the hands of a layman, to make application for it in the first place to a pious and good man, a professor of the same faith, and a member of the same communion. At worst, if, in case of extreme necessity, even such a layman cannot be had, and a schismatic or heretic be employed, as I conceive S. Gregory's limitation did not, so I presume Mr. W.'s principles will not condemn a Baptism, administered, with water, in the Name of the Trinity, even by such a one, as utterly "null and void purely upon the account of his being a schismatic or heretic."

25. And now we come to S. Jerome, who lived in the latter end of the same century. Sir, notwithstanding the great pains which Dr. Brett has been at, and the very plausible account which he gives us of S. Jerome's conference with the Luciferian, as if the principles maintained in it were altogether in favour of his hypothesis; yet I find by experience it is possible to read the piece of S. Jerome over without falling into the

Doctor's opinion. Particularly as to his judgment of what Mr. Bingham has quoted[p] from thence in favour of Lay-baptism, viz. that it was a lapse of S. Jerome's pen or memory, and that through want of care he transscribed more from Tertullian than what was for his purpose, I must ask his pardon that I dissent from him. Whether he transcribed at all from Tertullian, neither he nor I know. But I find, upon reading the place, nothing but what is very much for S. Jerome's purpose, and extremely proper to support what the Catholic asserts in the former part of that chapter. And it is a fine art the Doctor has, to spirit away the testimony which stands against him, and which he cannot surmount, by making us believe S. Jerome did not mind what he was doing. It is like the other sovereign remedy used upon such occasions against a stubborn evidence, viz., "He speaks not the sense of the Church, but his own private opinion." But it has happened very luckily, that just now Mr. Bingham's Second Part of his Scholastical History is come to my hand, wherein he has sufficiently justified this part of the evidence. To whom therefore, and to S. Jerome himself, I shall refer you.

26. S. Austin, lib. vii. de Bapt. contra Donat. cap. 53, mentions cases which had been sometimes put concerning ludicrous and mimical Baptisms, Baptisms given by those that are unbaptized, or with a fallacious intent, or administered in jest to those who, being suddenly moved by the grace of GOD, have received it

---

[p] S. Hieron. adv. Lucif. c. iv. Ecclesiæ salus in summi sacerdotis dignitate pendet : cui si non exors quædam et ab hominibus eminens datur potestas, tot in ecclesiis efficientur schismata, quot sacerdotes. Inde venit, ut sine chrismate et Episcopi jussione, neque Presbyter neque Diaconus jus habeant baptizandi. Quod frequenter, si tamen necessitas cogit, scimus etiam licere laicis. Ut enim accipit quis, ita et dare potest.

faithfully and devoutly. These are cases, which he owned no general or provincial council had determined: and therefore with very great caution and deference to the opinion of others, he gives us his own in these words: "Nequaquam dubitarem habere eos Baptismum, qui ubicunque et a quibuscunque illud verbis evangelicis consecratum, sine sua simulatione, et cum aliqua fide accepissent, quanquam eis ad salutem spiritalem non prodesset, si charitate caruissent, qua Catholicæ insererentur Ecclesiæ."

27. The same Father, lib. ii. contra Epist. Parmen. cap. 13, speaking of Baptism administered by lay-hands, expresses himself thus; "Sed et si nulla necessitate usurpetur, et a quolibet cuilibet detur, quod datum fuerit, non potest dici non datum, quamvis recte dici possit illicite datum. Illicitam ergo usurpationem corrigit reminiscentis et pœnitentis affectus. Quod si non correxerit, manebit ad pœnam usurpatoris quod datum est, vel ejus qui illicite dedit, vel ejus qui illicite accepit; non tamen pro non dato habebitur."

28. Give me leave to suppose it hardly possible S. Austin should be ignorant what was the practice of the Church in his time; nor at all likely, that he himself would go about (had it been in his power) to change the usages and traditions which former ages had recommended, or innovate anything in the rituals or discipline of the Church. I say, it is not likely that S. Austin should attempt this, whose deference for the authority of the Church was so great, that he said, he would not believe the Gospel itself without it. Had this Father then known, that the Church disowned the *validity* of Baptisms administered by *lay-Christians*, is it at all probable, in the first place, that *he* would *put* such cases as above mentioned; or so much as possible

to imagine, *he* would *give his opinion* upon those cases *as he does?* that he could so much as hesitate, or give a doubtful uncertain answer upon the most *extravagant* of those cases? and *determine* the last of them in language so diametrically opposite to what he knew, could not but know, to be the practice of the Catholic Church? Believe it who can: it must be stronger evidence that can force my belief of it, than I ever expect to see.

29. And that Lay-baptism (in cases of necessity) was a thing frequently practised in his time, we have positive evidence from S. Austin himself, as I find him quoted from Gratian by Mr. Bingham, in the first part of the Scholastical History, chap. i. sect. 12, whose words concerning the custom in those cases are, " Etiam laicos *solere* dare sacramentum, quod acceperunt, *solemus* audire."[1] Dr. Brett does not give his reader a fair account of these words, (which he writes not,) when he tells him, " that S. Austin had only heard so." I think the words will imply, that he had *often* heard so, had *frequently* been informed, that it was *a usual custom* among the laity so to do. What else can be the English of *solere* and *solemus?* In the following part of the same quotation, S. Austin adds, that the custom took its rise from apostolical tradition.[2]

30. Sir, I promised to pursue this matter no further than S. Austin, and therefore shall rest here, only refer you for fuller satisfaction to Mr. Bingham. Else it were easy to show, besides divers of the ancients already quoted, that Isidore Hispalensis also, and others in the following ages, confirm my foregoing

---

[1] When a man says that he "has often heard" that certain people do so and so, we do not usually call this "positive evidence;" it is commonly called "hearsay."

[2] S. Augustine does not say any such thing. (Vide Waterland's answer, p. 199.)

notion of the sense and limits of the baptismal commission, and upon it so expounded ground the validity of Lay-baptism, and the power of the Church to judge of Baptisms administered in an irregular manner. If I be not mistaken, our adversaries agree, that, after S. Austin's time, the use of Lay-baptism in cases of necessity prevailed universally, not only in the Western Church, but the Eastern too, where S. Austin's authority was nothing, his name scarce known, and the correspondence for some ages between the East and West not so good as to afford any ground of conjecture, that the East might (as if by infection) receive an irregular custom from the Latins. So that, were there no positive evidence of it, yet it seems most reasonable to believe they had the custom among them long before S. Austin. Dr. Smith, in the account he gives of the present state of the Greek churches, assures us the custom continues yet among them; Epist. de Ecclesiæ Græcæ Hodierno Statu, p. 74. "Hoc in casu, at solo quidem, (neque aliter omnino fas erit,) si ingens neutiquamque fictum moriendi periculum immineat, seculari personæ, qualiscunque sit sexûs, cui intervenire contigerit, moribundum infantem tingere permissum est."

31. That I am not deceived in these evidences from antiquity, which I have here produced, I am the more inclined to think, because I find the greatest men of our own holy Church concur in opinion, that the primitive Church did allow Lay-baptisms to be valid, viz., Dr. Cave,[p] Bishop Sparrow,[q] Mr. Thorndike,[r] Mr. Hooker,[s] Archbishop Whitgift,[t] and others.[u]

32. And now I have done with the ancients. Mr.

---

[p] Prim. Christ. P. i. c. 10.
[q] Ration. on Common Prayer, in Private Baptism.
[r] Epilogue to the Trag. of the Church of England, book ii. chap. 19.
[s] Eccl. Pol. book v. sect. 61, 62.
[t] Defence against T. C. tract. ix. chap. 5, p. 518.
[u] Bishops Bancroft and Bilson, in the Conference at Hampton Court.

W. in one part of his letter promises "to be thankful to me, if I will give him but one plain authority, except Tertullian, for the validity of Lay-baptism, as such, before S. Austin."

33. I know not what he means by his restriction [*as such*]. Else I would promise myself, that I have a just claim to his thanks, if the Fathers of the Illiberitan Council, if the commentator upon S. Paul's Epistles under the name of S. Ambrose, if S. Gregory Nazianzen, if S. Jerome, (not to mention Ruffinus, Optatus Milevitanus, &c.) lived and wrote before S. Austin.

34. And I reciprocally promise to be thankful to Mr. W. if he will produce within a thousand years after CHRIST, either one single canon of any council to confront that of the Eliberitan Fathers, or so much as a testimony of one single Father that speaks home on his side of the question.[1] S. Basil bids the fairest: but I think he is fairly made at least to stand neuter, if not to list on the other side. The Fourth Council of Carthage (about S. Austin's time) can. 100, (apud Carranzam,) does indeed forbid *women* to baptize, (*mulier baptizare non præsumat,*) but does not declare a Baptism even so administered to be utterly *null and void*. It is not improbable, that the Council might intend only to prohibit their baptizing in ordinary cases,

---

[1] Waterland has taken up this challenge (vide p. 207), but he was not bound to do so; for there are innumerable false doctrines, and evil practices, which are not *expressly condemned* by "any council," "canon," or "single Father," "within a thousand years after CHRIST," or beyond that limit. But it would be evidently unwarrantable to conclude from this that the Church accepted those doctrines, and approved of those practices. Even if it could be proved that no council or Father ever condemned unauthorized baptisms, this would go very little way towards proving that they were allowed.

or in public, and leave cases of necessity to be provided for according to custom. However, their forbidding *women* only, and not *laymen*, (at a time when laymen were known frequently to do it,) is a very plain, though tacit, allowance of the latter.

35. And I will be further thankful to him, if within that period he will produce so much as an instance of any one Christian rebaptized by or in an episcopal church, purely upon account of his having been before only baptized by *lay-hands*. I would not have set him such *narrow bounds*, but for the Constantinopolitan Council of 1166, mentioned by Mr. Bingham, (first part of his Schol. Hist. p. 106,) except that Council, and I shall content myself with an instance of it so much as fifty years old, or even later, done by the authority of any Bishop, whom the Rubric directs us to consult upon such occasions.

36. On the contrary, we can produce instances of the Church's receiving the Baptisms of those whose ordinations she had before declared void.[1] I shall not here concern myself with Mr. Bingham's argument, in the second part of his History, relating to Baptisms administered by degraded clergymen, further than asking, 1. Whether the same LORD and Head of the

[1] Kelsall here introduces (as Bingham had done before) the moot point of whether a priest can be, for heresy or any other cause, so degraded from his office that he ceases to be a priest, or whether he can be only forbidden to exercise his office, and deprived of all its privileges. The most prevalent view of this controversy has found expression in the proverbial saying, "once a priest always a priest;" and the doctrine of the indelibility of holy orders is largely accepted in the Church. This may conceivably be a mistaken view; but Mr. Kelsall has no right to assume that the opposite view is unquestionably the true one, and then make his unwarrantable assumption an argument in support of Lay-baptism.

Church Who gave, cannot withdraw a commission? 2. Supposing He can, how this can be done, otherwise, than by the Church's acting in His name and by His authority, as well in withdrawing as granting the said commission? 3. Whether the Church have not full authority to do this, considering the large and full promises her LORD has made to her, of ratifying and confirming all matters of discipline, which she shall think fit to transact in His name? And, 4. Whether the Church has not upon divers occasions expressed herself in such language towards heretics, schismatics, and delinquents, as if she thought she had such a power? particularly, whether she *can* express herself in higher language, supposing she has it? For answer to which last queries, I refer myself to those passages which Mr. Bingham has quoted, in the second part of his Scholastical History, from her general, her patriarchal, and provincial councils.

37. Only I must observe, that the Church has been troubled with *counterfeit priests* (I mean persons pretending to be priests who never had any ordination) in ancient times, as well as of late. Ischyras, in the time of S. Athanasius, is one instance of this. He, being never ordained, usurped the office of Presbyter. Being called to account for this by Athanasius, and thereupon flying to the Eusebian faction, he was by them made Bishop of Mareotis, a place in Egypt within the diocese of Alexandria, without being previously ordained either Priest or Deacon. This man, among other enemies of the Nicene faith and accusers of S. Athanasius, was condemned and excommunicated by the Sardican Council. But no decree was made for annulling the Baptisms administered by him either after or before his pretended consecration to the Bishopric

which he had usurped. You have the story in Socrates Scholasticus, Hist. Eccles. lib. i. cap. 27, and lib. ii. cap. 20.

38. The same Council declared all, whom Musæus and Eutychianus had pretended to ordain, not to be Clergymen, because they themselves were usurpers and unordained, as we learn from M. Blastares's Syntagma Alphab. B. cap. iii. and Balsamon's Comment upon the eighteenth and nineteenth Canons of that Council. And yet the Council made no order for rebaptizing those who had been baptized by any of these usurpers. It is not unlikely, but more instances parallel to these may be found by those that are skilful in the antiquities of the Church. But these are sufficient to show the sense of that bright age to which they belong.

IV.

1. The Church of England practises exactly by the same rule.[1] She receives foreigners baptized by men

[1] Waterland has replied (vide p. 226 et seq.,) to the main argument of this section, making to his opponent concessions, larger perhaps than he was warranted in making, but yet arriving at a conclusion as to the authorized teaching of the Church of England, the opposite of that which Mr. Kelsall asserts. Indeed this section of Mr. Kelsall's letter is so bold a misrepresentation that no one, fairly acquainted with the history of this controversy in the English Church, could be taken in by it. To specify only one prominent point—Mr. Kelsall illustrates the teaching of the Church by the history of the rubric (quoted by him in paragraph 2,) which in the First Book of Ed. VI. prescribes the manner of private baptism, and he says, quite truly, that in this rubric, there "is no mention of a lawful minister;" then he states that this rubric remained unaltered "till the beginning of King James the First." This also is true; but not so at all his next assertion, "that in that

not episcopally ordained, as well as natives baptized by schismatical laymen, into her communion without re-baptization; but none, whether natives or foreigners, to the exercise of the sacerdotal office without episcopal ordination, which shows, that *she* makes some difference between the case of *Lay-baptism* and *Lay-ordination*:

period (i.e., the period of the Hampton Court Conference) laymen and women did baptize in cases of necessity, and justified themselves by the foregoing rubric, and *were allowed by the Church so to do, is a truth as plain as anything in history."* (p. 127.) This is certainly a bold assertion, considering that when this matter was under discussion at the Hampton Court Conference, the Archbishop of Canterbury (Whitgift) stated "that the administration of baptism by women and lay persons was *not allowed* in the practice of the Church; but inquired of by the Bishops in their visitations *and censured; neither do the words in the Book infer any such meaning."*

(Vide "Documents connected with the revision of King James. No. V." cited in Cardwell's "History of Conferences.")

These being Whitgift's words with regard to the practice, and the rubric of the Church of England, Mr. Kelsall ventures to say (p. 127,) "The great Whitgift, Bancroft, Hooker, and other zealous champions vindicated her, not by denying the fact (i.e., of baptisms by laymen and laywomen) *but by justifying it and her*, not doubting then but they did the Church good service, and little expecting to be traduced upon that account after their death!"

That Whitgift's own opinion was in favour of the validity of Lay-baptism is quite true; but that he asserted that the Church "allowed," or that the rubric "justified," the practice of such baptisms is exactly the reverse of true.

After this specimen of Mr. Kelsall's historical method, we need scarcely follow him any further in his account of the practice of the Church of England. That the practice of Lay-baptism, and many other more or less bad practices, have from time to time obtained place within the Church of England, is a fact which must sorrowfully be admitted; but that

of the Anglican Rubrics. 89

and believes she may on good grounds allow the first to be valid, without being obliged by any consequence deducible thence to allow the validity of the latter.

2. Early in the infancy of the Reformation, and since, she hath so plainly declared her sense of this matter in her ancient Rubrics and present practice, that I cannot but wonder to see it brought into question. 127 In the first Liturgy of King Edward the Sixth, the Rubric, which prescribes the manner of private Baptism, is in these words : " First let *them that be present*" [here is no mention of a lawful minister] "call upon GOD for His grace, and saye the LORDE's Prayer, if the tyme will suffer. And then *one of them*" [i.e., of them that be present] "shall name the chylde and dyppe him in the water, or powre water upon hym, saying these woordes: N. I baptize thee in the Name of the FATHER, and of the SONNE, and of the HOLY GOST. Amen. And let them not doubte, but that the chylde so baptized, is lawfully and sufficiently baptized, and oughte not to be baptized agayne in the Churche," &c. And the child being afterward brought to the Church, the Priest is directed, notwithstanding that the child

the Church has allowed, still less that she has "justified" such bad practices, is quite another matter.

As to the formal doctrine of the Church of England, and the fact that she has never determined that Lay-baptism is valid, it may be well here again to repeat the oft-quoted words of the Lower House of the Convocation of Canterbury, A.D. 1712, when that House declined to accede to a proposed motion, allowing the validity of Lay-baptism, and assigning the reason of refusal, " First, because the validity of such baptism is a point, which the Catholic Church, and the Church of England in particular, hath hitherto avoided to determine by any synodical declaration." (Vide Lathbury's " History of Convocation," ad loc.)

was baptized by a *layman or woman*, if all other matters were right, to *certify that in this case they had done well, and according unto due order concerning the baptizing of the child.*

3. In that reign there were afterward considerable alterations made in the Liturgy, but none in this part of the Rubric about private Baptism, which continued unchanged during the remainder of that and all Queen Elizabeth's reign, till the beginning of King James the First. That in that period *laymen* and *women* did baptize in cases of necessity, and justified themselves by the foregoing Rubric, and were allowed by the Church so to do, is a truth as plain as anything in history. The *then enemies of Lay-baptism and the Church*, the Puritans, Cartwright and others, reproached her with it. The great Whitgift, Bancroft, Hooker, and other zealous champions vindicated her, not by denying the fact, but by justifying it and her, not doubting then but they did the Church good service, and little expecting to be traduced upon that account after their death, by zealous sons of the Church, and zealous proselytes, as latitudinarians.

4. Archbishop Whitgift reckons this among the dangerous points of doctrine avouched by T. Cartwright, viz., that "not only the dignity, but also the being of the sacrament of Baptism dependeth upon this, whether he be a minister or no, that doth minister it;" and says, that the consequence hereof is "plain Anabaptism." See his note of such dangerous Points of Doctrine, &c., prefixed to his Defence of the Answer to the Admonition, &c.

5. In the book itself, (Tract. ix. chap. 5, p. 519,) he thus addresses himself to his adversary T. C. "Whereas you say, that the minister is one of the

chief parts, and as it were of the lyfe of the sacrament; in so weighty a cause, and great a matter, it had been well if you had used some authority of Scripture, or testimonie of learned author: for so far as I can read, the opinion of all learned men is, that the essential form, and as it were the lyfe of Baptism, *is to baptize in the Name of the Father, and of the Sonne, and of the Holy Ghost;* which form being observed, the sacrament remaineth in full force and strength by whomsoever it be ministered," &c. He goes on in the next paragraph; "And certainly, if the being of the sacrament depended upon man in any respect, we were but in a miserable case; for we should be always in doubte whether we were rightly baptized or no: but it is most true, that the force and strength of the sacrament is not in the man, *be he minister or not minister*, be he good or evil, but in GOD Himself, &c. This I speak, not to bring confusion into the Church, (for, as I said before, let men take heed that they usurpe not an office, whereunto they be not called, for GOD will call them to an account for so doing,) but to teach a truth, to take a yoke of doubtfulness from men's consciences, and to resist an error not much differing from Donatism and Anabaptism."

6. Mr. Hooker is very large upon this subject. In the Fifth Book of Ecclesiastical Polity, sect. 62, he has these words: "If therefore at any time it come to pass, that in teaching publickly or privately, in delivering this blessed sacrament of regeneration, some unsanctified hand, contrary to CHRIST's supposed ordinance, do intrude itself to execute that, whereunto the laws of GOD and His Church have deputed others, which of these two opinions seemeth more agreeable with equity, ours that disallow what is done amiss, yet make not

the force of the Word and sacraments, much less their nature and very substance, to depend on the minister's authority and calling, or else theirs which defeat, disannul, and annihilate both, in respect of that one only personal defect, there being not any law of GOD which saith, that if the minister be incompetent, his word shall be no word, his Baptism no Baptism? He which teacheth, and is not sent, loseth the reward, but yet retaineth the name of a teacher: his usurped actions have in him the same nature which they have in others, although they yield him not the same comfort. And if these two cases be peers, the case of doctrine and the case of Baptism both alike; sith no defect in their vocation that teach the truth is able to take away the benefit thereof from him which heareth, wherefore should the want of a lawful calling in them that baptize make Baptism to be vain?"[1]

7. Bishop Bilson in the conference at Hampton Court declared, that "to deny private persons to baptize in case of necessity, were to cross all antiquity, and the common practice of the Church, it being a rule agreed on among Divines, that *the minister is not of the essence of the sacrament.*"

8. Archbishop Bancroft in the same conference affirmed, that the compilers of the Liturgy did by the forecited Rubric "intend a permission of private persons to baptize in case of necessity;" and to prove his assertion, produced some of their letters. He said, it was "agreeable to the practice of the ancient Church," and alleged "the three thousand baptized in a day," Acts ii., as an instance of it.

9. King James himself, who blamed this practice, and at whose instance the Rubric was qualified as it

---

[1] Vide Note at the end of this Letter.

now stands, declared at the same time his "utter dislike of all rebaptization of those whom women or laics have baptized." So that it is plain, he himself thought such Baptisms to be *valid*, howsoever, in respect of the administrator, *criminal and irregular*.

10. To this opinion of their validity, not one of the Church of England Divines then present offered the least contradiction. And whosoever at that time should have desired to hear it contradicted, must have fetched in one for that purpose from among the Puritans.

11. But now, how are we changed! Some, who call themselves the most zealous assertors of the rights of the Church and Clergy, have embraced this Puritanical notion, cast dirt upon the memory of those excellent men, and will hardly allow any, who come not into their measures, throughly to understand, or to be thoroughly well affected to the rights and interests of the priesthood. And all this, without regarding the unanswerable objections, (unanswerable, I mean, upon their hypothesis,) which hereby they put into the mouths of the Papist and Dissenter, against the *validity* of all our ministrations, that is, (as we stated the case in the former part of this letter,) against the very *being* of our priesthood, our sacraments, and of the Church itself. Believe me, Sir, if anything has prejudiced me [130] against this hypothesis, next to the novelty of it, and the authority of the Church both ancient and modern, which I verily think stands full against it, it is the horror I conceive at the sad and unsufferable consequences it is inevitably attended with.

12. But to proceed. It is plain from that conference, that the alteration of the Rubric thereby occasioned was not grounded upon the principle of the *invalidity*, but only the *inconvenience and indecency* of Lay-bap-

tism. And from thenceforth, what had been *canonical* and *lawful* before, became in this Church *unlawful* and *uncanonical:* and what was thought *valid* before, was still thought *valid.* The Church altered her Rubric, but not her judgment of this matter. I know it is of late pretended otherwise. But I shall not be easily persuaded, but that those gentlemen, who were concerned in the conference and in the alteration which ensued upon it, knew best their own sentiments and intentions.

13. Mr. L., who with a very authoritative air takes upon him to instruct and admonish the Clergy of their duty, and to interpret the Canons, the Rubrics, and Articles of the Church, undertakes from all these, and especially from the last, (the Articles,) to prove, that the *invalidity of Lay-baptism* is a doctrine espoused by her. To attend him in what he offers to this purpose, would be to trifle as much as he; I am too much tired for that work, as I expect by this time you yourself are. I shall only therefore observe, that had he accomplished what he undertakes from the Articles, he had then proved the Church to be inconsistent with herself: (for those Articles are above forty years older than the conference at Hampton Court:) an undertaking not very suitable to the character of so zealous a proselyte, as it is said he is! In the mean time, he has effectually shown the sense the Church then had of her own Articles, and his own sense of them, to be extremely different.

14. In his treatise called Dissenters' Baptism Null and Void, sect. 17, he does not disown that those great men concerned in that conference did countenance Lay-baptism in certain cases, but denies that they countenanced *unauthorized* Lay-baptism. In sect. 4, he is forced to the same refuge, viz., to shelter himself under

the word *unauthorized*, not denying that *laymen* were permitted and even *commanded* by King Edward the Sixth's Book, to baptize in case of necessity, but denying that to be any evidence of her believing that *unauthorized persons* could administer *valid* Baptism. Thus, when disputing against *Lay-baptism*, (not only in this, but in other writings of his,) he is pressed hard with authorities that he cannot get over, he puts his adversaries off with saying, their evidences reach not the case in hand, viz., the case of "Dissenters' Baptisms, Baptisms unauthorized, and administered against and in defiance of the Church's authority." And yet he hesitates up and down in his writings, he shuffles, is not free to grant that the Church or Bishops have power in any case to depute a Lay-baptizer, and thinks himself not obliged to declare his opinion upon it. What can be the meaning of this? Why does he not give up what he finds he cannot maintain, and so reduce the controversy into narrower bounds? Let him either own that the Church has such a power, or else prove she has not. He does own (sect. 17,) that she once had it in the persons of the Apostles; and gives an instance, Acts x. 48. Let him show, if he can, how she lost it. Or, if she has it still, let him find out a medium (if he can) to prove, that what is ever *regular* in the administration of Baptism, *with the leave of the Church*, is not only irregular, but so far *invalid* too *without* her leave, as to be incapable of being afterwards ratified by her authority. Every Lay baptist, since that alteration of the Rubric, hath acted *without her leave*. And yet she receives as *valid*, and hath never reiterated even such Baptisms, although administered without, and even against her authority. Further yet, she never made any canon or law for the punishment of a Lay-baptist, who shall presume to do that office upon charitable inducements and in extreme necessity. The Rubric indeed was altered: but so far is that alteration from decreeing any punishment for such an usurper, that it scarce amounts to a prohibition of the fact. It says, a *lawful minister* shall be procured; it does not say, that in case he cannot, no other shall be admitted. I insist not now, that the alteration (as we observed before) was proposed and received upon such terms, as rather confirmed, than any way prejudiced, the then received opinion of the *validity* of Lay-baptizations in cases of extremity.

15. Had the Church by that alteration intended to declare *Lay-baptism* to be *invalid*, it is strange, that for near a century of years not one of all her eminent and learned Divines should apprehend her meaning. Bishop Taylor, in his Ductor Dubitantium, twice argues against permitting women to baptize; and in his Discourse of the Divine Institution of the Office Ministerial, sect. 4, he disputes against *Lay-baptism* in general; but he doth not anywhere pretend that the Church of England hath rejected such Baptisms as *invalid*. So far from that, that in the last mentioned discourse, "he owns, that the Church of England hath not determined this particular:" (and what his own private opinions were, of which he had not a few singular, is not what we inquire for:) he professes, that "he cannot say the Baptism of a layman is null:" he owns, that the Greek Church permits laics, whether men or women, to baptize in case of necessity, i.e., in the absence of a Priest, as it is there expounded; and observes, "that the Nicene Fathers ratifying the Baptism made by heretics, (amongst whom they could not but know in some cases there was *no true priesthood or*

legitimate ordination,) must by necessary consequence suppose Baptism to be dispensed effectually by lay persons." Judge, Sir, whether his own concessions and testimonies (of which he has divers more besides these) for the validity of Lay-baptism be not of greater weight, than the objections which he brings against it; and whether he consulted well for his cause, who alleged such an advocate.^q

16. Excepting this great man, I know not any Divines of the Church of England, that have disputed the validity of Baptism administered by lay-hands, till the reviving of this controversy now of late.

17. Archbishop Abbott (as I find him quoted by Mr. Bingham) denies the minister to be of the essence of the sacrament, Præl. 2, de Bapt. p. 99. "Ministrantis personam non de *esse* sacramenti, sed de *bene esse* judicarunt.—Pie igitur fit, si minister tangat solus; at fit etiam, si tangat alius." The same learned author mentions a book, which I have not had the happiness to meet with; it is the Answer of the University of Oxford to a Petition of some Ministers of the Church of England, desiring Reformation of certain Ceremonies, wherein he tells us, that "whole University" defended "the validity of Lay-baptism." It was published anno 1603. Bishop Sparrow, in his Rationale on the Office of Private Baptism, cites the Eliberitan Canon, and in the very next words declares, "He cannot see what can be reasonably objected against this tender and motherly love of the Church to her children, who chooses rather to omit solemnities, than hazard souls: which indulgence of hers cannot be interpreted any irreverence or contempt of that venerable sacra-

---

^q Lay-baptism Invalid, part i. p. 110.

ment; but a yielding to just necessity, (which defends what it constrains,) and to GOD's own rule, *I will have mercy and not sacrifice*," Matt. xii. 7. Archbishop Bramhall, in his letter to Sir Henry de Vic, (p. 980 of his works,) speaking of the *essentials* of this sacrament, reckons as such only "the matter, which is water, and the form, *I baptize thee in the Name*," &c. In that paragraph of his discourse he argues, that martyrdom (although sometimes called Baptism, improperly and analogically, because it supplies the want of Baptism) is really no sacrament, no proper or true Baptism, because wanting the *essentials* of the sacrament, the matter and the form, as before expressed. Had he thought the *minister* also to be one of the *essentials*, no reason can be given, why he should not have added that defect also. For I presume martyrdom is (generally at least) administered by *lay-hands*. And to conclude this point, Dr. Fuller is of opinion,[r] that "our Church judgeth nothing to be of the essence of this sacrament, but the invariable form of Baptism;" and a little after gives such an account of this affair, as plainly argues him to be of opinion, that the question we contend about is a matter of discipline, rather than of doctrine, subject to and determinable by ecclesiastical authority. It remains, that the gentlemen who espouse the opposite side of the question, produce (if they be able) at least one Divine of the Church of England of equal standing with these whom I have here quoted, giving it as his opinion, that our Church, by altering her Rubric, or by any other act of hers, hath declared Lay-baptism to be invalid. I think it cannot fairly be denied, that she once declared the contrary since the

---

[r] Moderation of the Church of England, chap. x. p. 278, 281.

Reformation. If then it cannot be made appear that she ever retracted that declaration, we must look upon it as still in force, that is, that it is yet the declared sense of the Church of England, that a lay-administration of Baptism, howsoever *criminal* and *irregular*, is not altogether *null* and *invalid*.

18. To speak the truth, her constant and present practice is a sufficient declaration of this. In the time of the great rebellion, the sacrilegious invaders of our offices and revenues were men that had no ordination: (for we are all agreed, that *antiepiscopal* ordination is *none:*) by these men *very great numbers* of children were baptized, who were born in those miserable days: which children nevertheless, after the restoration of religion and royalty, were admitted by our holy Church to confirmation, communion, and all the privileges of Church-members, many of them doubtless to holy orders too, without being rebaptized. This all the world knows. And whosoever will dispute it, ought to produce some act of hers decreeing their rebaptization; ought to produce *some* instances (I shall be thankful, as I said before, to any that will show me so much as one) of persons rebaptized by her authority, or with the approbation and consent of at least some one of her Bishops (as the Rubric directs) upon that account. I am fully persuaded no such instance can be produced in all the time from the Restoration till now. Mr. R. L. it is true, was rebaptized,[s] I presume, upon that very account. But it was a *clandestine irregular* action; his second Baptism was *unauthorized* and *antiepiscopal:* for he waited not for the judgment of the Church upon his case, nor asked (as he, or some for him ought to

---

[s] Preface to the First Part of Lay-baptism Invalid.

have done) the opinion and consent of his Diocesan. How many more such late instances as these may be produced, I know not. But they are nothing to my purpose. They have not the concurring authority of the Church and of the Bishops. Without which necessary circumstances, instead of the judgment of the Church, such instances present us only with the sense of a few *uncanonical* members.

19. And unless some such instances as are here demanded can be produced, I do not see, but the gentlemen, who affirm the Baptism of those usurpers to be *invalid*, lie under a necessity, either of owning that they assert that for an important article of true doctrine which the Church of England denies, or of accusing their mother the Church of England of communicating and ordaining (for ends best known to herself) men, whom she knew at the same time to be unbaptized. I shall be heartily glad for the gentlemen's own sakes, many of whom are learned and eminent men, and some have done me the honour of a particular friendship, to see them get handsomely clear from this dilemma.

20. As the Church dealt with those who were baptized in the days of rebellion by lay-usurpers, so she deals still with those whom their successors in their usurpation, our lay-preachers at this day, baptize clandestinely, without and against the authority of her Prelates. She reconciles and admits them to communion, without requiring them to be rebaptized. And even thus, and upon no other terms, does she receive the foreign Reformed, who were baptized in communions where episcopacy is not in being. Their ordinations she rejects, but receives them all as lay Christians.

21. Sir, I have now finished this long epistle, and shall only beg your attention a very little longer, whilst

A Summary of "Principles." 101

I lay before you a summary account of the principles and grounds I have gone upon in the defence of my opinion.[1]

I am firmly persuaded,

1. That the Christian priesthood is only episcopal.
2. That it is of Divine establishment.
3. Consequently unalterable by any power upon earth;
4. And shall continue to the end of the world.
5. That whosoever among us shall act as a Priest, who is not consecrated by episcopal hands to that office, is a thief and a robber, a mere laic, and (what is much worse) a leader of schism, and a sacrilegious usurper, &c.
6. That whatsoever adult shall choose to receive Baptism from such an usurper, knowing that he is not episcopally ordained, receives only the outward sign, not the grace of the sacrament.
7. Because his choice of such a Baptism (preferably to one that is truly Catholic and regular) puts him into a state of schism.
8. Which state is an insuperable bar against the baptismal grace, till it be removed by repentance and reconciliation to the Church.

---

[1] Of these twenty-six "principles and grounds" the first seven, and those only, can be freely allowed, and all these, so far as they bear on Lay-baptism tell strongly not in favour of Mr. K.'s conclusion but against it. Of the rest, some express the opinion of Mr. Kelsall and those who agree with him, e.g., Nos. 10—14, but they are in no sense "principles," some are historical statements of questionable accuracy, e.g., Nos. 15, 17, 18, 24, 25. Others are doctrinal statements also of questionable accuracy, e.g., Nos. 19, 20, 21, 23. Therefore the conclusion which rests upon all these expressions of doubtful opinion, and all those questionable statements, is not a well grounded conclusion, and ought not to be allowed.

9. But such an irregular administration can be no prejudice to those who die in their infancy, because of the innocency of that age, and their not concurring in the irregularity.

10. Nevertheless, though in the case of an adult so baptized, the baptismal grace be wanting, the outward administration (if with due matter and form) is not altogether invalid.

11. Consequently I distinguish betwixt *an inefficacious* and *invalid* administration.

12. Inefficacious it is, when only the inward part, the grace of the sacrament, is wanting. Invalid, when the outward administration (through some *essential* defect) is necessary to be repeated.

13. I justify my distinction from the case of an hypocrite baptized by a lawful minister. You must grant that his Baptism is *inefficacious:* you cannot say it is *invalid*.

14. Every invalid Baptism is inefficacious; but not every inefficacious Baptism invalid.

15. Baptism hath not been usually thought invalid, that is, the outward administration hath not been usually repeated, except when either the matter (water) or the form (in the Name of the Trinity) hath been wanting.

16. Nevertheless, I am content that the validity thereof, when administered by *lay*-hands, should depend entirely upon the estimate which the Church (assembled in Council) shall set upon it;

17. Being persuaded, that the primitive Church was of that mind,

18. And that the Church of England is so:

19. For that the baptismal commission constitutes the Bishops, the spiritual heads and governors of the

Church, supreme judges in all matters and disputes of that nature;

20. And this under no other limitation, than what the edification of the Church, their own piety and discretion, and the *essentials* of the sacrament prescribe:

21. And that the minister is not one of those *essentials*.

22. Consequently, the Church being, as hath been declared, supreme judge of this matter, if she shall think fit to order those, who have been baptized by laymen, to be baptized again, I am not the man that shall gainsay it:

23. Because it is pure matter of discipline, not of doctrine.

24. But this the primitive Church did not do.

25. Nor hath the Church of England as yet done it.

26. And till then, private men must not.

22. Thus, Sir, I have given you a short, and yet a full view at once of what I think at present concerning this controversy. The proof of such of these propositions, as are disputed among us members of the same communion, I hope you have already met with in some or other of the foregoing paragraphs. If I have anywhere erred, which is very probable; or if the whole be an error, I am very willing to be convinced, and to retract what is amiss as soon as I am convinced; and shall most thankfully acknowledge the favour of Mr. W. or any else that shall do that good office for me, to set me right.

I pray GOD Almighty to set and keep us all right, and to avert those storms, which at this time threaten our holy Church, especially from our own intestine divisions.

Sir, I have no more to add, but to ask your pardon

for having detained you so long from your books by this tedious letter; and to assure you, that I am, with the most sincere respect,

     Reverend Sir,
    Your most obliged humble Servant,
       E. KELSALL.

It may be well here to call attention to a practice, often resorted to by the defenders of Lay-baptism, which is apt to mislead and confuse the reader. I mean the practice of comparing the ministry of Baptism with other ministries, e.g., that of teaching, *assuming that the two are "both alike,"* and then concluding that what is true in one case is true in the other. There is a striking instance of this fallacious argument in the foregoing letter (p. 92,) where Hooker is quoted as saying, "He which teacheth, and is not sent, loseth the reward, but yet retaineth the name of a teacher: his usurped actions have in him the same nature which they have in others, although they yield him not the same comfort. And if these two cases be peers, the case of doctrine, and the case of Baptism both alike; sith no defect in their vocation that teach the truth is able to take away the benefit thereof from him which heareth, wherefore should the want of a lawful calling in them that baptize make Baptism to be vain?"

The answer to this question is simple and conclusive. "The case of doctrine, and the case of Baptism" are not "both alike," but plainly different just in that very matter with which alone this controversy is concerned. Baptism is a Sacrament, doctrine is not. "The case of Baptism," whether it be "vain," or not, depends on the question whether the *donum spirituale Sacramenti*, the gift of remission of sin and of regeneration, is really given, or not. In "the case of doctrine" there is no such *donum Sacramenti*, because there is no *Sacramentum*, and therefore there is, in truth, no analogy whatever between these two cases, and instead of being "both alike" they are so different that we cannot even use the word "vain" in the same sense as applied to the one and the other.

DR. WATERLAND'S
SECOND LETTER

In reply to Mr. Kelsall's Answer.

―――

REVEREND SIR,

YOU was pleased some time ago to favour me with a letter relating to Lay-baptism, and to desire some further insight into a controversy of so great importance. The subject had been very near exhausted; and therefore I thought the best I could do was to send you all the books I had, that had been written either pro or con about it. With them I sent a short summary of one side of the controversy, to invite you to look further into it, and to prevent your leaning too much the other way; which I was somewhat apprehensive of from what you had written to me. This was the design of my letter; which was much too short, and too hastily drawn up, to give you a sufficient light into the matter, but might serve pretty well as an introduction to lead you into better writers, who had considered the controversy at large: that letter you was pleased to communicate to your ingenious and learned friend, who has since done me the honour to write a very handsome and particular reply to it.

I cannot but think myself obliged to him for that mark of his respect: though at the same time I am justly sensible what disadvantage I lay under, first, in having a few running thoughts so nicely scanned; and next, in having nothing but a short letter set against an elaborate treatise, as if the merits of the cause depended upon so unequal a comparison. When I came to read over your friend's papers, and saw what was in them, I soon perceived what I had brought myself into. Mr. K., to do him justice, is a powerful advocate for the side which he espouses; and I should not care to dispute with him on even terms, or where I did not think I had much the better of the argument against him. He has laboured the point with great dexterity; he has given it all the advantages one might expect from a person of his parts and reading; has embellished it with Scripture and Fathers, has laid the colours strong where they were most wanting, and has found out a plausible turn for everything: in short, he seems to have omitted nothing, that his cause could furnish him with, either to convince or move. Yet I must beg leave to dissent from him; and while I acknowledge him the better fencer, I presume to imagine I have the longer weapon. But that the sequel must show, and it must be left to you to judge of, if you think it worth while to give yourself the trouble of a careful perusal.

If you desire to have a distinct view of this controversy, (as I am sure you do,) I must beg the favour of you in the first place to consider well the state of the question. For that one foundation well laid will go more than half way toward solving the difficulties you will meet with in it. I never knew any controversy more entangled and confused than this has been, by wandering from the merits of the cause, and taking in many things which belong not to it.[1] The question is,

Whether those that come to us from our Dissenters, having been pretendedly baptized by men that never had episcopal orders, ought to be baptized by us or no?

This is all that it concerns us to dispute or know; and nothing ought to be taken into the question, that has not either a necessary relation to it, or connection with it. You certainly take that one point to be the matter of the whole dispute; and accordingly, if you think Mr. K. in the right, you would not baptize a person who had been pretendedly baptized among the Dissenters; if you thought me right, you would.

This then is the point in question. Yet you will find most of his arguments and authorities to be very wide of this question, so that, though he had really proved some points, (which remains to be considered,) yet both he and you would mistake in the inference and application from them. This will appear in due time and place. For the clearer and more distinct apprehension of what I mean, you may please to consider what is called *Lay-baptism* under different re-

---

[1] It will be observed that some of these "many things" have been made main points in the argument on behalf of Lay-baptism, e.g., notably the assertion made by Kelsall, (p. 96) and repeated as one of the so-called "principles," upon which his conclusion rests, that the Apostolic commission empowers Bishops to authorize *any persons whatever* to baptize, laymen as much as Clerics. There is not the smallest reason for supposing that this theory is true; but if it were ever so true, what bearing has it on the value of baptism administered by those whom no Bishop ever has authorized to baptize? and it is with unauthorized baptisms, and with these alone, that this controversy is, for any practical purpose, concerned.

spects, and, as it were, distinguished into these several kinds.

I. *Authorized Lay-baptism* (taking both these words in a large and popular sense) is such as is permitted or enjoined by episcopal license or authority; or by the express rules, orders, or canons of any Church.

Such may be supposed those within the Romish Church, which allows laics, and even women, in some cases, to baptize. Of the same nature were Lay-baptisms in England, before the alterations of the Rubric in the time of King James the First.

II. *Unauthorized Lay-baptism*, not founded upon any episcopal authority; not permitted or enjoined by any express rules, or orders, or canons of the Church; of which there may be three cases:

1. When it is administered by a person in communion with the Church, and only in cases of supposed necessity.

2. When administered by a person in communion likewise, but not in a case of necessity.

3. When administered by a person not in communion, nor in case of necessity; but in contempt of authority, and in schism; being not only non-episcopal, but anti-episcopal, as in the case of pretended Baptisms by our lay dissenters, about which we are now disputing.

From these several sorts and degrees may arise as many distinct questions; and there may be something peculiar to each, that the validity of one shall not necessarily infer the validity of another; and so likewise for the invalidity. *Authorized Lay-baptism*, for instance, might perhaps be valid, and *unauthorized* not so; because there is authority and commission, in some sense, to be alleged for one more than for the other.

Unauthorized of the first sort has a supposed necessity to plead for it, which the second wants; and even the second is more justifiable than the third, and has a fairer pretence for being valid, because not under the same circumstances of schism and contempt. This however is certain, that they differ in some peculiar respects one from another; and therefore the same arguments will not equally serve either for or against all. Indeed if the first (authorized Lay-baptism) be invalid, they are all so. And if the last be valid, they are all so; but not vice versa: i.e., if the best be bad, they are all bad; and if the worst be good, they are all good. The advocates therefore for Lay-baptism might fairly enough argue from the supposed validity of the lowest to that of the next above, and so on backwards; but not so certainly the other way; which yet has been their constant method, whereby they put a fallacy upon their readers. Indeed Mr. Laurence has for the most part mixed the three last together; and so disputed against them all under one common name of *unauthorized Baptisms;* which he has constantly distinguished from those of the first sort, having no mind to meddle with the point of authorized Lay-baptism, conceiving it very foreign to the case in hand; because it is certain we have no canon or rubric to authorize any layman, much less a Dissenter, to baptize. One thing further I must remark; that although in the proof of his position he takes in the three last, using such arguments as affect them all; yet in his answers to his opponents he often separates the second as well as the first from the last of all; as it were retiring hither, and here keeping his hold. For he thinks the case of necessity likewise foreign to the point in hand; because our Dissenters' Baptisms are utterly destitute of that plea, and must therefore be defended on some other principle, or not at all. It must be owned, that if the validity of *Lay-baptism* in cases of necessity could be proved, it would weaken the force of Mr. Laurence's main principle, whereby he would prove *Dissenters' Baptisms null and void;* and would therefore be so far pertinent to the case in hand: but it would not be a sufficient proof that the contrary opinion is true; and therefore is justly rejected by Mr. L. when used by his adversaries as an argument, that Dissenters' Baptisms are valid; and in this respect only I presume it is, that he sometimes seems to set it aside, as not affecting the question. In short then, it may be pertinently alleged by the patrons of Dissenters' Baptisms by way of objection to weaken their adversaries' principles, but not by way of direct proof to establish their own tenet.

Thus far I thought proper in vindication of my author, that Mr. K. may not again mistake his manner and method of reasoning, which is very just and accurate; nor call it shuffling and hesitating, only because he distinguishes very carefully, and will not suffer his adversaries to run off from the point in debate. As to myself, I shall endeavour to keep as close to the question as possible, or as the papers I am concerned to examine will give me leave: and if I sometime happen to make excursions beyond the limits of the question in pursuit of your friend; that cannot so properly be thought my wandering, as my endeavour to correct and reduce his.

Now to come to the point, we are to inquire whether persons that have pretendedly been baptized by dissenting laymen are really and validly baptized or no. Mr. K. says they are, and I deny it. The cause must be tried by *Scripture, antiquity*, and *reason*. He begins with reason: which, with submission, I take to be something wrong; because there is no reasoning to any good purpose in this question, till some foundation be laid either in Scripture or antiquity, or both, to reason upon: and I believe Mr. K. was pretty sensible of this, being frequently forced to appeal to the Fathers under his first and second heads, before he came to them. But I suppose he thought he had something more than an equivalent for that inconvenience, by beginning with what he calls his unanswerable objection, (as indeed it is the most material one,) that so he might probably dazzle his reader at first view with its glaring show, and so prepare him to receive what followed with less scruple and difficulty. I shall however, notwithstanding, beg leave to take the fairer and more regular method; beginning with *Scripture*, and under that head answering such exceptions as belong to it; then going on to the *Fathers;* and last of all managing the debate in point of *reason;* to which I shall subjoin something relating to the judgment and practice of our own Church, as Mr. K. has done before me.

I.

I begin then with Scripture: as to which I had observed formerly, that it confined the administration of Baptism to the Clergy only: which Mr. K. acknowledges as to the lawfulness and regularity of it in ordinary cases; but not with respect to its validity at all, nor even with respect to its lawfulness in cases extraordinary. That is, he imagines it may at all times be validly administered by a layman; and sometimes even lawfully too. And here he appeals to the ancients, Optatus, Gregory, &c. who shall be heard in their place. I shall only observe here, that if Scripture has left this business to the Clergy in all ordinary cases, and made no provision for extraordinary, nor given any intimation that she meant any; then the consequence is plain, that there is no warrant from Scripture for any such exceptions to make it lawful for laymen in any case to baptize. And since there is no Divine law or rule to found its validity upon, it can no more be valid than it can be lawful. For nothing is plainer to me, than that what has no foundation for its validity, has no validity at all; or that nothing can be valid, which has no sufficient authority to make it so.[1]

But Mr. K. observes, that even Calvin himself was not so strict in expounding the commission to baptize as this comes to; and from thence, together with what he had hinted of the ancients, infers that Mr. W. and Mr. L. &c. are the first, for aught he perceives, that have so rigidly expounded the commission, as to make the persons to whom it was delivered essential to everything transacted in it. And then after this, he makes the novelty of our interpretation an objection against it.

I concern not myself with Calvin, because it signifies

---

[1] This, as it has again and again been said, is the one primary and insuperable objection to Lay-baptism; and no serious attempt has been made to get over this objection except (i.) the entirely groundless assumption referred to in the last foot-note, and fully disposed of by Waterland (pp. 144, 145.) And, (ii.) the still more unreasonable assumption that Lay-baptisms must be valid unless "GOD is under the necessity" to "annul" them, (vide p. 105). As if every unauthorized act were valid unless it be expressly "annulled." One child taps another child on the shoulder, and says, "Rise up, Sir John," and that child becomes thereby truly a knight, unless the sovereign of the country "annuls" the act. It is difficult to imagine such an argument used seriously.

little: but I declare I am as much against novel interpretations of Scripture as any man, and am so well assured that mine is not novel, but perfectly agreeable to the principles and practices of the first and purest ages of the Church, that I would readily venture the whole cause upon it. But this is not the place to speak to that point, and so I proceed.

Mr. K. objects, that "if the words of the commission, *Go ye*, &c. were spoken to Apostles only, and their successors, viz. the Bishops; and if the minister be essential, then none but such, none but Apostles and Bishops, neither Deacon nor Priest," (for why laic should come in here I do not see,) "must baptize." In answer to this I observe, 1. That if this argument prove anything, it is that neither Priests nor Deacons have any right to officiate as Clergymen by the institution, any more than mere laymen; or that a Bishop may indifferently depute either, and their acts be equally valid. Here are two orders of the Clergy struck off at once, and the three reduced to one, which is pretty surprising. What led Mr. K. into it was, I suppose, his observation, that the "office of baptizing" (and the same may be observed of all the other sacred offices) "was so firmly tied to the episcopal chair, that no man could regularly baptize," (or otherwise officiate for the same reason,) "without leave from thence." Therefore any man might *with leave*, for that is his inference, or none at all; and so any layman might give the Eucharist, &c. with the Bishop's leave. I hope this does not need confuting. He should have distinguished between *sacerdotal* and *canonical* powers. A Deacon cannot *canonically* officiate amongst us without a license: therefore a Deacon has no more power of officiating than a layman by his instrument of orders. This is just his argument. But, 2. To clear the whole difficulty, the words of the commission do certainly imply more than they express; for otherwise I do not see how the Apostles themselves were empowered to ordain by it. The subsequent practice of the Apostles is the best interpreter of it: and that will afford us a sufficient demonstration of the three orders of Bishops, Priests, and Deacons; and of the offices appropriate to them, distinct from the laity. And therefore I hope the two last may be allowed to have something more to show for their pretended right of baptizing, than any layman can have, as such; though they are not expressly named in the commission or institution. And if they, and they only with the Bishops, have any right to baptize by virtue of the New Testament, I must still insist upon it, that they only can do it *validly*. There is no need of an express depriving law to exclude all other persons from the sacred offices, (though if there was, we might find enough in the New Testament to that purpose,) because the very appointing of officers is a virtual exclusion of all others not so appointed, and would be very insignificant without it. If therefore any, who are thus excluded by GOD's law, take upon them to minister in sacred offices, let them show by what authority they do it, or how an act can be valid without any sufficient authority to support it. To proceed.

Mr. K. takes the "commission to be a conveyance of power to the Apostles, &c. to appoint the ministers of that rite, not only Presbyters and Deacons, but (where these cannot be had) even laics too." But to this it is easily answered, that there is nothing in the words of the commission, nor in the whole New Testament, to favour this notion; no example, nor intimation of any such power; and therefore by the rule of the Church of England, as well as S. Jerome, (as Mr. K. speaks in another place,) "Quicquid de scripturis sacris autoritatem non habet, eadem facilitate contemnitur, qua probatur." But further: there is one particular method or rule which the Apostles and primitive Bishops observed in granting their commissions, as is clear both from Scripture and antiquity: and that was by *imposition of hands*, or *ordination*. Now if any such commission as this was given to laics, they certainly ceased to be laics from that moment. But if they had no such commission, I am afraid it will be hard to show how they could have any at all. I will allow Mr. K. that Bishops only have the original right and power of baptizing, and that therefore none can be authorized to baptize, but by a delegated power from them. But then I must observe, that the manner and method of delegation is already fixed in Scripture and apostolical practice; and it is not to be presumed that the Bishops of the Church have more power than the Apostles themselves had. It does not therefore appear that they can delegate a layman any other way than by ordaining him, i.e., by making him a Clergyman, which is the primitive way, and is sufficient; is a delegation *in perpetuum*, and impresses an *indelible* character. Any other pretended delegation *pro hac vice* is nothing else but a deviation from the apostolical rule, and a stretch of authority, which cannot be proved to belong to them. However, if this could be proved, I must observe, that it would not affect the question in debate; for it is certain that our lay dissenters have no manner of episcopal commission to baptize. I suppose Mr. K. might be sensible of this; and therefore he would fain persuade us, that there is something further implied in the commission; namely, that the Bishops, after the Apostles, are thereby "made the sole and supreme judges in case of any irregular disputed Baptism, to annul it, or receive it as valid. And all this under no other restraint or limitation, but what the analogy of faith, the needs of the Church, and their own discretion, shall impose upon them." In the next page, he makes it a question of discipline, whether Lay-baptism should be received; alleging, that "our superiors may admit a Baptism irregularly administered by a lay usurper, as valid, or, if they think fit, they may refuse to ratify such Baptisms, and order readministrations." So that, upon that hypothesis, if our superiors receive Lay-baptisms, they are valid; if not, they are not so. Very surprising! What a power is here lodged in the Bishops, and a momentous question about a venerable sacrament dwindled into the case of an indifferent rite or ceremony, dispensable at the will of our superiors! Can it be a thing indifferent in a case of everlasting concern, whether any such Baptism was antecedently valid or no? Either it was valid before, or it was not: if it was, how can any Bishop or Bishops *refuse to ratify it*, or by refusing it make it cease to be so! If it was not valid, how can any Bishop or Bishops admit of it, or, by so doing, make it to be what it is not? Take it as you will, you will find it hard to reconcile Mr. K.'s notion, that any Bishop or Bishops by admitting or rejecting can make or unmake at pleasure. Had this notion been thought of when Stephen and Cyprian had such warm debates about the validity of irregular Baptisms, or when the Catholics and Donatists differed upon the same question; had it been known that Bishops are the sole and supreme judges in case of any irregular or disputed Baptism, to annul it or to receive it at discretion; how easily might that have solved all difficulties, and have saved them the trouble of disputing! Both sides had done right upon that supposition, because either might have done as they pleased. But they were not so happy as to make this discovery: the point was then, whether the disputed Baptisms were Baptisms or no, antecedently to any judgment of theirs upon them; and the decision of the Church was not supposed effective or operative upon the disputed Baptisms, but declarative only of what they were before: if the disputed Baptisms were antecedently true and valid, they could not be reversed or annulled by any; and if they were not, not all the Bishops upon earth could make them such, or remedy the defect without baptizing. I allow Bishops under CHRIST to be the sole and supreme, but neither infallible nor arbitrary judges. Let them judge in such matters, but withal, let it be according to law, where there is a law in being to refer to, as the case is here. They cannot dispense with sacraments of Divine appointment, nor substitute what they please in the room of them. They cannot assume a power paramount to CHRIST's institutions, to make that to be Baptism which CHRIST has not made so, or to null what He has. I was in hopes that Mr. K. had not meant that the validity of Lay-baptism depended upon the Bishops' admitting or rejecting it; but only that their judgment should be a definitive rule to others, as the surest guide in doubtful cases. This would have looked plausible enough, and might have had some weight, could it have been shown that any general council of primitive Bishops had determined against us in the present question: for to the primitive Bishops we should certainly appeal from any modern authorities. But Mr. K.

means quite another thing: he founds his hypothesis upon the Power of the Keys, common to all Bishops ancient and modern. He does not look upon them barely as judges of controversy, and giving in their authoritative decision, (which yet would not reach the point, unless they were infallible,) but as acting with a plenitude of power, admitting into, and excluding out of the kingdom of heaven, with something more than apostolical authority. For I am very persuaded, the Apostles themselves had no such latitude, or, however, I think it cannot be proved that they had. The Apostles and their successors have without doubt a power of binding and loosing, and "whatsoever they shall bind on earth shall be bound in heaven; and whatsoever they shall loose on earth shall be loosed in heaven:" but to interpret this in such a latitude as Mr. K. imagines, would justify the Romanists in maiming the other sacrament, and in many other their deviations from the Scripture rule; and, in short, seems to be an hypothesis chiefly calculated for the infallible chair. Mr. K. refers us to Mr. Bingham[a] for a proof of this paradox; which was wisely done. I have carefully read over that part of Mr. B. He gives us a quotation from an uncertain author, supposed to be Hilary the Roman Deacon, in the fourth century, who shall be considered hereafter; and he adds several quotations from very ancient and good authors, to prove that Bishops had the supreme power over the Clergy, either to authorize and empower them, or else to limit and restrain them in the exercise of their function; which nobody denies: and it amounts to no more than that the Clergy in those times were under direction of Bishops and dependent of them, and

---

[a] See Scholast. Hist.

Of the Eucharist carried by Laymen. 119

were to pay a kind of canonical obedience to them. But how does this prove that the Bishops had any authority to declare Baptism valid which was not valid before, or to ratify and null at pleasure, which was the thing to be proved?

I shall add nothing here concerning the ancients, whom Mr. K. again appeals to, as if they were all of his side. They shall speak for themselves in their proper places. I have been hitherto vindicating the interpretation we put upon the words of the commission from Mr. K.'s exceptions to it, and should proceed to whatever else has relation to that point. But I must first step a little out of the way, to take notice of a remarkable apology, which Mr. K. is pleased to make for himself upon this occasion; being sensible, I suppose, that this plenitude of power placed in the Bishops, of dispensing with sacred institutions and ratifying nullities, would sound something strange; and therefore he adds, "I do not yet see that I hereby carry the power of the Church or of her prelates higher in this" (sacrament of Baptism), "than it ever was in the dispensation of the other sacrament, which &c.—I mean no more than that the Eucharist was wont to be sent home to those who could not be present at the public service, by the hands of the Deacon, or, in cases of necessity, by any other person." And he gives an instance of a little boy, who was ordered by the Priest, being sick and unable to go himself, to carry the Eucharist to Serapion, a lapsed communicant, but penitent, and then at the point of death. And this he calls "as large a stretch of power, and as great a variation from the primitive institution, as the permission of Lay-baptism can well be imagined." I wonder how he could think this at all parallel or pertinent to the case in hand. I readily own that the *consecrated elements* were often reserved in the Church or the Bishop's house, and sometimes too even in common houses by the laity; and that Deacons or even laymen might sometimes carry them. But of what use the observation can be in the present controversy, I do not see. Had he shown that laics could *consecrate* the bread and wine, which is giving the Eucharist, it had been to the purpose; to make the case of Baptism analogous to that of the Eucharist, he must suppose the water first *consecrated* by a *sacerdotal hand*, that the laics may baptize with it. And this would be a good argument for reserving consecrated waters for such purposes, as they anciently reserved the consecrated symbols for the other sacrament. And yet I am afraid this would not do; for in Baptism, not only the water, but the person himself to be baptized, is to be consecrated; and I cannot conceive how any laic can convey this consecration. Besides, if we suppose all this, yet what does it relate to *unauthorized Lay-baptism*, the matter in debate, which is neither performed with consecrated water, nor by sacred hands, nor has any sacerdotal benediction conveyed to it? Give me leave then to think, that the question of Lay-baptism is not a question only of discipline, but of doctrine. For I am still persuaded, that the point I am defending, being, as I conceive, founded upon the nature and tenor of Christ's institution, and confirmed in apostolical practice, "is one of those sullen things, that admit of no alteration or abatement for the sake of any inconveniences, how great soever."

And now to return to our argument about the words of the institution. I had said, "that the commission leaves no more room for Lay-baptism than for Lay-ordination, Lay-absolution, Lay-consecration of the Eucharist, Lay-preaching and praying; and that if we go from the institution in one case, we may as reasonably do it in all, supposing the like necessity." Against which Mr. K. is pleased to except as follows:

1. He denies *that admitting the baptism of a layman under the qualifications foregoing* (authorized, I suppose, by Bishops) as valid, is going from the institution. It seems then, admitting Lay-baptism not *under the qualifications foregoing*, not authorized by Bishops, as valid, *may be going from the institution,* notwithstanding; which is giving up the point in question; unless he means *authorized ex post facto;* which notion, I hope, I have sufficiently confuted in the foregoing pages, and shown it to be going from the institution. If assuming a power which does not appear to have been given, but would be of dangerous consequence, and defeat in a great measure the end and design of the institution, be going from it; then I do not doubt but that is so. But

2. Supposing this were so, that admitting Lay-baptism be going from the institution, yet he denies my inference, "that therefore in the like necessity we might as reasonably do it with respect to all the rest above mentioned;" because the like necessity cannot be supposed in the other instances. In answer to which I observe,

1. That there is one thing taken for granted in the objection, which can never be proved; viz. that Lay-baptism can be ever necessary to any one's salvation. For suppose that text of S. John[b] to be clear and decisive for the necessity of Baptism, (which it is not,)

---

[b] S. John iii. 5.

yet they must first prove that Lay-baptism is that true scriptural Baptism; or else citing this text in favour of it, is nothing but begging the question; or is as much as to say, it is necessary to be baptized, therefore it is necessary to be *washed* by a layman.

2. Abstracting from that consideration, why should it be denied, that there may upon the supposition be a like necessity for Lay-ordination, v.g. as for Lay-baptism? May not Clergymen happen to be wanting in some possible cases? and if so, will there not be the like necessity for appointing laymen to sacred offices, i.e. for Lay-ordination, as for Lay-baptism, when no Clergyman can be had? and is not the good of the whole Church as much concerned in one, as the salvation of a single person in the other? As to Lay-consecration of the Eucharist, why should it not be thought as necessary in some possible cases, as Lay-baptism? Both the sacraments are generally necessary to salvation; and therefore in want of Clergy, there may be as much reason for administering one by lay-hands, as the other. The whole Church of CHRIST, I think, for six or eight hundred years downwards from the third century, gave the Eucharist to infants upon this principle: they thought that sacrament as universally and absolutely necessary as the other, founding it upon a text[e] as full and positive for the necessity of it, as John iii. 5, for the necessity of Baptism.[1] But I do

---

[1] To make this comparison, and its bearing on the present controversy more clear, it might be asked, "why have lay persons never been allowed to attempt to consecrate the Holy Eucharist and administer it to dying people when no priest could be had?" I suppose the only true answer would be, first, because lay persons have no authority to do this, and

---

[e] S. John vi. 53.

not put the matter upon that foot; but suppose only, that it is absolutely necessary to adult Christians in general, as Baptism to infants. And therefore, if a regular Clergy cannot be had, there is as great necessity for Lay-consecration, as can be supposed for Lay-baptism. The like may be said of the other instances mentioned. I do not say that this necessity so frequently occurs, nor is my argument founded on that supposition: it is enough for me to suppose it barely possible, in order to show the patrons of Lay-baptism the tendency of their principles.

But still Mr. K. has a further evasion. He knows not what I mean by *Lay-preaching* and *Lay-praying;* and seems to wonder I should think either of them absurd in cases of necessity. I mean by *Lay-preaching*, a layman's taking upon him to preach *authoritatively* in GOD'S name, as GOD'S ambassador and as sent by Him, interpreting the supposed necessity to be an extraordinary call, and to supply the want of mission. And I mean by *Lay-praying*, a layman's taking upon him to be a mediator and intercessor between GOD and His people in public prayer, or pretending to bless in GOD'S name. Be not startled at the words mediator and intercessor: they are good words, when rightly understood, and properly applicable to Christian priests.[d]

secondly, because their action, if they did perform the externals ever so correctly, would be wholly null and void, and therefore useless to the recipient,—the second reason depending upon the truth of the first, and following of necessity, if the truth of the first reason is allowed. Do not the same objections to lay-action apply in case of one sacrament as in case of the other? And does not the same consequence follow as inevitably in one case as in the other?

---

[d] Ap. Const. C. ii. c. 25, cum not. Cotelerii.

Now if Mr. K. will suppose that any necessity can justify a layman in taking so much upon him, he must prove that such a one does not come with a lie in his mouth, while he pretends an extraordinary mission; which nothing can be a certain proof of, but the power of working miracles, or a revelation from heaven. In such a case I would allow lay-preaching and lay-praying, and in none else, whatever or how great soever be the supposed necessity for them. And if our lay-baptizers had any such warrant for what they do, they might go on for all me. The two noted instances of Frumentius and the captive woman of Iberia make nothing for your friend's purpose: divulging the Gospel and preparing converts is quite different from preaching. Frumentius did not officiate in his new raised church till he was ordained a Bishop;[e] and as to the captive woman, though Mr. K. would insinuate that she was a lay-preacher; or else I know not why she is brought in here; yet, you may observe, he is very shy of saying she preached, for fear, I suppose, of confronting S. Paul; and therefore cautiously words it, her divulging the Gospel; in which he is very right: for she did indeed divulge the Gospel, but they were ordained ministers, sent from Constantine, that first preached to the Iberians.[f] If it be objected, that Frumentius with the Roman merchants (Christian laics) had Divine service performed after the Christian manner, and therefore prayed at least, though they did not properly preach to the people; I suppose they might use such prayers as were suitable to Christian laymen, without the more solemn forms of intercession or benediction peculiar to

---

[e] Ruff. Eccl. Hist. C. i. c. 9. Theod. Eccl. Hist. C. i. c. 23.

[f] Ruff. Eccl. Hist. C. i. c. 10. Theod. Eccl. Hist. C. i. c. 24.

Priests.[g] However, this is certain, that in both the instances the necessity of a regular ordained Clergy was thought so great and apparent, that all possible haste was made both by Frumentius and the captive woman to obtain one. If this does not satisfy, let it be observed, that Mr. K. acknowledges that miracles were wrought in one of the cases, and it is not impossible there might be in the other also; which I have allowed to be warrant sufficient for what they did: and Mr. K. may infer as much as he pleases from these two instances, when our lay-baptizers bring miracles to attest their mission.

And let this suffice to have vindicated the commission for baptizing, and my reasonings upon it from Mr. K.'s exceptions. Now we proceed to another point. I had observed in my letter, that there were in Scripture some very remarkable examples of GOD's vengeance towards lay usurpers of ecclesiastical offices; and I instanced (as many have done before me) in Saul and Uzza. Mr. K. is of opinion that those instances are not to the purpose, and does indeed offer something considerable against them. The cause is but little concerned in it, and if he takes these instances from us, we can put other more unquestionable in their room, as Corah, Dathan and Abiram, and king Uzziah.[h] As to Saul, I find it a sort of a disputed case, a moot point among the learned, whether he sacrificed in person, or only ordered the Priests to do it. And as to Samuel, whether he sacrificed in person, or no, by virtue of his *prophetic character*, that set him above the ordinary and common rules, is another disputable point among the learned. I incline to the affirmative; and

---

[g] Dodwell de Jure Laico, c. 4.   [h] Numb. xvi. 30; 2 Chron. xxvi. 16.

if you please to see what may be said for it, you may consult Dr. Hickes's Christian Priesthood,[i] and Mr. Dodwell de Jure Laico Sacerdotali,[k] who has made excellent use of the observation in accounting for the difficulty, how it came to pass, that while there was standing ministry in the Jewish Church, yet our SAVIOUR and His Apostles were admitted to teach in the synagogue: but that by the way only. As to Uzza, I do not see why he may not well enough pass for an instance pertinent to the case in hand. We do not say that he was led by any *ambition*, or aspiring thoughts, to touch the ark of GOD; but he rashly presumed to touch *an holy thing*, which none but the family of Aaron were allowed to do;[l] and for this he died. And what could be the reason or design of this law, or of that vengeance, but to secure the greater honour and reverence towards the Priests? And if a Levite, and of the most honourable branch of the tribe, (being a Kohathite, and so next in rank to the Priests,) suffered so remarkably, only for rashly and incogitantly touching an holy thing, against the commandment; of how much greater punishment shall they be thought worthy, who shall presume designedly to invade any part of the Priest's office? We see by this how inviolable the office of a Priest was among the Jews. And if GOD thus fenced about the sacerdotal office in the Jewish Church, to prevent any profanation of it; what shall we think of the sacerdotal office in the Christian Church, of which the former was but a kind of type and shadow? Shall this be invaded and usurped at pleasure? No, that Mr. K. himself will not say, but "will willingly join with me in treating such acts of sacrilegious impiety and presumption with all the seve-

---

[i] P. 185. [k] P. 178. [l] Num. iv. 15.

rity of language I can desire." But that is not enough: while you suppose them *valid*, the rest will pass for little more than empty harangue; for it will be obvious to argue, that if they be valid, they are valid by some law, and if by any law, then by GOD's law, and what GOD establishes by a law, He will not disapprove in the main: or however it will be easy to find out an excuse for a few circumstantial irregularities. Thus the priesthood will be invaded, and its fences laid waste. So that this doctrine of the *validity of lay-ministrations* does not only rest men's salvation upon a precarious uncertain bottom;[1] but it also gives too great a countenance to usurpations and sacrilegious impieties; and opens a wide door to all imaginable confusion. Or if any one thinks all this may be prevented by supposing episcopal confirmation necessary to complete such acts, and to give them their validity; I refer him to Mr. Laurence's incomparable reasonings upon this very point;[m] which I despair of ever seeing answered.

[1] It would appear that the advocates of Lay-baptism, in their eagerness to prohibit the conditional Baptism by a priest of any who have received Lay-baptism, have failed to realize the great force of this argument from uncertainty. In a matter so important as Baptism, we should naturally think that if there were *the very least uncertainty*, every wise man would desire to remove that uncertainty, which can be done by conditional Baptism, and (so far as we know) by no other means. Admitting, for a moment, for the sake of argument, that Lay-baptism is most probably valid; still it cannot be denied that there is at least some "uncertainty" about it; and that uncertainty can be removed by an action, which, if not of any benefit, is at all events quite harmless—Does not every dictate of prudence say, "Take that action, and remove the uncertainty?"

---

[m] Suppl. Pref. p. 37, &c.

We have not yet done with the institution or commission for Baptism laid down in Scripture, till satisfaction be given to another exception, which may seem to weaken the force of it; and that is the noted rule, *quod fieri non debuit, factum valet*, though the Scripture forbids it, it may yet be valid; which I endeavoured to obviate and explain in my letter. And because this is true of matrimony, though the minister be no more than a layman, some might be apt to conclude it was true of Baptism too. So that this must lead us a little off from our point to discourse of matrimony. I thought I made that matter so plain and clear in a few words, that it was next to impossible to mistake it: yet Mr. K. has so perplexed and entangled a very easy case, that it must cost me some pains to set it right.

I could hardly imagine at first reading what it was he designed to prove, till, considering a little further, to my great surprise I found that he was attempting to prove the minister as essential to marriage (*a civil institution*) as to Baptism, *a Christian sacrament*. I shall speak to that point presently; but there are two or three other little matters to be first taken notice of. In order to weaken the force of the objection drawn from that rule, *quod fieri*, &c., I had observed that it was true only of *errors in circumstantials*, not of *errors in essentials;* and he is pleased to allow "the distinction to be very good; but excepts against it, that it will do me no service, till it be proved, that the minister is essential to Baptism." Yes sure, it may be of some service to show, that that rule is of no force to prove the contrary to what we assert, till it can be proved that the minister is not essential, (and then it is needless;) and that was all I was concerned to do in order to answer the objection drawn from that maxim.

Of the Marriage of Quakers.

And because some were willing to confound the case of marriage with this of Baptism, I thought it proper to show that they are by no means parallel. Upon which Mr. K. attempts to prove that the minister is as essential to one as the other; which, if allowed, will not hurt my cause, because I think I can prove the minister essential to Baptism; only the consequence then will be, that there can be no valid matrimony among Jews, Turks, and Pagans; and that adultery is a sin peculiar to Christians. Would not such a consequence startle a man a little, and incline him to think that the minister is not essential to marriage, but a circumstance only of decency, proper among Christians? But he "cannot see, but that upon this principle the pretended marriages among Quakers are as valid as ours." Who doubts it? or that a Quaker's concubine may not be guilty of adultery before GOD, as well as any other? But the civil legislature, it seems, looks upon them as no more than "pretended marriages, and subjoins a proviso, that nothing" (in an act concerning matrimony) "shall be construed so as to declare them good;" good, i.e., effectual in law, as the act itself referred to in the margin[n] expresses it, and it means no more: that is, such marriages shall not be received as good by the common or statute laws of England, nor plead any benefit of the law under that title. And this is a sufficient answer to his question, why the Quakers should be particularly careful not to die intestate. The same answer may serve in relation to the marriages in Cromwell's time before the justices. They were all afterwards confirmed by act of Parliament, and made legal;[o] and had

---

[n] 7 Will. III. c. 6. [o] 12 Car. II. c. 33.

they not been so confirmed, they had been *illegal*, not *invalid;* and could have claimed no benefit of the law. Every one must observe that it depends entirely upon the civil power, what sort of marriage shall be deemed or reputed legal or not. But the validity of it is quite another thing, founded upon mutual contract; and therefore perhaps a precontract is thought a sufficient impediment to marriage with another person; since that precontract is a kind of prior marriage, and wants nothing but the ceremony to make it legal.

I had said that marriage is a covenant between the two parties; that its essence is their mutual contract; and the minister is but a circumstance; whereas in Baptism there is a covenant between GOD and man. GOD is one of the parties; and therefore His consent in person, or by His commissioned proxy or deputy, where there are any such, is essential to it. Against this Mr. K. objects, "that in every vow GOD is party as well as we, being called not only as a witness, but as a judge too." Therefore say I no *party*. For to be *judge* and *party* at the same time are inconsistent; and therefore his speaking of a *third party* here, is nothing but playing upon a word. GOD's being a party in the sense that Mr. K. takes it, is equally applicable to every covenant, contract, or bargain; and yet I hope they may be valid enough without the assistance of the sacred order. His argument from the Divine institution of matrimony comes far short of proof. I suppose government is as much of Divine institution as marriage, and yet I presume kings have been validly married to their people, and may again, without the assistance of a minister. This is certainly GOD's own act, as much as the other, and is notwithstanding purely of a civil nature, and nothing sacerdotal or ecclesiastical is essential to it. I know not what Mr. K. means by insisting so much on the office of matrimony peculiar to the Church of England; unless he would prove that our particular method and manner of solemnizing be essential to marriage; which would make it necessary to be observed all the world over. The truth is, the minister is essential to *legal* matrimony with us, and so perhaps are several other little circumstances. The marriage is complete in the contract between the two parties; and the law only determines what shall be looked upon with us as a sufficient declaration of such a contract. And if joining of hands only was made as significant and effectual in law as the other, the marriage would be as complete and valid, though not so decent and Christian-like, as what we have now. Baron Puffendorf's observation relating to this point is worth reciting: "As the public laws of commonwealths are wont to invest other contracts with certain rites and solemnities, upon want of which they pass for invalid in *civil cognizance;* so in some states there are such ceremonies annexed to matrimony, as, if omitted, make it *illegal,* or at least deprive it of some effects, which would otherwise have sprung from it, according to the local customs and constitutions." This is exactly my sense of the matter. Laws and customs determine what marriage shall pass for legal or valid in civil cognizance. But the essence of matrimony is another thing, being the same in all places and ages; and is nothing else but a *mutual contract;* and is as binding in the nature of the thing before a Justice of peace as before an Archbishop. And indeed if it be performed only by a private engagement between the two parties, *remotis arbitris*, it

156

is as valid *in foro conscientiæ* as any, if they understand one another.

But Mr. K. adds, that "the minister acts for GOD, and in GOD's name, which Mr. W. says none can do without commission from Him: from which account he flatters himself that he has proved that the priest is at least as necessary in marriage as he is in Baptism." But I cannot flatter him so far as to believe it. That the *minister acts in God's name in both* I readily grant: and that he could not thus act without a commission from Him I allow also: only the difference is this, which is very considerable; it is necessary there should be one to act in GOD's name in Baptism, because there is no covenant without the explicit consent of both parties, whereof GOD is one; and therefore the minister, GOD's appointed proxy, is essential to Baptism: but it is not necessary there should be one to act in GOD's name in marriage; because the covenant is not between GOD and man, but between man and woman: and GOD's representative the minister is not essential to it. In Baptism then there must be one to represent GOD, in marriage there need not. Yet if any one will take upon himself to represent GOD under any capacity, either as a witness, or judge, or avenger, he must act by commission, otherwise his act is irregular, sinful, and null, and stands for nothing. Yet the acts of the two contracting parties are effectual and valid; because a contract is nevertheless a contract for the want of a proper person to represent GOD as a witness, or judge, or avenger to it.

I do not dispute, but that the general commission given to the Apostles, &c., reaches to all acts of religion, and consequently to the solemnization of marriage. For whoever acts in GOD's name in any case, must have GOD's authority and warrant for it. But this does not prove that it is absolutely necessary that any one should act in GOD's name in marriage, but only that if he does act in GOD's name, he must act by His authority and by virtue of His commission. And therefore if any layman does pretend, in GOD's name, to join two persons together in *holy matrimony*, he is an usurper of the sacerdotal function, and his part in the solemnity stands for nothing. Yet since the two parties have thereupon solemnly *plighted their troth to each other*, no matter whether the person had any authority to represent GOD or no; their act is valid, and GOD is witness to it in heaven. And now I hope I have sufficiently rescued the case from that confusion and perplexity which Mr. K. had left it in.

I shall beg leave here only to subjoin an observation relating to the point in hand. The celebrated Dr. Sherlock, supposed to be the author of the book noted in the margin,[n] though he was in the main pleading for the same side of the question with Mr. K., yet he thought the argument drawn from the nature of a covenant to be so strong and forcible against the validity of Lay-baptism, that he could find no surer way of evading it than by denying Baptism to be a formal covenant; in which I presume that great man was pretty singular, and only showed that he was hard pressed. To consider that point at large would be too great a digression. There is indeed another much more plausible solution of the difficulty, which he also has recourse to, viz. that circumcision was as much a covenant as Baptism, and *yet any Israelite might circumcise, that knew how to do it.* But to this he himself

---

[n] Vindication of Defence of Dr. Stillingfleet, p. 360, &c.

furnishes us in the same place with a sufficient answer. For he says the administration of Baptism is confined ordinarily to the governors of the Church, whereas the administration of circumcision never was the peculiar office of the priest. Where GOD has given orders for a thing to be done, and left the administration at large, there any man is His authorized proxy that does it: but where He has appointed proper officers, these and these only can act validly, as acting by His authority. It is sufficient therefore to our purpose, that circumcision was not peculiar to the priest's office by the Jewish law, whereas the administration of Baptism is confessedly confined to the Clergy by the Christian law in *all ordinary cases*. And it can never be shown, that it is not likewise so confined in the *extraordinary* too. And thus I have already in a great measure obviated what follows in Mr. K. relating to circumcision, the seal of the covenant to the Jews, as Baptism is to the Christians. The reason then why circumcision was not confined to the sacred order was, because GOD did not so confine it; there He allowed any person to covenant in His name; here He has appointed officers. I should make no further answer with relation to the case of Zipporah, but that Mr. K. has thence taken occasion to triumph over Mr. Laurence, as if he had given up all his principles at once; only because he happened to say, that Zipporah might circumcise in the right of her husband, his authority in his sickness, when he was not able to do anything, devolving upon her. He supposes it might possibly be thus; yet he does not lay the stress of his argument upon it. For in the same place he observes, that Zipporah's act was in a case extraordinary, and he resolves it into immediate revelation, which makes the case very different. But admitting the most Mr. K. would make of it, it can amount to no more than this; that laics or women may exercise sacerdotal functions in extreme necessity, and by the authority of the Bishops. This Mr. L. never directly affirms nor denies; it is beside the question, and his principles may stand good independent of it. But this is an instance of Mr. K.'s blending two distinct questions together, as if they were one; and not considering the difference between authorized and unauthorized Baptisms, while the latter only is the subject of the present debate.

What Mr. K. adds in relation to Zipporah, and the female administration of circumcision, I pass over, the cause being little concerned in it. The other particulars which he takes notice of in the following page will more properly fall in with the other head, whither I think best to refer them, that I may not be too long detained from the judgment and practice of the primitive Church, which is of so great moment in the present controversy, as well as in most others that concern the Church. Here Mr. K. seems to put the main stress of his cause, and here I am ready to join issue with him. I reject everything novel in religion, and for that very reason reject Lay-baptism; because I am persuaded it is novel, and was no current doctrine or practice of the Church for the first six hundred years at least. Mr. K. speaks excellently well in the entrance of his letter: "I believe every position in Divinity which is new, to be false; and that in all questions relating to religion, discipline, or government, *reason* ought to submit to *Scripture*, and Scripture be interpreted by the sense and practice of *antiquity;* and consequently that *history* is the best and shortest decider of this and of every controversy in religion."

Here I heartily close with him. To the Fathers we appeal, and to the Fathers let us go.

II.

He begins with *astonishment* that I should venture to say, that "the ancients do with one voice, for above three hundred years, (Tertullian excepted,) condemn Lay-baptism, not so much as putting any exception for cases of necessity." This was not, I confess, worded distinctly enough in a short letter, designed rather for hints of things, than for clear and full explication. I did not mean that Lay-baptism was *clearly and in terms*[1] condemned by the writers of the first ages; no more was transubstantiation or purgatory; and yet they are sufficiently condemned by them, inasmuch as they held principles inconsistent with them. In this sense I hope to make it appear that Lay-baptism also was condemned by the Church for more than three or four hundred years. It is enough for my purpose, if it was implicitly, virtually, or consequentially condemned; as negative prohibitions are implied in positive precepts, as drunkenness is forbid by commanding sobriety, and irregularity condemned by a precept to observe order. The ancients would be of little use to us in modern controversy, if we suppose them to condemn nothing but what they specify *in terms*. At this rate we might despair of confuting late inventions and modern corruptions from Fathers or Councils; for

---

[1] It is sufficiently plain that no false doctrine, or wrong practice, which is the growth of later times, *can possibly* have been "clearly and in terms condemned by the writers of the first ages." The only way in which such doctrines or practices *can possibly* be brought to the test of antiquity, is the way adopted by Waterland, i.e., an appeal to "principles."

it is evident they could not so *in terms* condemn what they never thought of. But notwithstanding, their very silence in some cases is a sufficient condemnation; and very often, the general reason they went upon in cases disputed in their times may be applicable to others afterwards: and so what they do by consequence or parity of reason condemn, they do as certainly condemn, though not so directly.

The use of the observation in respect to the point in hand will in part appear presently, and more in sequel. Mr. K. himself owns that it is easy to collect many passages of S. Ignatius and others of the ancientest writers, wherein the right of administering in religious matters is asserted to the priesthood, as proper only to them, and the people forbidden to meddle or do anything in holy things, without the concurrence and approbation of the Bishops. And he supposes that to be what I mean. I do indeed mean that, and something more. I mean plainly that according to the prevailing doctrine of the ancients for above three hundred years, the original power of baptizing was lodged solely and entirely in the Bishops, and derivatively conveyed by them to others; who do not appear to have been any, besides the standing ministers of Baptism: from whence I infer, that according to their principles, none could have a power of baptizing without a commission; and therefore if any had pretendedly baptized, their act would have had no authority, no right, or rule, to found its validity upon; and consequently would have been invalid. Therefore upon the principles of the ancients, *Lay-baptism unauthorized*, as that of our Dissenters, is invalid. Again,

By the principles of the ancients, as is confessed on all hands, laymen were always debarred from baptizing in all ordinary cases: therefore, had any laymen pretended to baptize in ordinary cases, their acts had been not only without, but against law, and consequently, as argued before, invalid.

Therefore again, the Baptisms of our Dissenters being done in ordinary cases, and not in any extreme necessity, are by the principles of the ancient Church for above three hundred years together invalid.[o] I observe further, that when laymen were debarred by the ancient Church from meddling with sacred offices, and particularly from baptizing; the prohibitions are general, no exceptions being put in for cases of necessity. Yet such cases might happen then as well as now; not only infants, but many adults might often be in the article of death, and no Clergyman near at hand to baptize them. And if the text of S. John was so rigidly understood, as Mr. K. supposes; strange that this so frequent a case should not have had as frequent provisos! Yet we find nothing of them, except a hint or two from Tertullian, which shall be considered by-and-by. There is no warrant therefore from the ancient Church for Lay-baptism even in cases of necessity; and yet if there was, our Dissenters' Baptisms might be invalid notwithstanding, because utterly destitute of that plea. Upon consideration of the premises therefore, I venture once more to say, that the ancient Church for above three hundred years condemned Lay-baptism, if not directly, if not in terms, yet implicitly, virtually, and consequentially.

As to Mr. K.'s excepting against this, that "no more is intended by it, but to set forth the dignity and pre-eminence of the priesthood, and that it relates only

---

[o] Ign. ad Smyr. c. 8. Cl. Rom. Ep. i. c. 40. Apost. Constit.

to ordinary cases;" and that they did not descend to speak of *extraordinary*, because it had been *highly improper;* all this is as easily denied as affirmed; and it may be observed of S. Chrysostom, (whom he supposes in the place cited to speak the sense of the ancients,) that when he does descend to *extraordinary cases* in another place, he allows not any layman to baptize, but Deacons only. "If there be a necessity," says he, "and a child be found ready to die, and unbaptized, it is lawful for a Deacon to baptize it." Strange he should not have added, or *even a layman*, had he known anything of such a power entrusted with laics. But to proceed from our general argument from the first writers to those of the following times, that speak more home to the point. We will begin with Tertullian.

A.D. 192.

Tertullian I had acknowledged to be for Lay-baptism in cases of necessity, but observed withal that it was only his *private opinion;* as indeed he had many strange ones. Upon this Mr. K. rallies me very pleasantly; he calls it a "modish sovereign charm," and soon after, "a nimble way of taking off an evidence we do not like:" and would have you imagine, that it portends something very dismal; and particularly, that "it makes all convictions from antiquity, except from general councils, impracticable and impossible." But, with submission, this sovereign charm is a very innocent thing; and is no enemy to anything, but to error, mistake, and false reasoning. This nimble way of taking off an evidence is a way used by the best and gravest writers in any controversy depending on the sense of antiquity. It is necessary in reading or quoting the Fathers to distinguish carefully what they give as their own *private judgment*, and what as their *testimony* of the doctrine of the Church. We admit their testimony, because we have all the reason in the world to believe they were honest men. But as to their own *private opinions*, they ought to weigh no more with us, than the reason on which they are founded. Thus the Fathers may always be of great use to us, as witnesses of the doctrine of the Church in their times; though not always as *private doctors*. And therefore I think your friend concluded a little too hastily, that we may hereby set aside all authorities of the ancients, except *general councils*. We set aside none; but we distinguish between what a Father tells us is the doctrine of the Church, and what he gives us as his own. Seeing therefore that the distinction is very good, I am next to show that it was rightly and properly applied. I grant that Tertullian does plead for Lay-baptism in cases of extreme necessity. His arguments are weak enough, and very easily answered: but that is not the point now; for the question only is, whether he speaks the Church's practice, or only delivers his own private opinion. There are two passages commonly referred to in this controversy: the first is this, [p]"Dandi quidem jus habet summus Sacerdos, qui est Episcopus, dehinc Presbyteri et Diaconi, (non tamen sine Episcopi autoritate,) propter Ecclesiæ honorem, quo salva pax est. Alioquin etiam laicis jus est; quod enim ex æquo accipitur, ex æquo dari potest. Nisi Episcopi jam, aut Presbyteri, aut Diaconi, vocantur, Dicentes," &c. The chief Priest, who is the Bishop, has power to give (Baptism), and next to him the Presbyters and Deacons, (but not without the authority

---

[p] De Baptismo, c. 17.

of the Bishop,) *because of their honourable post in the Church*, in preservation of which peace is preserved: otherwise even laymen have a right to give it, for what is received in common may be given in common. Except then that either Bishops or Presbyters or Deacons *intervene*, the ordinary Christians are called to it.

I have thrown in two or three words in the translation, to clear the sense of this passage; I have chiefly followed Mr. Bennet,[q] both as to the sense and to the pointing of them, and refer you to him for their vindication. What I am to observe from them is, that while he asserts an inherent right in laymen to baptize, he acknowledges the custom and practice of the Church to have confined it to the Clergy only for the preservation of peace and order; and he elsewhere[r] acknowledges the settlement of the Clergy to be of Divine institution, and to have obtained from the beginning. So that his assertion runs thus: "Were it not that CHRIST and His Apostles for wise ends and reasons had confined the administration of Baptism to the Bishops, Priests, and Deacons, even laymen might lawfully take upon them to baptize, having an inherent right to do it by virtue of their own Baptism; which right they are only now to use in cases of extreme necessity." Here is not the least intimation that the Church in his time either believed or practised thus. He appeals to no rule, order, or custom for the right of the laity, as he does for that of the Clergy; but, for want of it, sets himself to invent reasons, and goes on in arguing and debating the point for a good while together; which had been needless, had Lay-baptism

---

[q] Rights, &c., p. 118.   [r] De Præscript. Hæret. c. 21.

been the current doctrine or practice of the Church. And beside, the same Tertullian[a] marks it as a singularity of the heretics in his own time, that they made laymen perform the offices of the Clergy: "Nam et laicis sacerdotalia munera injungunt," are his words. He should have added, upon Mr. K.'s scheme, *etiam extra casum necessitatis;* or else what would it have signified to have made such a remark upon the heretics; when upon supposition that the Church allowed the same, it might easily have been retorted upon him? But since he remarks it as a singularity in heretics to allow of it in any case, it is evident Lay-baptism could not be the practice of the Church in his time. To return to the words we were before speaking of; Mr. K. observes from Mr. Bingham, that it "would be strange, if Tertullian, describing just before the practice of the Church in permitting Presbyters and Deacons to baptize, should invert his discourse immediately in the very next words," &c. But as Mr. Laurence in answer to Mr. B. more justly observes, "The word *alioquin* is a plain transition from his former subject of what had reference to the Church's law or custom; and evidently shows that he is going to say something that is separate and distinct therefrom. As much as if he had said, By the law and custom of the Church the Bishop has power to give Baptism, and after him Presbyters and Deacons, yet not without the authority of the Bishop, for the honour of the Church. Otherwise, distinct and separate from the consideration of this law or custom, *laymen* also have a right to give it."

Upon the whole then, it is so far from appearing

---

[a] De Præscript. Hæret. c. 4.

that Tertullian spoke the sense or practice of the Church in relation to Lay-baptism in his time, in the words cited, that the direct contrary may be reasonably inferred from them; and therefore Mr. K. will excuse me, if I repeat it again, that he spoke only *his own private opinion*. And though, for aught I know, Mr. Dodwell might be *the first man that thought so*, and might own it to be a *paradox*, being a very modest and ingenuous author, yet his reasons are good, and will abide the test; or however, we should have taken it kindly of Mr. B. and Mr. K., who join in the censure, if they would have told us likewise who shall be the first man that shall confute him. But I proceed now to the other passage of Tertullian relating to this controversy, where he is arguing against second marriages: "Vani erimus, si putaverimus, quod sacerdotibus non liceat laicis licere; Nonne et laici Sacerdotes sumus? Scriptum est, regnum quoque nos et sacerdotes Deo et Patri suo fecit.[u] Differentiam inter ordinem et plebem constituit Ecclesiæ autoritas, et honor per ordinis concessum sanctificatus, adeo ubi ecclesiastici ordinis non est consessus, et offers, et tinguis, et sacerdos es tibi solus—igitur si habes jus sacerdotis in temetipso ubi necesse est, habeas oportet etiam disciplinam sacerdotis, ubi necesse sit habere jus sacerdotis. Digamus tinguis? Digamus offers,"[x] &c.

Tertullian is here arguing against second marriages even in the laity. It was a rule in the Church in his time, and long after, almost universally held, and supposed to be founded in Scripture,[y] that no Clergyman should marry a second wife. Tertullian being now a

---

[u] Revel. i. 6.   [y] 1 Tim. iii. 2—12; Tit. i. 6.
[x] Exh. ad Castit. ed. Rig. c. 7, p. 522.

Montanist, and very austere in his temper and principles, had a mind to carry the matter further, and to bring even the laity under the same restrictions. It was a difficult matter for him to prove his point: however, being resolved to attempt something, he undertakes to prove that laymen are priests, and therefore ought to be subject to the same rules and the like restraints with them; and consequently not to marry twice. He endeavours to prove laymen priests from a text in the Revelation cited in the margin, from which he might as easily have proved them kings. But would it not from thence follow upon Tertullian's principles, that the laity and Clergy are all one, and might therefore indifferently officiate in the sacred ministrations? No. He was aware of that; and therefore very probably to obviate such a surmise he adds, "Differentiam inter ordinem et plebem constituit," &c., as much as to say, "Though laymen have an inherent right to officiate, yet the exercise of it is restrained so long as there is a particular order of men set apart for that purpose; upon whose rights and powers it would be an encroachment and usurpation for any layman to pretend to officiate, where there is any Clergyman to do it. But where there are no Clergy, there can be no encroachment upon their authority; and so the reason of the restraint ceasing, a layman may then freely exercise his inherent right, may baptize or give the Eucharist, and be his own priest." That this is the sense of Tertullian, and the substance of his reasoning upon the case, I make no doubt: but if you are not satisfied, I refer you to Mr. Bennet,[z] who has spent about thirty pages in interpreting this single

---

[z] Rights of Cl. cap. 9.

passage. That Tertullian here asserts, that laymen may baptize in want of Clergy, I readily allow: but that he lays it down as the doctrine or practice of the Church in his time, I utterly deny. It is all nothing else but his private reasoning; and that very probably in answer to a tacit objection, which he could not otherwise get rid of. So natural is it for a man, that will maintain absurd paradoxes, to fall from one absurdity to another. Mr. K. upon this passage makes a strong misrepresentation of the sense of the author, and fancies he sees such principles as Tertullian never dreamt of. He says, "Certainly no man of common sense would pretend to persuade men against second marriages, upon the topic of supposing them to be thereby unqualified to baptize, &c. in cases of necessity, if Baptism by laymen had at that time been never practised." But this is all a mistake. Tertullian goes upon no such topic. The topic he went upon was, that laymen had an inherent priesthood in themselves, which he founds upon a mistaken text in the Revelation; and what he asserts afterwards, of their right to baptize and give the Eucharist in case of necessity, is nothing but a forced inference, which his former premises necessarily drove him to, as has been before explained. However, that you may not suspect I assert anything confidently without some grounds, I observe,

1. That there is hardly a shadow of an argument to prove that he here spoke the sense of the Church. The chief thing commonly urged is, that *offers* and *tingis* are in the present tense, seeming to imply something then really practised: to which the answer is easy, that they are not to be understood *indicatively*, but *potentially*, as Mr. Dodwell and Mr. Bennet have suffi-

ciently shown.[a] They do not signify, *you do act thus*, but, *you may act thus*, or *have power to act thus*, in consequence of the principle before laid down, that laymen have an inherent priesthood. And that the words cited by Mr. K., *Digamus offers? Digamus tinguis?* are used potentially and not indicatively, is very plain: for as Mr. Bennet well observes, his friend had lately buried his wife, and was not yet married again; and therefore the words can bear no other sense but this, Would you baptize and administer the LORD's Supper, when married a second time? More might be added, but for brevity's sake I refer you to the forementioned authors, and proceed to show,

2. That there are good reasons to prove that Tertullian did not speak the sense or practice of the Church at that time. Observe the words, "Adeo ubi ecclesiastici ordinis non est consessus, et offers, et tinguis, et sacerdos es tibi solus." The *adeo* shows it to be an inference drawn from his former position, and not an assertion of any matter of fact in that time. Or if this does not satisfy, I shall add another consideration, which certainly must. Tertullian here joins the administration of the LORD's Supper with that of Baptism; and therefore if he spoke the practice of the Church in one, he did so in both; which I presume Mr. K. himself will hardly say: that the ancient Church ever permitted laymen to consecrate the Eucharist, can never be supposed by any man that knows anything of Church history. And yet Tertullian's words are as full and clear a proof of that, as of the practice of Lay-baptism. This is demonstration that he spoke not the sense of the Church, but his own. I know Mr. K. has here a sovereign charm, which he

---

[a] De Jure Laico, p. 53. Rights, p. 298.

had used before as well as now, and very unluckily in both places. He imagines that the word *offers* signifies no more than what Dr. Cave tells us, that laymen reserved consecrated elements in their houses, and so received at home: this is his sense, though not his words. But, with submission, I think it strange that Tertullian should mean no more than this: for not to mention that the word *offerre* absolutely put, answering to the Greek προσφέρειν, hardly ever signifies anything else in Church writers but to consecrate the LORD's Supper; is constantly used so by S. Cyprian,[b] and Tertullian[c] himself in other places: I say, not to mention this, which is so well known to the learned, that Dr. H. B. Johnson, &c. take it for granted that *offers* in this place signifies administering the Eucharist: there is another consideration offered by Mr. Dodwell,[d] decisive in the case, viz., that the whole scope and tenor of Tertullian's reasoning makes it absurd to take it in any other sense. For how ridiculous would be his whole reasoning, if, undertaking to prove that laymen had a proper inherent priesthood, and consequently might minister in sacerdotal offices, he should give an instance of an act not sacerdotal; not requiring any sacred character? From the whole then I think it is evident that Tertullian did mean the giving the Eucharist in the strict sense, as a sacerdotal act. For it is plain, that Tertullian upon his own principles meant not to exclude the laity from any clerical functions, how high and sacred soever; provided only, that they should not assume them, but in extreme necessity in utter want of a proper Clergy. If then he spoke the doctrine or practice of the Church in relation to Bap-

---

[b] Ep. l. 5, 17, 63, 69.
[c] De vet. c. 9; de exh. Cast. c. 11.
[d] De Jure Laic. cap. i. 2, 10.

tism being administered by laymen, I must insist upon it, that he spoke the doctrine and practice of the Church in relation to the Eucharist too. But because Mr. K. will, I am sure, deny it of the latter, I must beg leave to deny it of the former also; and consequently must still be bold to say, that Tertullian in this passage, as well as in the former, spoke only his own private opinion. Seeing then that Tertullian is thus singled out and separated, and has now nothing left to support him but his own slender reasons, it would be too easy a conquest to set upon him and confute him; which has been done so often: and therefore I leave him, only making these following observations in relation to him.

1. That he allows of Lay-baptism, but at the same time is forced to suppose laymen to be Priests in order to qualify them to baptize: so that, in the main, I take him to be of my side of the question; for if I could but prove that laymen are not proper Priests, (under this word we include Deacons,) which would be no hard matter; his own principles would lead him into my conclusion.

2. He founds his doctrine of Lay-baptism upon an inherent right of priesthood in every Christian. This can never agree with Mr. K.'s hypothesis; who founds it upon I know not what plenitude of power in the Bishops, inconsistent with Tertullian's principles: and therefore, with submission, while he rejects his principles, he ought not, I think, to allege his authority for the conclusion; because, if you disarm Tertullian of his premises, you do at the same time in effect make him disown the conclusion built upon them.

3. Tertullian allowed of Lay-baptism only in case of necessity: therefore his authority is not pertinently alleged in favour of Dissenters' Baptisms, which have

no such plea ; consequently whatever force there may be in the argument drawn from his authority, it is wide of the question.

4. Tertullian acknowledges, that in all ordinary cases the administration of Baptism is appropriate to the Clergy, condemns all Lay-baptism in such cases, as irregular and sinful. Whether he would have *pronounced them invalid* does not certainly appear ; though it might be probably enough argued that he would ; because it was his principle, as Mr. K. himself owns, to annul heretical Baptisms,[e] and probably schismatical too, (the same general reasons affecting both,) and such Baptisms would be schismatical. It is therefore reasonable to believe, that he must have pronounced Dissenters' Baptisms (such as among us) null and void. And therefore perhaps in the main I was a little too complaisant to Mr. K. to give him up Tertullian ; who, if he were to speak home to the point in debate, I am persuaded would be on our side. For the *inherent right of priesthood*, on which he founds the validity of Lay-baptism, has no place in ordinary cases, or however ceases in a schism ; and then there is nothing left upon his principles to render the thing *valid*. And now from Tertullian let us come to

S. Cyprian, 248.

From whom Mr. K. confesses he has no positive evidence. I should wonder much if he had ; because there cannot, I think, be a more positive evidence against him. You remember, I hope, that we are disputing whether the pretended Baptisms of Dissenters (i.e. of schismatical laymen) are valid. Now

---

[e] De Bapt. c. 15.

can any man imagine that Cyprian, who rejected the Baptisms of schismatical clergymen, should admit the pretended Baptisms of schismatical laics? Nothing can be clearer than that S. Cyprian would have nulled and vacated all such pretended Baptisms.

But it may perhaps be replied, that though S. Cyprian does agree with us in the conclusion, yet he differs from us in the premises, and condemns schismatical Baptisms, because *schismatical*, and not because they were Lay-baptisms. To which I answer, that he rejected schismatical Baptisms, because they were in his opinion *unauthorized uncommissioned Baptisms*, which was in effect to call them Lay-baptisms, or however upon the same principle that schismatical Baptisms were rejected, all unauthorized Lay-baptisms must be rejected also. Mr. K. thinks that Cyprian's silence on this subject, when he had such an inviting occasion to speak of it, will afford a fair presumptive argument, that Baptism administered by a layman was not thought invalid. I am not of Mr. K.'s mind, and shall show why, presently. Only first let me lay before you Mr. Bennet's reasoning from the like topic in this very case the other way: "Had any such thing (as Lay-baptism) been allowed before the controversy of rebaptizing heretics was managed by S. Cyprian, it is impossible (as every one may see) that it should never have been taken notice of by either of the contending parties, though the necessary inference from such a practice would have nearly affected that dispute —nor was any such practice ever heard of before the fourth century." Mr. Bennet is very right; for had Lay-baptism been admitted by the Church at that time, S. Cyprian's adversaries could not have failed to have taken advantage of it, in order to invalidate his reasonings against schismatical Clergy, (for as to heretical, they are of distinct consideration,) being founded mostly on this principle, that they had forfeited their orders, and had no sacerdotal powers left, being cut off from the Church: for if the Baptisms of laics in the Church, who never had sacerdotal powers given, be valid; why not the Baptisms of schismatical Clergy, who once had powers, but had lost them, according to Cyprian? The silence therefore of S. Cyprian's adversaries upon this point is a demonstration that no such practice as that of Lay-baptism was known in the Church in his time. But as to S. Cyprian's silence on the other hand, nothing can be inferred to the prejudice of our cause.

It was not necessary for him to say that *Lay-baptism* is allowed to be *invalid;* therefore so is the Baptism of schismatics; because this would have been begging the question, and proving idem per idem. The point was only whether schismatics had forfeited their orders or no; and how impertinent would it have been for S. Cyprian to observe that laymen could not baptize, unless his adversaries had allowed the schismatical Clergy to be no more than laymen, which they never did allow, but still contended they were priests? I say then that S. Cyprian had no occasion to take notice of the invalidity of Lay-baptism; because that, if granted, was wide of the point; since it did not appear that the schismatical Clergy were no more than laymen. But he set himself to prove that they were not Priests, that they had lost their commissions, that they had no sacerdotal power or character left; and that therefore their Baptisms were invalid. What was this, but in effect to prove them no more than laymen, and to reject their Baptisms on that very account; because, as to commission, they had no more than laymen, having lost what they had? What does it signify whether he called them laics or no; so long as he said what was tantamount to it in other words, viz., that they were not Clergymen, and consequently, and therefore had no power to baptize? And that this was said over and over by S. Cyprian and his adherents, is too plain to need proof. I expect here to be told, that the main principle on which the Cyprianists grounded their severe doctrine was, that schismatics were cut off from the Church; and therefore all they did was invalid. This I readily own; and it is very consistent with what I said before. For they reasoned thus: schismatics are *foris, extra Ecclesiam*, cut off from the Church; therefore, being divided from the fountain, they can convey nothing spiritual; therefore they have no power left of baptizing, their orders being as it were extinct, void, and null. So that the immediate reason why they could not baptize was, because their sacerdotal power was supposed to be lost and extinct, their right ceasing. But doth not this reason equally affect laymen, who never had this sacerdotal power or right given them? or does not the argument conclude as strongly against those that never had it, as against those that once had, but are supposed to have lost it? S. Basil[e] therefore was much in the right in saying, that Cyprian and Firmilian, with their adherents, rejected the Baptisms of schismatics upon this principle, that being cut off from the Church, and become laics, λαϊκοὶ γενόμενοι, they had lost the power of baptizing. For how does this differ from Cyprian's and Firmilian's own account of the matter, but in this small punctilio: according to S. Basil, they rejected

---

[e] [Migne, Patrol. Græc. Vol. 32, pp. 668, 9.]

the Baptisms of schismatics, because they judged them to be mere *laics;* according to their own account, they rejected them, because they judged them to be *no Priests, no proper or true Clergy.* I know that other arguments were used in the dispute beside this; yet this was the main argument, and most frequently occurs, except it be that schismatics had lost the power of remitting sins and conferring the Spirit, which almost amounts to the same thing. What I have here asserted is abundantly confirmed from S. Austin's management of this controversy with the Donatists afterwards. The main point, which he there undertakes to prove, and in which he prevails and triumphs over his adversaries at every turn, is, that heresy and schism did not null or vacate orders. For when the Donatists objected to him, that schism deprived them of the right of baptizing, he denies it utterly, and pleads strongly for the *indelible character.*[f] And he proves it unanswerable upon a principle which both sides acknowledged, viz. that *heresy or schism did not vacate Baptism before received in the Church.* If a layman by being a schismatic does not forfeit his Baptism, why should a Clergyman be thought to forfeit his orders? "Utrumque enim sacramentum est, et quadam consecratione utrumque homini datur, illud cum baptisatur, illud cum ordinatur, ideoque in Catholica utrumque non licet iterari." And he proceeds to observe at large, that when Clergymen who had deserted the Church were allowed again to officiate, (as they were sometimes,) upon their return they were never re-ordained, having the priestly character still residing in them. He repeats this argument in another place:[g]

---

[f] Contra Ep. Parmen. l. ii. c. 13.　　[g] De Bapt. l. i. c. 1.

"Nullus autem eorum negat habere Baptismum etiam apostatas, quibus utique redeuntibus et per pœnitentiam conversis, dum non redditur, amitti non posse judicant, ———— quod si haberi foris (Baptismus) potest, etiam dari cur non potest? Sacramentum enim Baptismi est, quod habet, qui baptisatur, et sacramentum dandi Baptismi est, quod habet, qui ordinatur. Sicut autem Baptisatus, si ab unitate recesserit, sacramentum Baptismi non amittit; sic etiam ordinatus, si ab unitate recesserit, sacramentum dandi Baptismi non amittit." And it is worth observing what he elsewhere observes of S. Cyprian in these words:[h] "Satis ostendit (Cyprianus) facillime se correcturum fuisse sententiam suam, siquis ei demonstraret Baptismum Christi dari posse ab eis, qui foras exierunt, quemadmodum amitti non potuit, cum foras exirent, unde multa jam diximus, nec nos ipsi tale aliquod auderemus asserere, nisi universæ Ecclesiæ concordissima autoritate firmati."

It was S. Cyprian's own principle, as well as that of the universal Church at all times, that no schism, heresy, or even apostasy, could take away Baptism once validly given; and therefore Cyprian himself[i] admitted all that returned to the Church (having been before baptized in it) without rebaptizing, and indeed constantly condemns rebaptization properly so called.

S. Austin argues upon this principle; if Baptism once validly given is alway valid, then orders once validly given are alway valid; therefore can never be *deleted by any heresy, schism,* or *apostasy;* therefore schismatical Clergymen still retain their *sacerdotal character*, therefore their ministrations, and particularly Baptism, are still valid, inasmuch as they could not lose

---

[h] De Bapt. l. ii. c. 4.   [i] Ep. lxxi. p. 194.

their right of baptizing given in their ordination. This is so clear all the way in S. Austin's dispute with the Donatists, that he that runs may read it. It is plain then, that he thought the strength of Cyprian's cause consisted in this one mistaken principle, that *schism and heresy nulled orders:* and that if S. Cyprian had been convinced of that mistake, he would have changed his *opinion.* What is this but asserting, or at least insinuating, the very same thing with S. Basil; that Cyprian rejected the baptism of schismatics, because he rejected their *orders,* and looked upon them, as to any sacerdotal power or right, as being no more than laymen? Upon the whole then, I venture to say again, and shall give further proof of it before I have done, " That the question in those times was not whether Lay-baptisms were null, both sides supposing that as an undoubted principle, (meaning by Lay-baptisms unauthorized Lay-baptisms,) but whether heresy and schism nulled orders."

I have mentioned S. Austin only as a witness of S. Cyprian's sense and meaning, whom he thoroughly studied, and as thoroughly confuted, with respect to that point on which Cyprian grounded his opinion, viz. that *heresy or schism nulled orders;* which being removed, there was nothing considerable left to support the doctrine of the *invalidity of heretical or schismatical Baptisms,* if administered in due form with water and in the Name of the Blessed Trinity.

For the clearer apprehension of Cyprian's principles, I shall just observe to you, wherein he and the other churches with him differed from the more ancient and universal Church with relation to schismatics. He thought they were entirely cut off from the Church, and therefore had nothing common with it, and consesequently their Clergy were not Clergy. The other churches thought they were not so entirely cut off, but were parts still, though unsound parts, and retained many things common with the Church; and so were still Christians in a large sense, as much as a baptized drunkard, idolater, atheist, or apostate, is such, or as much as a Judas or a Simon Magus.

Cyprian,[k] in consequence of his principle, thought that all the powers of the schismatical Clergy were extinct and dead, as rays separated from the sun, branches broken off from the body of the tree, streams divided from the fountain. But the Catholic Church, if we may allow S. Austin to be her interpreter,[l] thought the *waters of Paradise*, the spiritual powers of the Church, might flow in continued streams *beyond Paradise* itself, (by which is meant the Church,) and so spiritual powers might be conveyed and exercised *validly*, though not *savingly*,[1] so as the sacraments should not need to be

---

[1] This theory of S. Augustine's (which no one on either side of this controversy questions that he held) is a perplexing one, as it is difficult to understand in what sense he held Laybaptism to be valid. To ordinary minds a Baptism which is "valid" is a Baptism which conveys the grace of regeneration and the remission of sins, and a baptism, which does not convey this grace, is not "valid." But S. Augustine expressly states his belief that these unauthorized baptisms do not convey any grace, they are "of no avail for the remission of sins," (De Baptismo, lib. i. cap. 18.) They do "not avail for any spiritual profit," (Ib. lib. vii. cap. 53,) and yet they are "the Baptism of CHRIST," (Ib. lib. i. cap. 18,) and in some sense valid, but in what sense it is difficult to see. If such baptisms convey no grace, what do they convey? and if they convey nothing, how, and for what purpose, are they valid? This

---

[k] De Unit. Eccl. p. 108, ed. Oxon. Ep. 69, 73. Firm. Ep. 20, 202.   [l] Aug. de Bapt. l. iv. c. 1, passim.

repeated upon their return to the Church, but only to be made effectual to salvation by unity, repentance, and charity. You may observe then, that both of them supposed a necessity of a conveyance of spiritual powers to the administrators to make Baptism valid. And the only question was, whether in heresy or schism theirs was such a conveyance or no. S. Cyprian would not acknowledge any, S. Austin both asserted and proved 174 it. And so the doctrine of the indelible character, which S. Austin and the whole Catholic Church received at that time, was the main, if not the only principle, whereby they confuted S. Cyprian's tenets; whose authority the Donatists made great use of in that controversy against the Catholics. From whence, by the way, I cannot but wonder at Mr. Bingham's strange attempt, strange in a man of his learning and sagacity, to overthrow this so well grounded notion of the indelible character of orders, by which, whatever he pretends, he runs cross to all antiquity, (except the African Church in the time of S. Cyprian, and a few years before and after,) and not only so, but upon that principle leaves the arguments of the Cyprianists and Donatists incapable of a sufficient answer.

But to proceed. I hope I have said enough to show

is not a little obscure; but it is perfectly plain that the validity which modern advocates claim for Lay-baptism is something essentially different from that which S. Augustine claimed. These moderns make much of the great authority of S. Augustine, so long as he seems to hold with them, and to maintain a certain validity (though not *their* validity) in Lay-baptism: but where, at the root of the matter, he disagrees with them, they repudiate him utterly, and directly contradict his teaching; and then presently refer to him again, as if he were altogether on their side.

how much Mr. K. is mistaken in his judgment about S. Cyprian; and so might pass fairly to the next authority cited in this controversy; yet, that I may not seem to overlook anything that he has been pleased to urge on the other side, I shall just take some short notice of what he has excepted, before I go any further.

He thinks it highly probable that Cyprian was in the same sentiments with his master Tertullian. This argument is so inconclusive in itself, and so easily confuted by more than twenty instances, wherein Cyprian was wiser than his master, that I need not enlarge further upon it: beside that Tertullian himself, as I have observed above, was no great friend to Mr. K.'s hypothesis. He observes further, that probably among the heretics or schismatics some must be baptized by laics, and therefore wonders why S. Cyprian did not make that an argument against their Baptisms, if he disowned Lay-baptism: since that would have been the most plausible argument of all. But in answer to this, I am far from thinking that that argument would have been plausible, or so much as pertinent or proper to support S. Cyprian's cause; because it would not have affected the heretics in general, but only some part of them, viz. those that allowed women or laics to baptize. Besides, amongst those, all were not baptized by women or laics, but only some few, very probably an inconsiderable number in comparison. Consider then how Mr. K. would make Cyprian argue: "Among some heretics it may sometimes happen, that persons may have no other Baptisms but from the hands of women or laics; therefore I would have all that come from heretics (though most of them have been baptized by heretical clergymen) baptized in the Church." Would this have been a conclusion worthy of S. Cyprian?

Would this have been the most plausible argument of all, which is so manifestly inconclusive, and would only have exposed the cause? In a word, S. Cyprian's drift and design was to prove all heretical and schismatical Baptisms null; and so there is a plain reason to be given why he would not use Mr. K.'s argument, which is vastly short of the point. I may observe here, by the way, that when the Church came to distinguish between heretics, allowing the Baptisms of some and not of others, they rejected the Baptisms of the Montanists, (among which you may reckon the Pepuzians and Quintilians,) while they allowed of Arians and Macedonians, as great heretics as the other. See Gen. Conc. Constant. can. 7. Yet it was not given as a reason for rejecting their Baptisms, that women and laics among them baptized, because there were other general reasons that were sufficient, which affected them all. But from hence I remark, that it does not appear that the Church ever received the Baptisms of any of these heretics, who allowed laymen or women to baptize; so that nothing can be thence inferred in favour of Lay-baptism. To what has been said I may add this, that there might be another such argument, every whit as plausible as this now mentioned; that some heretics, particularly the Montanists,[m] did not baptize children, but delayed Baptisms a long time; from whence it might be that several heretics returning might happen to be unbaptized: yet neither did S. Cyprian use that argument; probably because it did not affect all, and such a particular case might be remedied as well as the other, only by demanding certificates of their Baptism before their admission into the Church.

---

[m] Hist. of Mont. p. 147.

Mr. K. next, in order to weaken the testimony of S. Basil, observes, that he does not give us the words either of Cyprian or Firmilian. But I have already proved that he gives us their sense, which is enough. And sure, if we could not prove it from Cyprian's or Firmilian's own works, so considerable a writer as Basil, who lived about a century after them, and was successor to one of them in his see, might be credited upon his bare word in a matter of testimony, as this is. As to the next exception, that Basil might mean, not Cyprian and Firmilian, but their adherents; I am persuaded upon second thoughts he will be inclined to believe that he meant both; especially if he considers that the tenet there laid down was the principle of the party, as I have observed above, was received by the Donatists, and does not appear to have been completely and solidly answered, before S. Austin undertook it. And then he did not pretend to confute the principle itself, (unless a few diffident conjectures brought in by the by may be called a confutation,) but in the main he confirmed the principle, and denied the inference drawn from it. And this is a sufficient answer to the other subterfuge, that S. Cyprian might perhaps "speak only his private opinion;" for though I readily own that the Church in a few years after determined against his principle of *heresy or schism's nulling orders:* yet they never so determined against his other, that *unauthorized Baptism is null.* And even as to the former principle, though in comparison it was novel, (since Cyprian himself could have it no higher than Agrippinus,) and never was general; yet the world was nearly divided into halves upon it in the time of S. Cyprian, and perhaps afterwards, till the Councils of Arles[n] and Nice[o]

---

[n] A.D. 314, c. 8.   A.D. 325, c. 19.

decided the question. What follows in Mr. K. has been answered already. And so I pass on to the Elvira, leaving S. Basil to come in again in due time and place.

COUNCIL OF ELVIRA, A.D. 305. 19 Bishops.

The thirty-eighth canon is what concerns our present dispute. The words you have in Mr. K. His reflection upon them is this. That the Fathers of that Council "do not so much assert, as *suppose and take for granted* the liberty of laymen to baptize in cases of necessity, (*nothing being more common in that age,*) but *restrain* the use of that liberty to such alone of the laity as had not unqualified themselves for holy orders." A strange account this of that Spanish Council, and in those few words no less than three either manifest mistakes, or at least groundless suggestions.

1. That "they supposed or took for granted" the liberty of laymen to baptize, how does this appear? Because they gave them such a liberty, therefore they supposed they had it before. The words of the canon are, "posse baptizare," i.e. such a person as is there described may baptize; he is empowered or authorized by this present canon to do it; therefore say I, he could not do it before, or else, what need of the canon?

2. "Nothing being more common in that age." Whence could Mr. K. learn this? We have seen what Tertullian's and S. Cyprian's authorities amount to; and shall inquire into the rest in order, who will be found to say no such thing: or does he ground it wholly on this canon? That is what I imagine; and then it is an inference from what he said before; because the Council took it for granted, therefore it must be "common in that age." But the first is so

far from being true, as I have observed, that the very words and intent of the canon rather prove the quite contrary. But he supposes the intent of the canon was,

3. "To restrain the use of some liberty" which they had before. This is very wonderful, that men upon a voyage and under great necessities, which might entitle them to the most favour and indulgence of any, should have a canon made on purpose to abridge them of a liberty, that any man might take at home. But waiving the unreasonableness of such a supposition, which seems as absurd as to say, *because you have more occasion for liberty, therefore you shall have less;* I say, waiving that, yet how is it reconcilable with the very frame and tenor of the canon, which upon Mr. K.'s scheme should have had a quite different turn, in the form of a prohibition, as thus: "Though it has been a custom for laymen to baptize in cases of necessity; yet in this particular case upon a voyage we strictly forbid it, unless with these provisos, &c.," and so it should have been worded *negatively*, "*Non posse* quenquam, qui sit bigamus, &c." which would, in my humble opinion, have suited much better with the wisdom and accuracy of the *Spanish Fathers*. But not to insist further in so clear a case; the truth is, here is a plain *permission* of Lay-baptism, though under several *restrictions;* and I wonder any man who is concerned for the credit of his cause should endeavour to make anything more of it, because it betrays a bias, and makes the argument look less considerable than it really is. But to come to the point, we may observe as to this canon,

1. It must be in a case of *extreme necessity*. This gives no umbrage to the Baptisms of Dissenting laymen with us, who can plead no such necessity. The

administrator *must be one of the faithful, who has his* own *Baptism entire*, i.e., probably confirmed, and one that is in communion with the Bishop. Therefore necessity alone is no sufficient plea, nor the *inherent right* mentioned by Tertullian; because if they were, there would have been no need of further restrictions. And yet besides the former, he was not to be a bigamist.

2. The most that can be made of this Council is, that the Spanish Fathers thought authorized Lay-baptisms valid; which does not affect our present question, as it has been observed.

3. It does not appear that this was the current doctrine of the Catholic Church at that time, but rather the contrary; because if it had been so, there had been no need of a particular canon to allow it.

4. It is not a testimony of fact, but the judgment only of a private council. However, I am willing to allow that a national council may afford as considerable an evidence of the doctrine and discipline of the Western Church, as S. Basil's single letter can of the Eastern and something more, provided it be meant only of the times when S. Basil wrote, and this Council was held. But then it is to be noted, that it does not appear that the Western Church ever received this canon of the Spanish Council,[q] nor was its authority ever urged, as Dr. Brett well observes, by any of the Fathers, who pleaded for the validity of Lay-baptism; whereas the epistle of S. Basil is a canonical epistle, and received by the Greek Church, and as such is put into the canonical code of that Church, as early as the sixth century at least. This so important and material

---

[q] Bingham, Schol. Hist. Works, vol. ix. p. 30. Oxford ed.

a difference between these two is of great force in the present argument, and should not, I think, have been concealed from the reader. When we quote the epistle of S. Basil, we give the authority of the whole Greek Church, who received it; but when we quote this canon, it is no more than the private opinion of one national church; and yet, to make the best of it, it comes not up to the matter in debate, but is wide of the question, since it allows no Baptism by laymen, but what is *authorized by Bishops*, done in *extreme necessity*, done by one in *communion* with the Church, and qualified for *orders*. Here are no less than four qualifying circumstances; none of which are applicable to the pretended Baptisms of our Dissenters, about which we are disputing; and therefore little use can be made of this canon in the present controversy.

COUNCIL OF ARLES, A.D. 314. 33 Bishops.

Having before mentioned this Council, it may be proper to observe, that the eighth canon determines the famous question about rebaptization of heretics; ordaining, "that if any one leave a heresy, and return to the Church, he shall be asked concerning the Creed; and if it be known that he was baptized in the Name of the FATHER, SON, and HOLY GHOST, imposition of hands only shall be given him, that he may receive the HOLY SPIRIT; but if he does not acknowledge the Trinity, he shall be rebaptized." I shall only observe here, that the question in those days was not about Lay-baptisms, but about the Baptisms of heretical and schismatical Clergy; and the Church still looking upon their *orders* as good and valid, and therefore operative and effective, even in heresy and schism, (contrary to what the *Cyprianic churches* before, and the *Donatists* then taught,) did of consequence receive their Baptisms, if administered in the Name of the Trinity. For if the orders of those who first left the Church were really valid and indelible, why should not all their acts be valid too, and consequently their Ordinations and Baptisms?

COUNCIL OF NICE, A.D. 325. 300 Bishops.

"The eighth canon declares, that the Novatian Clergy, who return to the Church, may continue in the Clergy after having received imposition of hands. This was determining the famous controverted point about the validity of the Orders of schismatical Clergy. The Novatian Clergy were allowed to be Clergy, that is, their Orders were pronounced valid."[r]

This is what I presume S. Austin might have in his eye, when he so often appeals to the Catholic decision of the Church on his side in his disputes with the Donatists; from whence I cannot but again observe, that this was the principal point in debate, and that the other question about heretical and schismatical Baptisms depended entirely upon it. They were looked upon to be either valid or invalid, according as should be judged of the orders of those heretics or schismatics; so that both sides supposed Lay-baptism to be null and void.

The nineteenth canon ordains, that the Paulianists should be rebaptized, and their pretended Clergy not received as Clergy, till rebaptized and ordained in the Church. By Paulianists are meant the followers of Paul of Samosata, who denied CHRIST's Divinity, and consequently did not baptize in the Name of the Tri-

---

[r] Brev. Not. ad Can. p. 61. Brett's Furth. Enq. p. 20. Laur. Suppl. p. 61.

nity: so that this canon agrees exactly with the eighth canon of the Council of Arles cited above; only in both it were more proper to say *baptize*, than *rebaptize;* because no more is meant than that such should be baptized in the Church as had not received true Baptism before, wanting the due form. Rebaptization strictly so called was never admitted in the Catholic Church. About this time comes in the fable of Athanasius's baptizing his playfellows, and the pretended determination of Bishop Alexander upon it. Mr. K. is too conscious to vouch for the truth of it, but he observes, after Mr. Bingham,[t] that "Ruffinus and Sozomen do not censure the decree supposed to be made upon it," nay, he adds of his own, that they seem to applaud it. This is largely and solidly answered by Mr. Laurence.[u] I shall observe from him in short, that Ruffinus, the first relater of Alexander's supposed determination, relates it with such diffidence, as if he did not firmly believe it. Socrates Scholasticus, who comes after him, leaves out the latter part of the story; probably because he thought it not worthy of credit. Sozomen copies the story from Ruffinus, and leaves it as he found it; nothing can be concluded from their passing no censure upon it, but that either they thought it too improbable a story to make any serious censure upon; or that they looked upon it, if true, as done by a Divine instinct, and carrying something supernatural in it, upon which Alexander's determination might be founded; or, lastly, that in a very particular and extraordinary case they chose to suspend their judgment, and so leave it to the reader to think as he pleased of it. Any of these is as probable as what Mr. K. would

---

[t] Schol. Hist. Works, vol. ix. p. 31, 32. Oxford ed.   [u] Part ii. p. 85, 88.

insinuate; or however are enough to show, that the argument is very weak and inconclusive; or if you are not satisfied, be pleased to consult Mr. L. in the places cited in the margin.

As to Mr. K.'s further remark in relation to S. Jerome, I suppose it will weigh little. Ruffinus's History might not perhaps be published, when S. Jerome wrote his answer to the other's *invectives;* and it was hardly worth the while to renew the quarrel afterwards, especially when he had been bitter enough before. Besides that Ruffinus's History is faulty enough in many other things, which yet were never taken notice of by S. Jerome. You may please to observe Dr. Cave's censure upon it, Hist. Litter. vol. i. p. 218. "In historia isthac concinnanda temporisque ratione digerenda credulum admodum fuisse Ruffinum constat, in fabulas et incertos plebeculæ rumores nimis propensum, quos e triviis et tonstrina petitos literis mandare temere solebat."

I need not have troubled you with so much about this, but that out of respect to your friend, I thought it good manners not to pass anything over without notice, which he had thought worth his remarking. The next writer in order of time may be

HILARY THE ROMAN DEACON, A.D. about 355.

Probably the author of the commentary passing under the name of S. Ambrose. By the way, this Hilary was a stiff and rigid Luciferian; not only rejected the Arian Ordinations, but their Baptisms too, and would receive none without *rebaptizing*, nor so much as communicate with those that received them; which was a step beyond the rigour of the Cyprianists. I suppose a person of this character and principle could be no great favourer of schismatical Lay-baptisms; or if he were, neither his authority nor judgment should weigh much with us. But let us hear what advantage Mr. K. can make of him. He observes, that Hilary "supposes the office of baptizing and preaching separable," though they are both joined together in the commission. I see no such supposition in Hilary's words; "Non omnis qui baptizat, idoneus est et Evangelizare." A man may be invested in both these offices together by ordination, and may be fitter to perform one than the other, without supposing them *separable*. The occasion of the observation was what S. Paul had said, that he "was not sent to baptize, but to preach the Gospel;"[x] i.e. not so much for the one as the other; preaching being his principal business. For he was certainly *sent* to baptize as well as to preach, was ordained and empowered equally to both, and so the offices were *inseparable;* but because he could do more good by one than the other, and was peculiarly adapted for it, he might leave the ministration of Baptism, more easily executed, to persons of inferior abilities, and who had less upon their hands than he had. How is this pertinent to our present case? or what would Mr. K. insinuate from it? That Baptism is not a clerical office, nor to be reckoned among the sacerdotal powers? That is what I believe he would almost find in his heart to intimate to us; but it was wiser not to speak out. To proceed. This Pseudo-Ambrose, or Hilary, it seems, tells us, that at first, for the swifter propagation of the Gospel, leave was given to all promiscuously to teach, baptize, and explain the Scriptures; and that too *in Ecclesia.* To all whom? Not to women, I presume.

---

[x] 1 Cor. i. 7.

By whom was this leave given? By GOD, I suppose, or by His representatives the Apostles; which, if true, (as it is not,) is little to the purpose. Show any such leave for modern Lay-baptisms, and we need not dispute. Well, but what does this counterfeit Ambrose ground his observation upon? Nothing but the instance of Cornelius and his company, whom S. Peter "commanded to be baptized." Here was therefore something more than bare leave. Here was express order from an inspired Apostle. Therefore the persons, whoever they were, that baptized Cornelius and his company, were authorized to do it. Show this our Dissenting laics. Further, it is not yet proved, nor ever, I believe, will, that those baptizers of Cornelius were laymen. Mr. Bennet thinks he has sufficiently proved them to be of the Clergy;[y] if so, the whole argument drawn from hence falls to the ground. But had we no certain proof of that matter, yet I should very much suspect the truth of the observations made by this author, "that at first leave was given to all promiscuously to teach." S. Paul does as good as tell us,[z] that all men were not teachers in his time; and why may not the author be as much mistaken in his other point in making all baptizers? S. Clement of Rome, a much more competent witness in the case than an author of the fourth century, takes no notice of this promiscuous company of Laics and Clergy empowered to teach and baptize; but expressly tells us,[a] that the Apostles, as they went forth to preach the Gospel, constituted a Clergy, "appointed the firstfruits of their conversions to be Bishops and Ministers over

183

---

[y] Rights of the Clergy, p. 236.   [a] Clem. 1 Ep. ad Cor. sect. 42.
[z] 1 Cor. xii. 29.

such as should afterwards believe:" and that the distinction between Clergy and Laity was early settled in the Apostles' days, is so clear from the Acts and the Epistles, that I need not prove it.

This author himself however is pleased to allow, that when the Church was spread, "ubi omnia loca complexa est Ecclesia, conventicula constituta sunt, et rectores et cætera officia in Ecclesia sunt ordinata."[b] Very inaccurately expressed, if he means it of the times of the Apostles, a few years after our LORD's ascension; but perhaps he thought it later. He proceeds, "Ut nullus de Clericis auderet, qui ordinatus non esset, præsumere officium non sibi creditum vel concessum: et cœpit alio ordine et providentia gubernari Ecclesia." Though this author is something mistaken in his chronology, (not fixing the distinction of Clergy and Laity early enough,) yet he reasons very right; that after proper officers were once appointed, none should dare to usurp upon the sacred inclosure. And it is worth observing what he adds; "Hinc ergo est, unde nunc neque Diaconi in populo prædicant, neque *Clerici vel laici baptizant.*" He may be a good witness of what was done in his own time, though a bad reasoner about the practice of the Apostles: so that at last this author, where he talks of matters he knew little of, is of Mr. K.'s side; but when he speaks of matters within his own knowledge, he is of mine. But Mr. K. observes, that the words above cited do not imply that laics were under a *total prohibition* from baptizing in all cases, but that they do not baptize *in populo*. This is his sense, and a pretty strained construction it is, to fetch *in populo* from its proper place, and put it in an-

---

[b] Com. I. in Ephes.

other not very proper, and which, I am sure, he can never certainly prove to belong to it. But his hypothesis required it, and that solves all. I cannot however but with some pleasure observe, that this anonymous author, who at first setting out seemed to threaten us terribly, appears at length so gentle and favourable to us, that he can hardly without violence be kept from declaring on our side of the question. But Mr. K. observes, that "much less do his words imply that Lay-baptism is not valid." I am content that the words should not of themselves imply so much: but they certainly do imply, that the practice of the Church was against Lay-baptism, as irregular and sinful at that time; and this is a better argument to prove it invalid, than any the author has furnished us with for the contrary opinion; and is sufficient to show, that what Mr. K. thinks the Council of Eliberis took for granted, and what he takes to have been very common in that age, was not the general sense and practice of the Church fifty years after, nor then neither, since this testimony of Hilary looks backward to the time when he supposed the distinction of the Clergy and Laity first fixed. But enough of this: the next in order may be

PACIAN, A.D. 360.[c]

The most remarkable words in him are these: "Generat Christus in Ecclesia per suos sacerdotes—atque ita Christi ocmcn, i.e. Dei Spiritus novum hominem alvo matris agitatum, et partu fontis exceptum *manibus sacerdotis* effundit.—Hæc autem compleri alias nequeunt, nisi lavacri et Chrismatis et Antistitis sacramento.

---

[c] De Bapt. Biblioth. Patrum, tom. iv. Lugd. p. 318.

—Lavacro peccata purgantur, Chrismate Sanctus Spiritus superfunditur, utraque vero ista *manu et ore Antistitis* impetramus." To these we may add what he says in another place, speaking of the power of baptizing and remitting sins :[d] "Totum hoc non aliis quam Apostolis imperatum est ;" but at the same time observes, that it must extend to their successors. From the whole we may remark,

1. That the right of baptizing belongs only to persons of sacerdotal character; this right or power being committed to the Apostles only, and therein to those who derive it from them, viz. the Episcopal Clergy. This wholly destroys any pretended inherent right of laymen.

2. That the efficacy and validity of the sacrament depends upon the commission of the administrator, "Hæc compleri alias nequeunt." This leaves no room for any plea of pretended necessity without episcopal authority; and so utterly invalidates all unauthorized Lay-baptisms.

3. It is highly probable that laymen in S. Pacian's time had no episcopal power or license to baptize in any case; because no mention is here made of any such power; the administration is confined to the Sacerdotes.

4. The least that can be supposed from it is, that it was so confined in all ordinary cases : so that whether you consider Dissenters' Baptisms as destitute of the plea of necessity, or as *unauthorized*, not to say *antiepiscopal*, they are by the principles of that age, so far as S. Pacian may be allowed to have understood them, null and void. If you desire to see more about Pacian,

---

[d] Ad Sempr. Ep. i. Ibid. p. 307.

and what may be collected from him, I refer you to the second part of Lay-baptism Inv. p. 99, and shall pass on to

OPTATUS OF MILEVIS, A.D. 368.

What Mr. K. has observed of this author is very just and right. For though I once was of opinion, that Optatus meant no more than our twenty-sixth Article teaches, that "the holiness of the Minister is not of the essence of the sacrament," (which was all that he needed to have said, or should have said,) yet, upon second thoughts, and a more careful perusal of him, I do find that he carries the point further. The words which Mr. K. cites from him, "Non dixit (Salvator) Apostolis, Vos facite, alii non faciant. Quisquis in nomine Patris et Filii et Spiritus Sancti baptizaverit, Apostolorum opus implevit;" I say, these words, besides others in that discourse, are too plain to admit of any other construction; and yet, what you will wonder at perhaps, Optatus's reasoning would necessarily imply, not only that Lay-baptism, even by women, by Jews, Turks, and Pagans *in the Name of the Trinity* is valid, but that it is lawful too; since he supposes that by the institution of Baptism any man has an equal right to administer it, as being not excluded by CHRIST from doing of it. This is contrary to Scripture, to antiquity, to reason, to Mr. K.'s scheme as well as to mine, and is too weak and groundless a notion to deserve any serious confutation. All that can be said is, that the good Father overshot himself, and in order to keep from one extreme in the heat of his dispute, as is very usual, run into another. He had not so clear and distinguishing a head as S. Austin, who engaged in the same cause, but came off much better; and knew how to prove the Baptisms of Catholics valid upon juster principles, viz. the *undoubted validity of their ordinations*. Though he likewise sometimes run into the same topics with Optatus, but as it were *ex abundanti*, not being willing to lay the stress of his cause upon them. For he first secured his point from the other topic, and would never lay himself so far open as to rest his cause upon such principles as would in their consequences overthrow all distinction between Clergy and Laity. Those who are for judging most candidly of Optatus are willing to think he designed no more. It was enough for him to prove that the personal faults of GOD's ministers did not null their orders, or hinder the effects of their ministrations. If he used an argument to prove this, which proved too much, he is blamable for it, and only shows that he reasoned ill, though he meant well.

However, be that as it will, I am not concerned to show, that he or any other always reasoned right. He has honestly given his reasons, and any man that understands them has a right to judge of them. In a word, he spoke the judgment of the Church in his conclusion, that the "Donatists did ill to rebaptize the Catholics," but not in his premises from whence he inferred it, defending her on such principles as she had never owned. Upon the whole, I allow Mr. K. to have one beside Tertullian before S. Austin favouring his cause, not plainly and in terms, but implicitly and consequently; not as a witness of the doctrine or practice of the Church in his time, which was contrary; but as an author pressed in dispute, and delivering very unwarily "his own private opinion," his unaccurate determination about the "Baptism of heretics, and the faith of the recipient" in that sacrament:[e] points which were handled in a quite different manner, and differently determined by the acute S. Austin,[f] sufficiently show that he came unprepared to his subject, before he had well considered of it, and engaged in an argument that he was not master of. And now we come to

S. BASIL, A.D. 370.

He was called in before only as an evidence for Cyprian and the Cyprianic age; now let him speak for himself, and the sense of the Greek Church in his time upon the present case. Mr. K. is of opinion, that if we wrest S. Cyprian from him, "we must give him Basil in exchange." I am far from thinking there is any such necessity for it, hoping to make it appear that Basil is a very clear uncontestable evidence, as any can be, on our side. Mr. K., in order to draw him from us, observes,

1. That Basil took heretical and schismatical priests to be no more than laymen.
2. That notwithstanding he was willing to comply with the custom of the Church in receiving their Baptisms. Here he has so blended and confounded S. Basil's true meaning, that it will take some pains to set it in a true light. The truth is, S. Basil in his own opinion looked upon heretical and schismatical priests as laymen; but yet was willing to submit his judgment in that matter to the judgment and practice of the Church, which did not look upon them generally as laymen, but owned the validity of their Orders, and sometimes received them again, permitting them to officiate by virtue of the Orders they had during their heresy

---

[e] C. i. cont. Parmen. p. 37, 38. ed. Par.   [f] C. v. p. 91.

or schism; and upon this foot it was that S. Basil was willing to allow their Baptisms; not that he thought Lay-baptism valid, as Mr. K. mistakes the case, but because their Orders were looked upon by the Church as valid, he concluded their Baptisms were so too. To make the whole clearer, let it be observed, that S. Basil, going to declare what Baptisms should be valid, and what not, makes in the first place a distinction between heretics and schismatics; the pretended Baptisms of the former he rejects utterly, and observes, "that Cyprian and Firmilian and their adherents went further, rejecting the Baptisms of the Cathari, or Novatians, who were only schismatics, upon this principle, that they being no longer members of the Church, they had forfeited their Orders, and had no more power to baptize, &c. than mere laymen: yet since the Asiatic churches had received the Baptisms of such schismatics, he was willing to submit his judgment." I suppose he might have the determination of the Nicene Council in his eye, cited above, that declared the Ordinations of the Novatian Clergy valid, and consequently their Baptisms; and so the Church received both. He proceeds next to consider the Baptisms of the Encratitæ, another sort of schismatics, and seems inclined to reject them, but thinks there may be some reasons in some cases why they should be received. At length he concludes, with this remarkable observation: "But I know that we have received our brethren Zois and Saturninus, who were of that sect, into the episcopal chair: wherefore we can no longer separate those from the Church who were joined to them, having already made a kind of rule for their communion with us by receiving their Bishops."

You see from hence the rule and standard which

S. Basil goes upon as to receiving of schismatical Baptisms: if their Orders were received, he would receive [188] their Baptisms, and makes the latter depend upon the former. He still adheres to his principle, that Lay-baptism is null; only, because he was willing to think that the Orders of schismatics were good, and that therefore their Baptisms were not Lay-baptisms, he is content to receive them. Can anything be a clearer evidence for the invalidity of Lay-baptism than this is?

Gregory Nazianzen, A.D. 370.

Mr. K. having only a Latin version of the author, therein, it seems, reads these words: "Tu vero neminem non satis dignum et idoneum ad Baptistæ munus obeundum existima: qui modo inter pios censeatur, ac non aperte condemnatus sit, atque ab Ecclesia alienus—omnes citra ullum discrimen vim perficiendæ animæ habere existima, qui modo eadem fide sint informati." And these he would interpret in favour of Lay-baptism, though it be clear to a demonstration, from what goes before and after, and from the whole scope, drift, and design of the place, that Gregory meant nothing like it. Read the whole passage, (but in English, because of its length,) and tell me if a man must not wink very hard to mistake it. Gregory is advising his catechumens not to be fanciful or curious in the choice of a minister to baptize them.[g] "Say not thou, a Bishop shall baptize me, and he a Metropolitan, or one of Jerusalem. For grace is not the gift of the place, but of the Spirit. Say not, I will be baptized by one of noble birth, and that it will be a reproach to my quality to be baptized by any other. Say not, if a

---

[g] Orat. xl. de Bapt. p. 656, ed. Paris.

Presbyter is to baptize thee, that he shall be one that is unmarried, and one of the continent and angelic order; as if thy Baptism were defiled, when administered by another. Make not thyself a judge of the fitness or qualification of the preacher or baptizer; for there is another that judges of these things. Σοὶ δὲ πᾶς ἀξιόπιστος εἰς τὴν κάθαρσιν, μόνον ἔστω τὶς τῶν ἐγκρίτων καὶ μὴ τῶν προδήλως κατεγνωσμένων, μηδὲ ἐκκλησίας ἀλλότριος. μὴ κρῖνε τοὺς κριτάς. Every one is qualified to thee for thy purgation, provided only he be one approved, and not under public censure, nor cast off from the Church; judge not thy judges, thou that hast need of healing. Tell me not of the dignity of thy purgators, make no difference between one spiritual father and another; one may be of more or less dignity than another, *but any of them is superior to thee:* if there be two seals, the one of brass, the other of iron, but both bearing the same royal image upon them, and so making the same impression upon the wax, what difference can you find between one impression and another? None at all. Οὕτως ἔστω σοὶ πᾶς Βαπτιστὴς, κἂν τῇ πολιτείᾳ προέχῃ, ἀλλ᾽ ἤγε τοῦ Βαπτίσματος δύναμις ἴση, καὶ τηλειοποιός σοι πᾶς ὁμοίως ὁ τῇ αὐτῇ πίστει μεμορφωμένος. So as to the ministers of Baptism, though one be a better man than another, yet the power and efficacy of the Baptism is the same; and any of them indifferently may give you Baptism, that *is of the same faith with you.*" By which I suppose he means one that is not an heretic. That all this relates only to the Clergy, as the proper administrators of Baptism, is, I think, evident beyond dispute;

1. From the comparison made between Bishop and Bishop, and between a Presbyter and Presbyter, not between Priest and laic, or one laic and another; intimating that men should not be too curious in the

choice of their ministers, since all had the same authority.

2. From that it must be a person approved by the Church. Now I hope that Mr. K. will not say, that laymen were approved by the Church as the ministers of Baptism in ordinary cases, to which these words plainly refer.

3. From the administrators being here called the judges, implying some authority over them, which cannot be said of lay-administrators; but it may truly and rationally be said, that catechumens should not pretend to judge of the qualification of those whom GOD had appointed to the office. And S. Gregory would argue very weakly and inconclusively on the other supposition.

4. Gregory mentions no administrator lower than a Priest. He begins with Bishops, bidding them not be curious whether this or that Bishop, and then proceeds to Priests, giving the like direction about them. Why did not he go on to Deacons, and so at last to laymen, or even women, upon Mr. K.'s hypothesis? In short, from Gregory's words we may sooner prove that even Deacons did not administer Baptism in his days, than that laymen did. And indeed that I take to have been the standing rule in the Greek Church especially, that none but Priests should ordinarily administer Baptism, nor any lower than Deacons in the greatest necessity; which seems to have been the rule of the Church also in the time of S. Chrysostom.[h] Believe me, Sir, these good Fathers were men of true Church principles, and would have sooner laid down their lives than have betrayed the rights of their order. To proceed.

---

[h] De Sacerd. lib. iii. Hom. 61, tom. vii. ed. Savil. 423.

Mr. K. imagines that Nazianzen "gives such advice as any of us would give to an adult in the like case." I hope so too: and sure any of us in the like case would advise an adult to go to the minister of his own parish for Baptism, and not to ramble I know not whither for a gifted man to do it; much less should any of us advise him to take up with the first layman he could find, and to ask Baptism of him. But Mr. K. adds, "if any emergency should drive him to desire Baptism at the hands of a layman, then, &c.," but not a tittle is there of any such supposed *emergency* in S. Gregory. He is putting the case, that some may be scrupulous, nice and humoursome, that any Priest would not satisfy them, unless it were an unmarried Priest, nor that neither, unless he were a Bishop, or even an Archbishop, or a Bishop of such a particular place as Jerusalem, or so and so qualified. Do not you see plainly by this time what an imaginary construction Mr. K. had been making from plain words, that bear quite another meaning, and are as far from countenancing Lay-baptism, as preaching or praying in a schismatical conventicle? For the purpose: might not you or I advise any person not to have *itching ears*, not to be nice and curious about their ministers, but to be content to edify under any, and submit to such as GOD has appointed them, without making themselves judges of things and persons beyond their proper sphere: I say, might we not fairly offer such advice without being suspected of any design to commend Lay-preaching? And yet I am confident there would be as much ground for such a supposition, as there is for what Mr. K. would insinuate from S. Gregory about Lay-baptism.

Apostolical Constitutions.

I shall here insert a few passages relating to our subject from the Apostolical Constitutions; not laying any great stress upon them, because of the uncertain authority of that work. [i]"As it was not lawful for a stranger that was not of the tribe of Levi to offer anything, or approach the altar without a Priest; so do ye nothing without the Bishop. For if a man does anything without the Bishop, εἰς μάτην ποιεῖ αὐτὸ, *he does it in vain.* It shall not be imputed to him as any service. As Saul, when he had offered sacrifice without Samuel, was told, μεματαίωταί σοι, that it was of no effect: so whatever layman does anything without the Priest, (or Bishop,) μάταια ποιεῖ, *he does it in vain.*" See Second Part of Lay-baptism Invalid, p. 117.

[k]"We suffer not laics to usurp any of the sacerdotal offices, as the Eucharist, Baptism, imposition of hands, &c., for no man taketh upon him this honour, but he that is called of GOD.[1] For this dignity is given by the imposition of hands of the Bishop. But whosoever hath it not by commission, but seizes it to himself, shall bear the punishment of Ozias."

All I shall observe from hence is, that no exception or proviso is made for cases of necessity. The prohibition is general and full. The first quotation seems directly to make Lay-baptism invalid; the other is clear for the unlawfulness of it: both suppose Baptism a sacerdotal act, and found it upon sacerdotal powers, conveyed by episcopal ordination; so interpreting the commission to baptize, as to preclude the laity.

S. JEROME, A.D. 384.

Great dispute has been about the sense and meaning

---

[i] Ap. Constit. lib. ii. c. 27.
[k] Ap. Constit. lib. iii. c. 10.
[1] Heb. v. 4.

of S. Jerome in relation to the present controversy; both sides contending that he is expressly for them, and both having something very plausible to urge for their respective opinions. I have considered this matter very carefully, and shall state it very fairly and impartially, as far as I am able to judge of it; and perhaps in conclusion Mr. K. himself will have no reason to complain of me. His Dialogue against the Luciferians is what we are to examine. The Luciferians, as is well known, so called from Lucifer Bishop of Caralis, (now Cagliari in Sardinia,) the head of the schism, separated from the Catholic Church, because they had received the Arian Bishops; yet they scrupled not to receive the Arian laymen to communion. S. Jerome undertakes to confute them upon their own principles, by showing them how inconsistent they were in rejecting the Bishops, and yet receiving the laics, and how they must upon their own principles either be obliged to receive or reject both. The Luciferians pretended that the Arian Bishops were by their heresy and crimes utterly disabled from acting *in sacris* to any purpose, that their ministrations were ineffectual, their light extinguished, their powers deleted, in a word, they unbishoped them. S. Jerome confutes their pretences by this single argument; that since they allowed their Baptisms, they must of consequence admit of their other sacerdotal ministrations as effectual and valid, and therefore own their character not to be extinct, nor their sacerdotal powers deleted. The most remarkable words of the Dialogue to this purpose are the following:

m" Quamobrem, oro te, aut sacrificandi ei licentiam

---

m Dial. adv. Lucif. i. c. 2.

tribuas, cujus baptisma probas, aut reprobas ejus baptisma, quem non existimas sacerdotem."

[n]"Arianus baptizat, ergo Episcopus est: non baptizat: tu refuta laicum, et ego non recipio sacerdotem."

[o]"Tu eum Episcopum probas, quia ab eo recipis baptizatum—Christianus non est, si non habuerit sacerdotem, qui eum faceret Christianum."

From these words, and from the whole scope and drift of S. Jerome's argument, Dr. Forbes and Mr. Reeves, and after them Dr. Brett and Mr. Laurence, thought it reasonable to assert, that the invalidity of Lay-baptism was the undoubted principle upon which the *orthodox* confuted the Luciferians in S. Jerome's times. For it is very plain, that the validity of the Arian Baptisms is here made an argument of the *sacred character* still residing in the Arian Bishops; from whence it may seem reasonable to infer, that according to the principles of that age the validity of Baptism depends upon the *sacred character*, and consequently *Lay-baptism is invalid.* S. Jerome seems plainly to suppose a reciprocal connection between the validity of Baptism, and the validity of the Orders of the baptizer; and it is very certain, that the Donatists afterwards laid a great stress upon this principle in their disputes against the Catholics, which made S. Austin labour hard to prove the validity of Orders once given,[p] and that they could never be extinct or deleted afterwards, in order to establish the validity of the Baptisms of the Catholics. And it is worth remarking what he says relating to Fælicianus and those baptized by him, whom the Donatists received inconsistently with their usual stiffness and severity.

---

[n] Cap. 5.   [o] Ibid.   [p] Cont. Ep. Parm. lib. ii. c. 13.

"In honore quippe suo sicut exierat, ita receptus est cum his omnibus quos ipse foris positus baptizavit, nullo eorum rebaptizato; quia si aliquem eorum, quos foris baptizaverat, rebaptizandum esse censerent, judicarent eum amisisse jus dandi, cum foris esset; et propterea consequens erat, ut ipsum quoque iterum ordinarent, si illos iterum baptizarent."

You may please to observe from hence, that the Donatists in S. Austin's time founded the validity of Baptism upon the right of the administrator. If the baptizer had not *jus dandi*, a right to give Baptism, it was looked upon as null. By the *jus dandi*, they meant the power received in ordination; for so S. Austin understands and explains it in the place cited, and in the other parts of the chapter. Therefore they founded the validity of Baptism on the validity of the baptizer's Orders; and therefore Lay-baptism in ordinary cases at least, upon their principles, was null and void. Now if you please to compare thus far the principle of the Donatists with what we have seen from Cyprian and Basil before, and now again from Jerome; you can hardly believe otherwise, than that that had been a standing rule of the Church at least in ordinary cases; and that the Donatists were so far Catholic in their principles, though they drew wrong conclusions from them. I know S. Austin endeavoured to resolve the validity of Baptism in another principle, as being CHRIST's Baptism if done in due form by any administrator. But this was *ex abundanti*, more than he needed to have done, having before sufficiently vindicated the validity of heretical or schismatical Orders, which was the main point. And what he adds further is a new notion of his own, unless Optatus may be said to have broached it before him. S. Jerome indeed in this very

Dialogue has these words in relation to Baptism: "Quod frequenter, si tamen necessitas cogit, scimus etiam licere laicis, *ut enim accipit quis ita et dare potest.*" A very wise reason! I hope the Church had a better, if that were her practice. However, I will not say, with Dr. Brett and Mr. Laurence, that this was a slip of his pen, and inconsistent with the rest of the Dialogue. I will suppose that the practice of Lay-baptism in cases of necessity had got some footing in the Latin Church about his time. But then I say it was by the permission of the Bishops, whenever it was, and was not *unauthorized Lay-baptism*, nor was any such permitted in ordinary cases, or allowed to be valid: and so to make S. Jerome coherent and consistent, he might perhaps think Lay-baptism unauthorized, and in ordinary cases invalid; and yet allow of the validity of authorized Lay-baptism in cases extraordinary; or else, he might think that the *sacerdotium laici*, which he speaks of, might take place in such circumstances, and consistently enough allow laymen, when necessity makes them Priests, as he seems to imagine, to execute the priestly function: or, in short, he might suppose Lay-baptism *lawful*, and therefore *valid*, when permitted by the Church in case of necessity; and yet think it *unlawful*, and therefore *invalid*, in other cases. And indeed I take it for a certain truth, which I shall explain and prove in the sequel, that wherever Baptism is unlawful in the *whole act*, not circumstantially, but essentially unlawful, it is also invalid.

Thus I think the good Father is clear enough from contradiction; and yet nothing can be drawn from him in favour of our Dissenters' Baptisms, which have no permission from the Church, nor any plea of necessity: and therefore we are still as much at a loss as ever to find any principle of the ancient Catholic Church whereon to found their validity. And now let us take leave of S. Jerome, and come to

S. AUSTIN, A.D. 400.

I have mentioned this Father more than once already. I shall now lay before you so much out of him, as may give you a sufficient idea of the principle he went upon. It was objected to him by the Donatists, that heretics or schismatics had forfeited their Orders, and therefore could not validly baptize. Now observe how he answers this objection.

1. He absolutely denies the very supposition on which the objection was founded,[q] proving that heresy and schism did not vacate Orders for these reasons, because neither heresy nor schism could vacate Baptism once truly given; and he thought there was a plain analogy between the *sacrament*, as he calls it, of Orders, and that of Baptism.[r]

195 Because the Catholic Church always thought that Orders once truly given could never be deleted by any heresy or schism, or indeed by anything. And here he observes, that if any of the heretical or schismatical Clergy upon their return to the Church were allowed to officiate again as Clergy, they were admitted without any new ordination; a plain argument that heresy or schism had not deleted their Orders: nay, he observes further, that though they were often not allowed to officiate, but only admitted to Lay-communion; yet even then they were not looked upon as laymen, and therefore did not submit to penance and receive imposition of hands, which was the usual

---

[q] Contr. Ep. Parm. lib. ii. c. 13.
[r] Ibid. De Bapt. lib. i. c. 12, et alibi passim.

discipline for returning laics. "Non eis ipsa ordinationis sacramenta detrahuntur, sed manent super eos; ideoque non eis in populo manus imponitur, ne non homini sed ipsi sacramento fiat injuria." To this answer, though full, plain and unexceptionable, and agreeable to the known rules and practice of the Catholic Church, he subjoins another of his own with great diffidence and modesty.

2. He denies the consequence, that Baptism must necessarily be null upon supposition that heresy or schism did vacate Orders; and he brings it in as it were by the by, and *ex abundanti*.

"Quanquam etsi laicus aliquis pereunti dederit (Baptismum) necessitate compulsus, quod cum ipse acciperet, quomodo dandum esset addidicit, nescio an pie quisquam dixerit esse repetendum?"

Does this look as if Lay-baptism even in cases of necessity was a customary practice in the Church in his time? Would he have spoke with such diffidence, "nescio an pie?" would not he rather have urged the authority and custom of the Church, as in the case before mentioned, and have said, instead of *nescio an pie, certe impie* or *temere?* But he is here offering his own private conjecture in a case that had not been expressly determined in any council, though the reason of the thing, and the custom of the Church, were sufficiently against him. He has neither rule nor instance to plead in his behalf, and therefore endeavours to supply that want by his own private reason; and so he goes on to give his opinion that Lay-baptism may be valid even in ordinary cases, though irregular and sinful, upon this principle, "quod datum fuerit, non potest dici non datum:" which is either begging the question, or arguing thus: A per-

son is washed in the Name of the Trinity, therefore
196 he is baptized. After he had wandered awhile in the
dark about this question, indulging too far his own
private conjectures, he returns at length to his first
answer, as being more just and solid, and abides by it;
insisting again upon it, that heretical or schismatical
Clergy had not lost their Orders; and he appeals to
the decision of the whole Christian world in proof of
his assertion, and so goes on triumphantly on that point
to the end of the chapter. By the way, it is very
apparent, that S. Austin never imagined that the Baptisms of the schismatical or heretical Clergy were Lay-baptisms, nor that the Council of Arles, or Nice, or
any other, meant any such thing. That was what none
but the Donatists pretended in that time, or since, till
Mr. B. was pleased to oblige the world with the second
part of his Scholastical History, which I heartily wish,
for his own sake, and for the sake of his other excellent works, he had never published, so much to the
discredit of himself and them. But to proceed.

It may be observed of S. Austin, that though at
first in his disputes with the Donatists he was very
modest and diffident in proposing any of his own
private conjectures, keeping close for the most part to
the known rules and principles of the Church; yet
afterwards in the progress of the dispute, as men are
apt especially when flushed with victory to grow both
warmer and bolder, he ventured to proceed further,
and to lay it down for a maxim, that any Baptism was
good by whomsoever administered in the form of
words, in the Name of FATHER, SON, and HOLY GHOST.
This was a short and easy solution for any difficulty;
and were it as solid too, would justify all the lengths
of Popery in the matter of Baptism, would not only

prove that heretics or schismatics, whether of the Clergy or Laity, may validly baptize, but that women and children, and even Jews, Turks, and Pagans, either seriously or in sport and mockery, may administer true Baptism. But as that maxim of his was novel, and only founded on this weak pretence, that it is CHRIST's Baptism whenever it is administered in His form, (which is nothing but a *petitio principii*, or taking for granted the thing to be proved), I shall not think it worth the while to say anything further to it: only observing this, that S. Austin, in his management of the controversy with the Donatists, says enough to silence and confound his adversaries without it. He proves unanswerably, that the validity of the sacraments does not depend upon anything uncertain and precarious, as the personal qualifications of the minister, either known or secret, and neither the intention of the minister, nor his orthodoxy, nor his life and manners, can come into the question. But to infer further, that the validity of the sacraments depends entirely upon GOD, and not at all upon the administrator, is carrying the point too far; is dissolving all rule and order in the Church; is frustrating CHRIST's commission to His Apostles, and melting down all distinction between Clergy and Laity. He might safely enough have said, and consistent with his other principles, that GOD had tied down the efficacy and validity of His sacraments to regular and authorized ministry, acting in His name and by His commission. This hypothesis is not uncertain and precarious, but clear, certain, and evident, by a perpetual succession from the times of the Apostle; which can never fail, while the Church stands, or the world lasts. This secures all that S. Austin was contending for, and at the same time keeps up the honour and respect due to GOD's holy ordinances and institutions. In short, it is a middle way between the two extremes; ascertaining to us the validity of the sacraments without any diminution of the priesthood, or any breach of rules and orders. And here I might dismiss S. Austin, but perhaps Mr. K. may expect I should take notice of what he has said in relation to him, which I shall do in short.

He can hardly believe it possible "that S. Austin should be ignorant what was the practice of the Church in his time:" nor do I think it possible, or however not likely; and his proposing his opinion so modestly and with so much diffidence is to me a plain argument of it. But Mr. K. adds, that he would not "go about to innovate anything in the rituals or discipline of the Church." Truly I believe not, upon his own authority. But he might nevertheless humbly offer his own private opinion; and it is no strange thing for great men to have some particular fancies to themselves, or to think out of the common road; and there is no harm in it generally, if they be but modest and humble withal, and be willing to submit to lawful authority and decisions of the Church. However, it is fact, that S. Austin had his *nostrums* and particular opinions. He often left the notions of his predecessors to follow a path wholly new, as Dupin has judiciously observed of him, applying to him the character that Cicero gives of himself, that he was *magnus opinator*. After all, suppose it could not be proved, that the invalidity of Lay-baptism was the doctrine of the Church in S. Austin's time, must it therefore follow that they held the contrary opinion? Might not they be silent as to either side of the question, or think little of it, having no occasion to dispute it? It is as plain and clear as possible from S. Austin, that he knew of no determination of the Church in favour of Lay-baptism. He would never have hesitated, as he does upon the case, had he known of any such decision, but would have appealed to the declared judgment and practice of the Church, as he does in many other cases, had there been the least ground or pretence for it. It is enough then for us to say, that in S. Austin's time there was no rule of the Church, no warrant for the validity of Lay-baptism. They that say there was ought to prove it, and not to put it upon us to prove that the Church had determined expressly against it. We have enough from Scripture and from the reason of the thing for our side of the question, though antiquity had said nothing of it: and therefore they who make their boast of the ancients should show plainly that the ancients are for them; otherwise their cause drops, and has nothing left to support it. And yet when they come to speak of the ancients, the most that is commonly attempted is, to show that they have not spoken expressly on our side; which yet they can never show; but if they could, this would be only an artful way of turning the tables upon us, and, instead of proving their pretences good, is presuming groundlessly they are so without proof, unless we demonstrate them to be false. So that the greatest pretences to antiquity, when they come to be examined, amount only to this; that the Church has not in every age determined expressly against them in this point; when they ought to have shown that it always determined for them; or that it did so at least some time or other within the first six hundred years, which I am persuaded they can never prove.

But I must not forget to take notice of what Mr. K.

subjoins, that he has *positive evidence* from S. Austin, that Lay-baptism in cases of necessity was a thing frequently practised. Let us see what this *positive evidence* is; for I much suspect it: the words are, "Etiam laicos solere dare sacramentum quod acceperunt solemus audire." It seems some reports were spread abroad, and came to S. Austin's ear, (whether true or false is not said,) that laymen (in cases of necessity) were somewhere used to baptize. Suppose I deny the truth of the reports, how will any man prove it? And what becomes of the *positive evidence?* Suppose I grant it; what does it signify with regard to the general sense and practice of the Church, when it is not told, either how many laics were concerned in the practice, nor by what authority? Yet Mr. K. immediately advances this hearsay story into *a custom*, (of the Church, I suppose, he means,) and tells us that S. Austin adds, that the custom took its rise from apostolical tradition. This, I confess, amazed and confounded me. What, S. Austin say it! *Believe it who can* that knows S. Austin. Pray let him speak for himself, if the words be really S. Austin's;[s] "Sanctum est Baptisma per seipsum, quod datum est in nomine Patris et Filii et Spiritus Sancti, ita ut in eodem sacramento sit etiam autoritas traditionis per Dominum nostrum ad Apostolos; per illos autem ad Episcopos et alios sacerdotes, vel etiam laicos Christianos ab eadem stirpe et origine venientes." You see the word *traditionis*, which there signifies CHRIST'S commission; and all that can possibly be drawn from the words is, that Bishops act by virtue of that commission, and may communicate the like power to laymen; which is an

---

[s] Apud Grat. de Consecrat. dist. iv. c. 36.

assertion precarious enough. But where does Mr. K. find that the custom of Lay-baptism took its rise from apostolical tradition? Where is there a word of *custom* or *tradition* in his sense in the whole quotation? To do Mr. K. justice, I believe Mr. Bingham led him into his mistake, who has these words relating to this passage of S. Austin. [t]"This custom he founds upon authority descended by Bishops from the Apostles," which being a little crudely and obscurely expressed, might lead a man to say what Mr. K. does; though their assertions are very different from one another, and are both wide of the sense of the author, who has not a syllable about anything of *custom* in the passage quoted: which notwithstanding is the most material word of all, upon which the argument depends. Having now done with S. Austin, we may take our leave of the ancients, after we have summed up their evidence.

1. As to authorized Lay-baptism in cases of necessity, you may observe, there is some plea for it in antiquity, from Tertullian, the council of Eliberis, S. Jerome, and S. Austin; but all together make no proof of the *general sense and practice of the Church* in favour of it, but rather the contrary implicitly; as Cyprian, Basil, Pacian, and the Apostolic Constitutions do more plainly. And yet had all these authorities been for Lay-baptism in cases of necessity authorized by Bishops, it would make little for Mr. K.'s purpose, being wide of the question.

2. As to unauthorized Lay-baptism in ordinary cases, which is the point in dispute, there are Cyprian, Basil, Pacian, directly and expressly against its being valid;

---

[t] First Part of Schol. Hist., Works, vol. ix. p. 35. Oxf. edit.

and the rest implicitly and consequentially; not one directly or implicitly for it, except Optatus and S. Austin; and that not as witnesses of the Church's general sense or practice, but as disputants in a nice and difficult controversy; or as private Doctors. However, I am willing to admit, though not easy to be proved, that the doctrine of Lay-baptism's being valid in some cases crept gradually into the Western Church from the time of S. Austin, and, like other corruptions of Popery, came to its height in the following dark centuries; though it does not appear that it ever prevailed in the Greek Church so early as the twelfth century. However, I do not think it material to make any nice inquiry into the notions or practices of later ages, which must stand or fall by the ancients, and are of small authority without them.

To what has been said upon particular Fathers, I shall here subjoin two probable presumptive proofs to confirm the foregoing observations.

I. The first assertion I lay down is this; that there was no universal standing principle among the ancients, whereon to found the validity of Lay-baptism.

II. There were some general standing principles universally held, which do by consequence overthrow it.[1]

---

[1] The reasonableness of this mode of combating certain false doctrines is evident, if we for a moment consider (1) that it is impossible that all false doctrines should have been expressly condemned in the primitive Church; and therefore the mere fact that some particular doctrine was never "expressly condemned" is no proof that it was received, (2) that every doctrine, which is false, can be shown to be false because it is either inconsistent with some other doctrine, admitted to be true, or in violation of some general principle universally held to be sound.

I. As to the first point; in proof of it I shall examine the chief principles that can be supposed to have any weight in the case, and show why I think none of them were universally held.

1. *The plea of necessity* could not be a principle universally held as sufficient to warrant Lay-baptism, or to make it valid; for we find no mention of it in the earliest writers, and but little afterwards. Besides that the Baptism of women was always absolutely disallowed by all, as well as that of Jews and Pagans; which shows that necessity alone was not thought sufficient; and Tertullian, who is the first that mentions it, yet does not found the validity of Lay-baptism upon that only, but upon the inherent right, or baptismal priesthood of laymen.

2. That principle of inherent right of priesthood seems to bid as fair as any, several of the early writers having mentioned it besides Tertullian and Jerome. But there lies this presumption against the ancients giving universally into that notion, that they never allowed the Eucharist to be consecrated by laics in any case of necessity; which they certainly would have done, as well as Tertullian, had they been of the same principle with him as to the inherent right of priesthood. For indeed it would have been a plain necessary consequence resulting from it.

3. The third principle upon which S. Austin founds the validity of Lay-baptism after Optatus, viz., *its being Christ's Baptism*, entirely GOD's and not man's, and therefore not depending at all on the administrator, is no principle of the primitive Church. We find no author mentioning it, before the two just named. We find as many against it as confine the administration to the Clergy only. Most of the ancients held principles

that were inconsistent with it; such as utterly disallowed of women's or Pagans' Baptism; such as held Lay-ordination invalid, which indeed were all to a man; and yet S. Austin's principle would make that as valid as the other. The like may be said of Lay-consecration of the Eucharist; which all the ancients with one voice reject. And yet the same reasons that S. Austin gives for Lay-baptism upon that principle would nearly affect the other too.

4. Another principle, mentioned by S. Austin, is, *quod datum datum;* and therefore Lay-baptism is Baptism, and must be valid. This would equally prove that orders given by laics are nevertheless Orders; and consecration of the Eucharist by laics is nevertheless consecration; which is contrary to all antiquity, as was before observed.

5. Another principle, which Tertullian, Jerome, and Austin advance, is, that every one may give what he himself has received; and therefore every baptized person may baptize. This we never meet with in many of the earliest; nor could they hold it consistently with their other principles, that a Deacon could not make a Deacon, nor a Priest a Priest, nor a layman give the Eucharist, though he may receive it.

6. Another principle, whereon some would found the validity of Lay-baptism, is, the permission or authority of the Church, or of the Bishops, as in the Council of Eliberis. There is the most to be said for this of any. Yet there is no proof that the general sense or practice of the ancient Church ever countenanced it. S. Austin seems to have known nothing of it. It has never been shown, nor, I believe, ever will be, that this principle was general or universal, or if it

could, it does not affect our present question, as has been often observed.

7. The last principle which seems to prevail most now, and is contended for by Mr. K., is, that a subsequent act or ratification of the Church supplies all deficiencies, and renders any pretended Baptism valid. This I do not meet with in any of the ancients, I mean Catholic ancients. I know the Luciferians had a notion very like it, and were confuted by S. Jerome. None ever that I know of among the orthodox pretended that any subsequent act of the Church could make that valid which was not so. It might make Baptism before valid, effectual, and saving; that is the most the ancients ever thought of it. Confirmation was a distinct thing from Baptism, and not an essential of it; and it was always supposed that Baptism was complete and entire as to essentials without it. Confirmation helped to improve and advance what was begun in Baptism; and the same may be said of the Eucharist. And so either, or both, might contribute to make Baptism more effectual to the purposes of salvation, but not to supply anything wanting in the essentials of it. Having seen then, that there was no general universal principle whereon to found the validity of Lay-baptism in the ancient Church, I beg leave to infer from hence, that the ancients never universally held any such doctrine, or gave into such practice; unless you would imagine they might come into it by apostolical tradition, without any other reason; which it will be time enough to consider, as soon as any one of the ancients can be brought to vouch for any such tradition. I proceed now to show,

II. That there were some general standing principles almost, or entirely universally held by the ancients, which seem by consequence, or virtually or implicitly, to overthrow the pretended validity of Lay-baptism.

1. I observe that laymen were absolutely forbid to intermeddle in sacred offices, as we learn from the earliest Christian writers, *no proviso* being inserted for cases of necessity. Lay-baptism therefore was certainly upon these principles sinful and criminal, and therefore probably null. And it is very observable, that not one writer before S. Austin ever thought Lay-baptism valid, but what thought it lawful too, and so probably founded its validity upon the supposed legality of it. This were easy to show of Tertullian, the Council of Elvira, Optatus, Jerome, or any other. If it be objected, that the Church admitted the Baptisms of degraded clerks, heretics, and schismatics, and yet did not think it lawful for them to baptize, having forbid them the exercise of the sacred function; I must distinguish between what is essentially and what is circumstantially unlawful; and between an absolute prohibition to act at all, or only to act in such and such circumstances. It is well and judiciously said by S. Austin, with respect to the Baptisms of such persons, "Non eis dicimus, Nolite dare, sed Nolite in schismate dare." The Church thought such Baptisms to be legal, authorized, and warrantable in the main; and only illegal, unauthorized, and criminal in some particular circumstances. That is, in short, they were what the persons had a right to do, and were so far lawful, and therefore valid; but at the same time they should not have been done in that manner. Or to be yet plainer, the fault lay not in the exercise of the sacerdotal function abstractedly considered, for they were priests; but in the heresy, schism, &c. It was therefore a rule of the Church, as far as appears, till S. Austin, that no

Baptism was valid, but what was for the main lawful, or what the baptizer had a right to execute in the general, though forbid to do it in some peculiar circumstances. Seeing therefore that laymen were entirely and absolutely forbidden to intermeddle with the sacred offices by the earliest Christian writers, as persons who had no right at all to do it, no title or claim to such offices, either in whole or in part; I must conclude from thence, that the Church upon these principles looked upon all pretended Lay-administrations as null and void.

2. Another avowed standing principle of the primitive Catholic Church was, that the Christian Clergy were proper priests, or that their priesthood was as well mystical as mediatory, as truly and properly as the Levitical priesthood, though not of the same kind or order. For proof of this I refer you to Mr. Dodwell, Of one Altar, &c. and De Jure Laico Sacerd. p. 30: Dr. Hickes's Christian Priesthood Asserted, chap. ii. sect. 4, p. 315: Johnson's Unbloody Sacrifice. From this principle I infer, that no ministration can be valid that is not sacerdotal, or is not performed by GOD's designation, commission, or appointment. The sacrament loses all its virtue and efficacy, or rather is no sacrament, if administered by profane unauthorized hands. This argument against the validity of Lay-baptism appeared so strong and forcible to a learned writer,[u] who was in the main of Mr. K.'s opinion, that he could find no other way of getting clear of it, but by denying the Christian Clergy to be proper Priests, against all antiquity. And indeed it seems to me very plain, that if the Clergy act *in sacris*, as GOD's peculiar priests, proxies, or representatives; the validity of the

---

[u] Vind. of Def. of Dr. Stillingfleet, p. 350.

sacraments must depend upon GOD's commission, which laymen are supposed to want. If therefore the primitive Church took Baptism to be a sacerdotal act, and the Clergy to be proper Priests, both which are very certain, they did by consequence disallow and invalidate all pretended Baptisms by laymen.

3. Another general prevailing principle of the primitive Church was, that the consecration of the Eucharist was so entirely a clerical act, that there could be no such thing as Lay-consecration. If you want to see this proved, I refer you to the forementioned authors, Dodwell, Hickes, and Johnson. Now the inference drawn from it is, that Lay-consecration of water, or of the person baptized in it, (i.e., Lay-baptism,) must upon that principle be null too; since the reason is much the same in both. If the Eucharist be a sacrament, so is Baptism; if the virtue and efficacy of the Eucharist depend upon CHRIST's commission given to the administrator, why should not the virtue and efficacy (by which I mean the same with the validity) of Baptism depend upon the commission also? or if the latter be supposed valid without commission, why should not the former also?[x] Further, that there is a mysterious change wrought upon the bread and wine in the Eucharist upon the prayer of invocation, is the unanimous doctrine of the ancients;[y] and the like mysterious change in Baptism upon the water by the prayer of invocation is taught by the ancients also. Seeing then there is so plain resemblance and analogy between the two sacraments, both being of a very sublime and mysterious nature, and therefore proper to be administered only by sacred hands; it would be very

---

[x] See Johnson's Unbloody Sacrifice.   [y] See Bing. Orig. vol. v. part xv.

strange, that the ancients should think one appropriate to the Clergy, and not the other. It seems to have been a disputed point among the ancients, whether Deacons could baptize; and that they did not do it ordinarily is plain enough from many authorities cited by Mr. Bingham;[z] which I do not so much wonder at, as that they ever were allowed to do it at all. But I suppose the Scripture instances of Philip and Ananias, and the ancients looking upon Deacons [a]as *priests of the third order*, might reconcile them to it. But then this makes nothing for the Baptisms of laics. There are no Scripture instances of these, nor are they in any strict sense Priests.

4. Another general principle of the ancients was, that Lay-ordination was null and void. This need not be proved directly. It is very certain, that no pretended ordination less than episcopal was ever admitted as valid in the Christian Church; and therefore certainly there could be no such thing as Lay-ordination. And does not this principle equally affect Lay-baptism? Why cannot laics ordain, but because they have no commission or authority to do so? And there is the very same objection lies against their baptizing. It were easy to show, that most of the arguments brought in vindication of Lay-baptism would be equally forcible in favour of Lay-ordination. For the purpose; if it be so, that Baptism is GOD's act, so is ordination; if necessity be pleaded in the former, so it may happen also in the latter; if *quod datum datum* be a rule, it is as good for one as for the other; if a subsequent ratification of the Church would do in pretended Baptism, it might as well in pretended Ordination; and so

---

[z] Schol. Hist. part i. Works, vol. ix. p. 14. Oxf. edit. Hieron. Ep. [a] Optatus, lib. i.

the ancients need not have ordained any that had been pretendedly ordained before, but only have received them. Since therefore there appears the same or the like reasons for nulling Lay-baptisms as for Lay-ordinations; and since the latter was the undoubted practice of the Church, it may reasonably be inferred, that the general practice and judgment of the Church was alike in both.

These may serve as probable arguments, or indirect proofs of what I am contending for; and are, I think, far more considerable than anything that I have yet seen urged from the ancients in favour of the contrary opinion. However, I lay not the stress of the cause upon them, because it does not want them. Two inferences I draw from the whole.

1. That it is very certain that the *general sense and practice of the primitive Church* did not countenance or establish the validity of Lay-baptism.

2. It is more than probable, that they did both in judgment and practice favour the direct contrary to it. And the chief, if not only reason why we have not fuller and more repeated proofs of it is, because the matter came not into dispute; no laics ever attempting to baptize, except among heretics; nor then without the countenance and approbation of the Bishops. For any company of laics to pretend to be a church, or to act independently upon their Bishops, would have been thought as absurd and strange among the ancients, as if so many women only had pretended to be successors to the Apostles, and to ordain, baptize, and teach, &c.——Pretty remarkable are the words of S. Jerome, in relation to Hilary the Roman *Deacon*,[b] who was therefore a degree above a laic.

---

[b] Dial. adv. Lucif.

"Hilarius, cum Diaconus ab Ecclesia recesserit, solusque, ut putat, turba sit mundi, neque Eucharistiam conficere potest, Episcopos et Presbyteros non habens, neque Baptisma sine Eucharistia tradere; et cum jam homo mortuus sit, cum homine pariter interiit et secta, quia post se nullum Clericum Diaconus potuit ordinare. *Ecclesia autem non est, quæ non habet sacerdotes.*"

But it is time now to return to Mr. K. I had said in my letter, that I should be thankful for one *plain* authority (except Tertullian) for the validity of Lay-baptism, *as such*, before S. Austin. Upon this Mr. K. thinks he has a just claim to my thanks, if he knew but what "I meant by the restriction (as such)." That is easily known: I meant *unauthorized* Lay-baptism. If any be authorized by Bishops, and thereupon be valid, it must be on this account, that it is an act of the Bishops by lay hands, and so a *clerical* act interpretatively, and not properly a lay act. Whether such acts may justly claim the benefit of such an interpretation, and whether that would make them valid, I dispute not here; it being foreign to our debate about Lay-baptism as such, i.e. unauthorized Lay-baptism, such as that of our Dissenters undoubtedly is: and Mr. K. has not yet brought any one plain authority before S. Austin for such Baptism. Pseudo-Ambrose's notion has been shown to be a gross mistake of that author. Gregory Nazianzen has not a word to the purpose, but means a quite different thing. Ruffinus only gives you a hearsay story of a very improbable fact. The Eliberitan Council, and perhaps Jerome, are to be understood of authorized Baptism. Optatus is no *plain* authority; it being highly improbable that he meant the words in that gross sense (attended with all its consequences) in which Mr. K. takes him. It is plain, however, that he supposes no Baptism valid, but what he supposes lawful. S. Austin is the first that ever presumed to think that illegal unauthorized Lay-baptisms are valid; the first that ever spoke home to the purpose on Mr. K.'s side of the question; and his reasons on which he built it have been shown to be weak enough.

Mr. K. has been pleased to promise me his thanks, "if within a thousand years after CHRIST I produce either one single canon of any council to confront that of the Eliberitan Fathers, or so much as a testimony of one single Father, that speaks home to his side of the question." By the way, it is their business to produce Councils and Fathers for the validity of unauthorized Lay-baptism, who assert it. *Affirmanti incumbit probatio.* It would be but small satisfaction in a case of everlasting concern to a considerate man to be told that Fathers and Councils had not expressly declared against it, while there appears little or no ground anywhere for it. However, Sir, I think, besides Scripture and the reason of the thing, the Apostolical Constitutions, the Cyprianists, and S. Basil, have *expressly* declared against it; and the main stream of Christian writers before S. Austin, *implicitly*. This is enough, especially against a thing which because of the great moment of it ought not to be admitted without clear and certain proof on that side. Let us see how they can answer it, who would rest men's salvation upon such weak and precarious foundations; especially when the remedy, the certain remedy, is near at hand, and may be easily applied. I have often observed that the Eliberitan Council is not pertinent to the case of unauthorized Lay-baptisms; or if it was, such a particular case as that was not of weight sufficient to rest a cause of such importance upon. Mr. K. says further, that he will be thankful "for so much as an instance within that period, (a thousand years,) of any one Christian rebaptized by or in an episcopal church, merely upon account of his having been before only baptized by lay hands." But we should first have an instance, I do not say within that period, but within five or six hundred years after CHRIST, of any being so baptized and received into the Church without another Baptism. (I take Baptism here in the large sense.) Strictly speaking, neither Catholics nor heretics (except the Marcionites) ever allowed a second Baptism; but when they gave a second, they understood the first to be none.

Mr. K. says, "Instances may be produced of the Church's receiving the Baptisms of those whose Ordinations she had before declared void." That we deny utterly, and challenge any man to give but one instance in all antiquity.[1] I know what Mr. K. means, viz. that degraded Clergy became laymen, and yet their Baptisms were received. I deny not that their Baptisms were received in most churches, especially after the determinations of the Councils of Arles and

[1] On this point, as a matter of historical fact, Mr. Elwin, in his very candid and impartial inquiry, says, "It is a fact, whether it was intentional or not, that Baptism was in no case allowed to a body which had not started in episcopacy, with the possibility therefore of an ordained priesthood." ("The Minister of Baptism," p. 80.) He is speaking of the discussions in the primitive Church, as to the validity of Baptisms administered within various heretical and schismatical communions; and certainly, if the validity of Lay-baptism was generally allowed in those ages, then this fact, which Elwin notices, was a most remarkable, and indeed, an inexplicable fact.

Nice: but then these churches did not think the degraded Clergy, or heretical and schismatical Clergy, were laymen. For a confutation of Mr. Bingham's notion, that the censures of the Church null Orders, I refer you to S. Austin[e] particularly among the ancients, who is very full and positive against it; and to Dr. Potter amongst the moderns, and to Mr. Bingham himself, who is an ingenious and a learned man, but cannot reconcile contradictions. As to Mr. K.'s queries,

1. The first is, "Whether the same LORD and Head of the Church, Which gave, cannot withdraw His commission?" I answer, Yes, He may.

2. "How can this be done otherwise than by the Church's acting in His name, &c." I answer, By express order from CHRIST, revealed from heaven. The Bishops have a delegated power to give Orders, but none that I know of to take them quite away: it is no strange thing for a man to be able to do what he cannot undo.

3. "Whether the Church has not full authority to do this," &c. I answer, No; at least it does not appear that she has.

4. "Whether she has not expressed herself in such language, as if she thought she had such a power?" I answer, None but the Cyprianic churches, and those who comply with them in nulling the heretical and schismatical Baptisms. The main body of the Church, both before and after, were of another judgment, as is plain from S. Austin.

In short, it is as clear as the sun, that whatever churches looked upon degraded Clergy as Clergy, re-

---

[e] Cont. Ep. Parm. lib. ii. c. 13. De Bapt. lib. i. c. 1, 2.

ceived their Baptisms; and whatever looked upon them not as Clergy, rejected their Baptisms. This latter was the case of the Cyprianists, who acted consistently enough, but went upon false premises; and it is pleasant to observe how some would now lay down the same premises, and yet reject the conclusion; blame Cyprian for what was right, and admire him for what was wrong. He was right in his conclusion, and wrong in his premises; but these will be wrong in both, as if resolved to be inconsistent, and confute themselves to save others the trouble of a confutation. All Mr. Bingham's quotations prove no more, than that the degraded Clergy were reduced to Lay-Communion, were suspended *ab officio*, either for a time, or deprived for life; and if they were excommunicated too, they still retained their Orders, as much as they did their Baptisms, and could not in any strict sense forfeit either.

Mr. K.'s next attempt is to prove by instances that the primitive Church sometimes received the Baptisms of those whose Orders she rejected as invalid. And his first instance is of Ischyras, once a pretended Presbyter, afterwards a Bishop. To make this matter serve his purpose, he has first strangely misrepresented the case, mingled very foreign and distinct things together, supposed some things without any certain ground, drawn wrong inferences from them: and yet if you grant him all he would have, his whole argument is inconclusive.[f] Ischyras, he observes, was made a "Bishop, without being previously ordained either Priest or Deacon." This certainly made his consecration uncanonical; but he might be a Bishop notwithstanding, and undoubtedly was so. Next, he observes,

---

[f] See Bingham's Orig. Eccl. book ii. ch. x. sect. 6, vol. i. p. 129, &c. Oxf. edit. 1855.

"that this man among other enemies of the Nicene faith and accusers of S. Athanasius was condemned and excommunicated:" right, for being an enemy to the Nicene faith, and a false accuser of S. Athanasius: and many other Bishops, as Theodorus,[g] Narcissus, Ursacius, Valens, &c. were condemned by name: Ischyras himself is not named among the persons anathematized, though I grant it reasonable enough to conclude him among the rest. But Mr. K. adds, "No decree was made for annulling the Baptisms administered by him." No, it would have been strange if there had; for it is not at all necessary that, as often as Bishops are deposed or excommunicated for crimes or heresy, as the case was here, that their ministrations, which were not affected by it, should be nulled. It would have been more to Mr. K.'s purpose to have alleged that the Council of Alexandria eight years before declared this *Ischyras*[h] to be no more than a pretended Presbyter, a mere laic, without making any decree to annul his Baptisms. But these negative arguments prove very little generally: besides, if it was a rule of the Church before, there was no need of a special decree to annul those Baptisms, which were void of course; and after all, it does not appear how long, or in what instances Ischyras officiated as a Presbyter, or whether he baptized any at all. The like answer may serve for the two other instances of Musæus and Eutychianus, whom the same Council declared not to be Bishops, and those pretendedly ordained by them not to be Clergymen, without adding any decree to annul their Baptisms. And it were to be wished that when Mr. K. cited Balsamon in favour of his

---

[g] Theod. Ec. Hist. l. ii. c. 8.   [h] Athan. Ap. 2, cont. Arian. p. 784, ed. Par.

interpretation of the Canon, in order to prove from thence Lay-baptism invalid according to the principles *of that bright age,* he had observed withal, that the very same Balsamon does from the same nineteenth canon infer the quite contrary, arguing by parity of reason from the invalidity of Lay-ordination, or non-episcopal, to the invalidity of Lay-baptism.[1] So easy is it for ingenious men to draw contrary conclusions from the same premises.

And now let us take our leave of antiquity; the tracing of which, though it be something tedious, is of great satisfaction, and carries its reward along with it. I promise your friend to abide by it, and to throw up all my reasonings as uncertain conjectures, rather than run cross to it. I hope he will be so kind as to do so too, and after this view of the ancients not lay so great a stress upon some very uncertain reasonings in the present case, which he has advanced with pomp and triumph, as if they had never been considered, nor were capable of any just and solid answer. These I have had in my eye, and reserved them for this place under a third general head, after what related to Scripture and Fathers.

III.

We are now then to manage the debate in point of reason. We have, we imagine, many and great reasons for our side of the question. We think it very absurd that anything should be valid without some certain principle to found its validity upon; especially a thing of this moment, wherein the everlasting salvation of thousands is concerned. We think it very

---

[1] See Bevereg. not. ad Can. 19, Conc. Sardic. p. 201.

unreasonable to rest a matter of such importance upon weak and precarious foundations; and should expect, if it were true, to find it writ in legible characters in sacred Scripture, or at least in the judgment and practice of the ancients. On the contrary, we find nothing but obscure hints, and dark and remote inferences that look that way. Nay, so confident are some among us, Mr. Laurence in particular, that he thinks our side of the question demonstrable; and has laid down five or six reasons in the way of *mathematical demonstration* to prove his opinion.[1] We think it a little strange, that, among so many adversaries as that gentleman

---

[1] Laurence begins his argument by laying down five "axioms, or undeniable maxims," viz.:

I.

The essential parts of anything are of the same nature as the whole.

[From which it follows, that we have as much right to dispense with the whole ordinance of Baptism, as with any single part which is essential.]

II.

GOD Himself may dispense with any of His own positive institutions, either in whole or in part; and bestow the benefits annexed to them when, to whom, and how He pleases.

[From which it follows that the denial of the validity of Lay-baptism is not at all any denial that GOD may, if He will, bestow the "benefits" of Baptism on those who are lay-baptized, or on any others, whether baptized in any way, or not.]

III.

No ecclesiastical or civil authority can dispense with any divine positive institution, either in whole or in any essential part, so long as it is binding and obliging to us.

[From which it follows, that if an ordained minister was an "essential part" of the "institution" of Baptism, no huhas met with, no one has yet given himself the trouble to unravel those reasons; to show where they are fallacious; where he has laid down false premises, or

man authority can dispense with such a minister, or substitute any other in his place.]

IV.

The only way to determine whether an act is valid or invalid, for the purposes of a divine positive institution, is to know whether that act be lawful or unlawful, agreeable or contrary, to the will of GOD: which is to be found nowhere, but either in the institution itself, or in some other part or parts of His written Word, relating to the same institution.

[From which it follows, that no sacrament can be "valid," unless the minister thereof is a "lawful" minister, and "agreeable to the will of GOD," and that no minister can be "lawful" and "agreeable to the will of GOD," unless he is duly authorized to that office either "in the institution" of such sacrament, or "in some other part" of GOD'S word relating thereto.]

V.

No power or authority on earth can, by any after act, not appointed by GOD for that purpose, make that which before was invalid to become as valid as conforming to the divine institution itself would have made it.

[From which it follows, that if Lay-baptism is *per se* invalid or defective, that defect or invalidity cannot be removed by Confirmation, or by any other "after act, not appointed by GOD for that purpose."]

These "axioms" appear to be, as Laurence calls them, "undeniable;" and the conclusions to which they inevitably lead are so vitally important to the controversy on Lay-baptism that it seems well here to quote them at length. The "axioms" are in Laurence's own words: the conclusions, given within brackets, are brief summaries of his extended arguments on the several points involved.

drawn false conclusions. It is a little surprising that the advocates of Lay-baptism should raise so many scruples and difficulties on one side, and yet pass over in silence those many and great difficulties which are urged on the other; as if it concerned them not to answer objections sometimes, as well as to make others. Yet it is usual with them after this partial management of the cause to cry victory and to triumph; whereas at best they ought only to suspend and to leave the matter undecided. For suppose their objections were really such as we could not answer, yet as long as they do not answer the difficulties on the other side, which seem equally forcible, at least must be thought so till we see them answered; the utmost that they ought to conclude from it is, that we are upon a par, and that the cause is doubtful. I speak this of the advocates for Lay-baptism in general, not including therein Mr. K. I must do him the justice to say, he has managed the debate fairly, so far as he undertook in answer to my letter; and has not only given his own reasons, but has also considered mine. I shall first endeavour to vindicate the reasons hinted at in my letter from his exceptions, and then let you know what I have to say further in answer to his.

I argued from the nullity of subjects acting in a civil government without a competent authority, viz. levying soldiers, naturalizing strangers, &c. in the name of the sovereign without orders or warrant. To which Mr. K. answers, that "he knows not in what sense levying of soldiers without authority can be said to be null and void." To which I reply, I know not how he can mistake or want to understand so plain a thing. May not a man pretend a commission from his majesty, call himself an officer, beat a drum, and list men in the usual form into the king's service? But as soon as the cheat is discovered, the whole engagement is dissolved, the listed men are set at liberty, and *the imaginary contract null and void.* Apply this to the case of listing men into CHRIST's service by an imaginary Baptism without a competent authority, and you will find it parallel and to the purpose, or I am very much mistaken. But, says Mr. K., "does the consequence hold from things civil to sacred? Are the reasons the same in both?" Yes, I humbly conceive it does hold, and the reasons are the same in both, because drawn from one and the same general principle, that no man can act under another and in his name without his leave or order. But Mr. K. excepts "that all grants, commissions, &c. from earthly princes ought to appear genuine and voluntary, and must therefore pass under forms of law to ascertain the rights of the parties concerned, and to prevent mischiefs which may accrue through fraud and forgery." And so likewise all grants from GOD ought to have His seal and stamp, and pass under such forms as He has appointed to ascertain the rights, &c. Are not our Christian rights as dear to us and as valuable as any; and as much want to be ascertained in a regular and uniform method to prevent tricks and frauds and counterfeits from such as would beguile the simple, and take the honour upon them of being ambassadors from heaven without being sent? "But may we not trust GOD without such securities?" No: because it is presumption to slight such securities as He has appointed, or to expect His favours without them. Mr. K. adds, "GOD is not under the like necessity with earthly princes to annul what is done, much less to do it to the prejudice of an innocent person." True, GOD is under no absolute necessity; and He might have contrived many other methods in His infinite wisdom. But He is a GOD of order and not of confusion, and, in a moral sense, is under a necessity of acting wisely; and therefore will not leave the weighty business of the priesthood in common to all, but is pleased to confine it to a select body of men that shall act by His authority. But will He annul any usurped acts "to the prejudice of innocent persons?" I presume He will annul the acts, i.e. the acts shall stand for nothing; but He may possibly receive the innocent persons, not upon the account of these acts, but of His own free mercy. And is it not better to trust GOD without doing an unwarranted thing, than to run the risk of offending Him to no purpose, but what may better and more safely, for aught we know, be had without?[k][1] Cannot GOD be merciful to the innocent without our presumption? Is He less concerned for them than we? Or does He stand in need of our sins? What does all this mean? May we not trust GOD without such wretched securities? What Mr. K. adds about an adult's receiving Baptism of a schismatical usurper, if he means of a schismatical Clergyman, it is

---

[1] In this same way Bishop Jeremy Taylor replies to the argument that it is "safer" to have a child lay-baptized rather than to let it die unbaptized; he says, It is "unreasonable" to imagine that GOD is better pleased that His ordinance should be ministered in a manner, which He has not commanded, rather than that it should be reverently left alone unless it can be ministered according to His command. ("The Office Ministerial." Vol. xiv. iv. 5.)

This notion that it is "safer" to have the outward form of Baptism *si possis recte, si non possis, quocunque modo*, may well be called "unreasonable."

[k] See Bennet, p. 342.

true, but not to the purpose; if he means it of a schismatical layman, or any layman, we want proof. His next observation about an infant "being as sure of the grace attending (Christian Baptism), as all the promises of the New Testament can make him," though washed by a layman only, is only so many words put together; unless it can be shown that there is any one promise in the whole Old or New Testament annexed to such pretended Baptisms. True, there are many promises annexed to Baptism; but the question is, whether what we are speaking of be Baptism or no; and it should not be taken for granted that it is, when a disputant is concerned to prove it. He says "he can by no means think it all one to the future condition (of an infant), whether he be baptized or not, as some notions lately advanced would incline us to believe." I do not say or think it is all one whether an infant be baptized or not. But a pretended Baptism and no Baptism are so much alike, that upon either supposition, as I take it, the infant dies unbaptized. I see not therefore to what purpose all this is, till it be proved that Lay-washing is Christian Baptism. As to the doctrine of the absolute necessity of Baptism, whether it be true or false, it concerns not the cause. Let Baptism be ever so necessary, yet till you prove Lay-washing to be Baptism, or a counterfeit seal to be a true seal, we are just where we began. However, if Baptism be so absolutely necessary as some suppose, great care should be taken that every man may be certain that he is baptized; and then I am sure Lay-baptism must be out of doors, which at best has but a chance whether it be Baptism or no. Not that I think Baptism, truly such, so absolutely necessary to salvation as some have pretended; and if you please to consult Forbes's Instruct. Hist. Theolog.[1] upon this question, or only observe from Mr. Bingham[m] what allowances the ancients used to make in some cases for persons dying unbaptized, you may possibly incline to be of my mind. It would be needless and tedious in me to enter into that dispute here; and so I choose to waive it, and to come to another point.

I had argued in my letter against the validity of Lay-baptism from the unlawfulness of it; thinking that if it was sinful *in the whole act*, i.e. such as could never in any case be done by a layman without sin, it must be void. Here Mr. K. is pleased to mistake me for near a page together, till at last he comes to understand me, and to put the case right, and then he is of my mind; that supposing Lay-baptism to be valid, which is the same in effect with what he says, ("supposing the principle they act upon to be no mistake,") there is neither sin nor danger in a layman's administering in extreme necessity. Which was the same thing I had asserted, only I inferred further from it, arguing backwards; that if there were sin and danger in a layman's administering in such a case, then Lay-baptism could not be valid. And I am now fully satisfied, though I spoke of it before with some diffidence, that the argument is just and right. If the validity of Lay-baptism in a case of extreme necessity necessarily implies it to be lawful; then its unlawfulness in the same case necessarily implies its invalidity. It is an established rule in logic to argue as *a positione antecedentis ad positionem consequentis*, so *a remotione consequentis ad remotionem antecedentis*. And the reason of it is plain; for if the antecedent cannot be without the consequent,

---

[1] Vol. i. l. 10, c. 6.   [m] Vol. iv. p. 25, &c. Oxf. edit. 1855.

it is evident by taking away the consequent you take away the antecedent also. So that now the first question between Mr. K. and me is, whether the validity of Lay-baptism in a case of extreme necessity does not necessarily imply that it is lawful in that case: but this I think he has given up. And next, whether its being sinful even in this case does not imply that it is invalid, cannot be a question between us, since it evidently follows from the former. The only question then is, whether in such a case it be a sin or no. I think it is, because it seems to be an unwarrantable usurpation of the priestly office, a breach of rules and orders, a bold presumption without any leave, command, or commission for doing it, or in Mr. Bennet's words,[n] "a downright lying and forgery, a cheat upon one's neighbour, and an affront to GOD." Seeing therefore that it is a sin for a layman to pretend to baptize, even in cases of necessity, as they are called, though improperly, it follows by what has been said, that it is null and void. Not that every sinful act is always void; for "we were in an evil case," as Mr. K. justly observes, "if every sinful circumstance in the administration should make the administration itself null and void." But I had guarded against this by calling it *sinful in the whole act;* not accidentally, nor circumstantially, but entirely and essentially, as having no manner of plea, pretence, or warrant, to justify it either in whole or in part. A Clergyman may baptize a person against the order of the Bishop. He sins in doing so; not as to the act of baptizing, for that he has authority to do as a Clergyman; but in that circumstance of disobedience to his Diocesan. So the schismatical and

---

[n] P. 336.

heretical Clergy formerly were guilty of a sin in baptizing, in such manner, and in such circumstances. But separate these circumstances from them, and it was no sin for Clergymen to baptize. But as to a layman's baptizing, the flaw is in the act itself, not in the circumstances; as having no power or authority to do it in any circumstances whatever. The fault is not only in doing it at a wrong time, or in a wrong manner, but in doing it at all. And I am persuaded it will be difficult to show how any act can be valid, where a man has no power, right, or authority to act at all: which is certainly the case of *unauthorized Lay-baptisms*, about which we are disputing.

Having thus endeavoured to vindicate and clear up the reasons hinted at in my letter against the validity of Lay-baptism, I now come to consider Mr. K.'s reasons for it. His reasoning part chiefly consists of one argument drawn *ex absurdo*, and may thus be represented in his own words:

"To suppose (Lay-baptism) altogether null and void, must needs have a terrible influence upon the state, not of the Church of England alone, but of all the churches in Europe: for if the Baptism of such Clergymen as we now speak of (Clergymen baptized by lay-hands) was invalid, so was their Ordination too. They could not have the keys of the Church delivered to them before they were members of it; the effect whereof must be an endless propagation of nullities, &c."

This is the terrible objection against us, so often boasted to be unanswerable; wherefore I shall not attack it all at once, but try if I can weaken it, and break the force of it by degrees.

1. I observe, that every difficulty urged against an opinion that is supported by great and solid reasons,

ought not presently to make us conclude that that opinion is false. A man may prove his position, and not be able always to answer the objections on the other side.

2. However certain and terrible this consequence[1] may seem against us, there are others as certain and terrible against those who hold the contrary opinion. Hear Mr. Laurence urging consequences against them :[o] "If baptism performed by persons who were never really and truly commissioned to baptize, and who act herein rebelliously against and in opposition to the Divine right of Episcopacy, be good and valid; then authoritative preaching, administering the other sacrament, the power of binding and loosing, of retaining and absolving men's sins, and all the spiritual functions of the Clergy are good and valid also, when attempted by unauthorized, never commissioned lay-persons; the consequence of which is the utter dissolution and taking away the necessity of the *Christian priesthood*, therefore of *Christ's authority here on earth*, and so of all *revealed religion* too, which is a dreadful consideration." Thus far Mr. Laurence. And being called upon by

[1] Would it not be wise to abstain from this argument from supposed "consequences" on both sides? It is our duty to deal with the mysteries of GOD'S Grace according to His revealed will and commandment, and to presume no further. It is therefore our concern to find out what GOD has commanded and authorized us to do, and faithfully to do it. What may be the speculative "consequences" of doing, or leaving undone, something else, which is not commanded, is an inquiry upon which we merely waste our words, since it is an inquiry where there is no possibility of obtaining any information.

[o] Pref. Second Part of Lay-baptism Inv. p. 20.

Mr. Bingham to prove it,[p] he does it most admirably in one continued chain of close reasoning, too long to be here inserted. Here then I set consequence against consequence, equally dreadful and terrible, and not less certain; and had I nothing more to say, yet I think we should be pretty even, and it would be but a kind of drawn battle betwixt us; but this is not all, for,

3. I do not think the objection in that latitude which Mr. K. gives it comes up to the point of *unauthorized* Lay-baptism, about which we are debating. All that Mr. K. himself pretends is, that the Church, from the time of S. Austin, has generally permitted Lay-baptism in cases of necessity, which might perhaps be denied; but however, if it has been so for five hundred years, it is enough for his purpose, and that I will readily allow. But then what is done by permission of the Church, and stands upon canons and episcopal license, is not wholly unauthorized, and so does not affect the question. We are disputing about pretended Baptisms, unauthorized, uncommissioned by Bishops. Will Mr. K. show that such ever obtained in the Church, I do not say from S. Austin's time, either in East or West, but that they were any where received, except in this island, scarce an hundred years upwards? Lay-baptisms in England had some authority from the Church, till the Rubric was altered in the reign of King James the First: from that time they have been wholly unauthorized; and all such we pronounce invalid, neither affirming or denying anything of the other, till it can be shown that the case is the same in both. So that if Mr. K.'s charge should chance to fall heavy on those who reject all Lay-baptism,

---

[p] Pref. to Suppl. p. 59.

authorized or unauthorized, without distinction; yet it does not affect us who confine our dispute to *unauthorized* only, such as those of our Dissenters have certainly been ever since the Rubric was altered; and what the consequence of disallowing them only would be, I hinted in my letter, and am satisfied that the objection so stated as it ought to be with regard to the point in question, *neither deserves nor requires a better answer.* We condemn none absolutely by this doctrine but those who are culpable, those who want true Baptism, or at least may suspect they want it, and yet will not have it, though it be easy to be had.

4. Suppose the objection to be ever so much to the purpose; yet the whole force of it depends upon one uncertain proposition, viz. that one not validly baptized cannot have valid orders, or cannot validly baptize others. As to which give me leave to observe, that the advocates for Lay-baptism have not yet offered anything that amounts to a proof of that proposition; which it is their business to do who press the objection. Mr. K. asks, can any one that is no Christian be a Christian Priest? One that is not of CHRIST's family be a steward of it? One that has no right to partake of the body of our LORD be a sufficient dispenser thereof? One that is not a member of the Church be a *governor of it?* for so it should be put, and not a *governing member of it.* We ask, why not, and demand a reason; but all that we find alleged amounts to this only, that an unbaptized person is utterly uncapable, because he is so: and that he cannot administer, no, that he cannot. The very same questions which Mr. K. asks may be applied to heretical, or wicked, or excommunicate Priests, who are Priests notwithstanding, as appears from S. Austin, as cited [218]

above.^q Besides that I hope such Clergy as we are speaking of may have as good a right to the title of Christians as catechumens had formerly; who, though unbaptized, were reckoned Christians in a large sense. This might be enough to show the supposition not to be so very absurd as he thought; which is all we are concerned to show in point of reason; and there is no need of Scripture proof, which Mr. K. calls for, to ward off an objection of little weight, unless it appear to involve us in a contradiction. Yet I shall say something from Scripture by-and-by. That there is no contradiction or absurdity in the supposition appears further from hence, that it is not a man's Baptism, but his commission, that empowers him to act as GOD's minister. They are things of a very distinct nature, and given for different ends; and it cannot be shown that they are essential parts, or at all parts of each other. A personal qualification may be often wanting, where the authoritative one stands good. A man may be a Heretic, a Deist, an Apostate, an Atheist, and yet be a Christian Priest; and it will be hard to prove that the validity of his ministrations depends any more upon his Baptism than it does upon his faith or manners.[r] A man may be an instrument of conveying that to another which he does not enjoy himself; and nothing more usual than for proxies and representatives to confer rights, privileges, and powers, to others, which they have not of their own. A person need not be married to be capable of marrying others, nor be free himself to enable him to make others so: provided he has but a commission (ordinary or extraordinary it

---

[q] Bingham's Orig. Eccl. vol. iv. p. 27. Oxf. edit. 1855.
[r] See App. to Lay-bapt. Invalid, p. 130.

matters not) to empower him to do it. And why may not the case be the same with regard to Baptism, that any person commissioned to baptize may do it, whether he himself be baptized or no? Besides, it seems not only the safest, but the only certain rule we have in such cases, to look to the visible commission and authority, and to inquire no further. Whatever becomes of this point of Lay-baptism, if secret nullities affect the succession of the priesthood, and render all their ministrations afterwards invalid; there is no being secure of any such thing as a visible uninterrupted succession at seventeen hundred years' distance from the time of the Apostles. Who can assure us that there have not been several in pretended Orders, who have acted as Priests or Bishops, who really had no Orders; or several that have had no Baptism of any kind, who had done the same? From a few such instances might ensue an endless propagation of nullities in Mr. K.'s scheme; and we should now be to seek for a succession in the Church. But such nullities I take to signify little, when either past discovery or past remedy. If we know of any such instances, we must pronounce such ministrations null; if not, there is no remedy for invincible ignorance; GOD will mercifully ratify and make good all such secret nullities, nor are they such to us till they appear such. Dr. Hickes[a] gives a very good resolution of this in the case of "an unbaptized Clergyman believing himself to have had valid Baptism through invincible ignorance. I make no scruple to tell you, that a Priest in this case is in the eyes of GOD a valid Priest; and that all his priestly administrations by His merciful allowance are also valid

---

[a] Letter to Mr. L. p. 38.

and effectual, and as acceptable as those of other Priests to Him, Who can make allowances where men cannot, and ratify what men, if it came to their knowledge, *could not ratify, but must pronounce null.* The priesthood was hereditary among the Jews; and it is not unreasonable to suppose that one priest or other in such a long tract of time might without any suspicion have an adulterous son; upon which supposition I believe you will not doubt, that when he was at age to administer, GOD would reckon him among the Priests, and accept of all his ministrations at the altar; or if such an one happened to be high priest, even in the very holy of holies, though, if his incapacity had been known, he must have been deposed."

This is a very clear and sufficient answer to Mr. K.'s grand objection, and it ought the rather to satisfy him, because it puts the succession of the Clergy upon a right foot, and secures all that is worth contending for: whereas his way of reasoning would leave it liable to a thousand doubts and scruples, and not only strike at the doctrine we assert, but at the succession *itself abstracted from the consideration of the present subject.* Supposing then, but not granting, that their ministrations are not good and valid in themselves, yet they may by an all-merciful GOD be reckoned to us as such; and that serves the purpose as well. If we know of the defect, we should be obliged to do our best to remedy it; but upon supposition that we are invincibly ignorant of it, it may be construed to us as no defect at all, while we are supposed to have done our best.

The like sort of reasoning may be applied to the case of such as have received no valid Baptism, yet have believed they had, and lived and died in invincible ignorance: it would be hard to call them heathens,

Waterland's doctrine not "so terrible." 225

or no Christians, and harder to suspect that they should suffer eternally for no fault of theirs. I should be willing to think with S. Cyprian in a case of this nature: [s] "Potens est Dominus misericordia sua indulgentiam dare, et eos, qui ad Ecclesiam simpliciter admissi in Ecclesia dormierunt, ab Ecclesiæ suæ muneribus non separare; non tamen quia aliquando erratum est, ideo semper errandum est."

Upon the matter then, our doctrine of the invalidity of Lay-baptism need not appear so terrible and shocking as some would represent it. I have shown that it does not necessarily affect the succession of the Clergy, even though want of Baptism might incapacitate a man for Orders; much less can it affect it on the other supposition, that a visible commission is all that is required to make orders good and valid. I have hinted further, that our doctrine does not necessarily condemn all that have lived and died without any other Baptism but what they had received from lay hands. Indeed it condemns none but those who are either culpably ignorant of their duty in that respect, or wilfully neglect it. Those that will not examine what sort of Baptism they have had, or content themselves knowingly with a pretended Baptism, when they may have a true one; I have nothing to say for such persons, and I leave it to Mr. K.'s coolest thoughts to consider whether he shall think it reasonable, prudent, or pious, to plead for them. All that we desire is, that persons in that case be baptized by a lawful Minister. There is no comparison to be made between the hazard of one and that of the other. A man in these circumstances may be only *hypothetically* baptized, as one

---

[s] Ep. ad Jubaianum.

that doubts whether he has been baptized or no. There is a rule laid down for Baptisms in doubtful cases by canon 72 of Conc. 5 of Carthage, held A.D. 401 : and the Church of England in her Rubric to the Office of Baptism has in a manner adopted it for her own, by ordering in doubtful cases a conditional form, " If thou be not already baptized, I baptize thee, &c." There is no danger at all in this, if done with a religious and pious intent. But as to the danger of leaving persons in so uncertain and doubtful a condition, as every man must be in that has no other Baptism but Lay-baptism, which it is impossible for any man to demonstrate to be true, and which has hardly any probable ground for its being so, I tremble to think on it. Judge then, Sir, with yourself, whether it be more advisable to take Mr. K.'s scheme or mine. If it is not probable, if it is not certain that Lay-baptisms are good, it is of the last moment not to trust to them : but if it be barely probable, or even possible that they should be null, what wise man would not choose the only certain and secure method, to be conditionally baptized by a proper Minister, which is all I am pleading for ?[1]

And here I might take leave of the great unanswerable objection so much insisted on, having, I hope, sufficiently disarmed it. But the regard I have for two very worthy gentlemen, Dr. Brett and Mr. Laurence, obliges me in this place to do justice to them, and to wipe off the suspicion of mistake and fallacy which your friend has been pleased to fix upon them. They give two Scripture instances to show that a man

[1] It would be impossible more fairly and truthfully to sum up the practical results of this inquiry as it bears upon those persons who know themselves to have "no other than Lay-

may be capable of valid Orders that is not baptized. Dr. Brett's instance is S. Paul,[t] whom he shows to have been ordained before he was baptized. Mr. K. denies the fact, not conceiving how a miraculous call from Heaven (the design of which was to make S. Paul *a minister* and *a witness*,[u] and upon which he was immediately declared a [x]"chosen vessel to bear GOD'S name before the Gentiles") should amount to an ordination: though for that very reason most probably S. Paul calls himself [y]"an Apostle, not of men, neither by man." But he thinks his "solemn consecration to the apostolical function came afterwards, and is recorded Acts xiii. 2, 3." That is, after he had been preaching and making disciples about ten years, according to the best chronologers, at Damascus, Tarsus, Cilicia, Antioch, Jerusalem, &c., he came, it seems, to Antioch, and was there first ordained by his own converts. I hope this does not need confuting. Dr. Brett's instance therefore may stand good yet for anything that appears to the contrary; and may still "be a demonstrative argument, that the want of Baptism does not render an ordination null and void." S. Paul indeed did not execute his commission before he was baptized; but when he did officiate, he did it by virtue of that commission which he had before Baptism; and

222

baptism." And if the duty of this wiser choice is incumbent on such persons, it is plain that a corresponding duty rests upon the clergy to assist and encourage all such persons, under their care, thus "to be conditionally baptized by a proper Minister," and any refusal on the part of a clergyman to administer such Baptism would be not only a neglect of duty, but an act of very great injustice.

---

[t] Acts ix. [u] Acts xxvi. 16. [x] Acts ix. 15. [y] Gal. i. 1.

therefore want of Baptism did not void it; which is all that Dr. Brett meant to prove.

So much for him. I come next to Mr. Laurence; who according to Mr. K. urges "the similitude of circumstances betwixt a person uncircumcised and one unbaptized, and *pretends* that as the want of circumcision during the forty years' abode of the Jewish Church in the wilderness did not vacate the ministry of those Priests and Levites who were born in that time; so neither can the want of Baptism now vacate the ministration of one that is consecrated to the Christian priesthood."[a] Under favour he does not pretend quite so much. He does not bring the instance to prove the want of Baptism *cannot* vacate Orders, but that it *need not*, or always *does not*, i.e., they may be consistent; which was all that Mr. L. was concerned to prove. Against which Mr. K. objects thus:

1. "Admitting the fact to be true, it was an extraordinary case, and proves only this, that GOD may dispense with His own institutions, though we must not, and so ratify things transacted in His name by persons unbaptized. But that He does so, it is presumption in us to imagine, without Divine warrant, signifying His will and pleasure." By the way, could Mr. K. write this, and at the same time remember that he was pleading for the validity of Lay-baptism? Is it not as great *presumption* to imagine that GOD will ratify what is transacted in His name by persons *unordained*, as by persons *unbaptized?* Is not the reason equal, nay stronger in one case than in the other? and does not the argument recoil strangely? But to let that pass. With submission, he mistakes Mr. Laurence: his argu-

---

[a] Append. to the First Part of Lay-bapt. Inv. p. 137.

ment proves something more. It proves that want of circumcision (or Baptism) is not in the nature of the thing inconsistent with valid Orders; as it certainly is not, if GOD allowed both: whether ordinarily or extraordinarily is not the point. But,

2. Mr. K., to make all sure, denies the fact. Why? because the Priests and Levites born in that time *needed not* to exercise their function, there being enough besides to do it without them: therefore they *did not*. Is this any consequence? Does this make Mr. L.'s supposition *evidently false?* I do not find that he ever went upon a supposition that the whole number of Priests and Levites must necessarily officiate, or that otherwise there would be wanting men for the service. All that he supposes is, that in forty years' time many born in the wilderness might grow up to the age for service, and be admitted to serve, having an hereditary right to it; and there is all the reason in the world to believe they did so, notwithstanding their want of circumcision. And Scripture says nothing to the contrary, which makes me wonder at Mr. K.'s attempt to prove what it is impossible for him to know, upon nothing but very uncertain and precarious conjectures against the highest probability imaginable. How shall we know precisely how many or how few Priests or Levites might be needful for the service? What probability is there that such a number as this supposes should be excluded from their birthright, and discarded only for not being circumcised, when it does not appear that GOD required it? Or how is it possible that so remarkable a matter of fact, and so instructive, if true, should be passed by in silence, and no notice taken of it by the sacred writers? Is it reasonable to call Mr. Laurence's stating the case "altogether

fictitious and imaginary," upon no better grounds than this, that possibly there might be circumcised Priests and Levites enough to do the business all the forty years, without any of those who were born in the wilderness? But let us hear how he attempts to prove it. First, he observes that Aaron lived almost to the end of that period, which is very true, and that "he had to assist him Eleazar, Ithamar, Phinehas, &c." I put Phinehas last, because he was the youngest, and, for aught that appears, born in the wilderness; and if so, he should be struck out of the account. But what do we do with that *et cætera* at the end? Can Mr. K. or any man else name ever another Priest born in Egypt besides these? Yes, he adds, "such in general of the tribe of Levi as came out of Egypt, and were afterwards consecrated to the priesthood." But how could he imagine that the Levites *in general* could be consecrated to the priesthood; which everybody knows was confined to the family of Aaron only, which family was no more than a branch of the Kohathites,[b] who were a branch of the tribe of Levi? All Priests were indeed Levites, but yet no Levites could be Priests, but those of the race of Aaron. So here is a fine argument spoiled at once by an unlucky mistake at first setting out, which renders all the rest a mere airy speculation. We have found then but three Priests that could have been born and circumcised in Egypt, or at most four, Aaron, Eleazar and Ithamar his sons, and Phinehas his grandson. Nadab and Abihu perished soon after they came into the wilderness; and these are all we read of: yet it is reasonable to believe that Eleazar and Ithamar, not to mention Nadab and

---

[b] Numb. iii.

Abihu, might have sons born to them in the wilderness, who officiated as Priests, as soon as they came to be twenty, or however thirty years old.

This, I believe, is what Mr. Laurence supposed; and he might very reasonably do so: or however I am sure Mr. K. has not disproved it. Mr. L.'s observation takes in the Levites as well as the Priests, and either is sufficient for his purpose. Mr. K. seems to think that there must have been Levites enough without dispute, and is therefore chiefly concerned for Priests. But I must ask his pardon, and beg leave a while to try if I cannot show, that there would have been wanting Levites for the ordinary service upon Mr. K.'s supposition.

The number required for the ordinary service may best be known from the number first appointed by GOD Himself, viz.,[c] eight thousand five hundred and eighty, all that were between thirty and fifty years old. (This is to be understood of the most laborious and burdensome part of the Levites' service, to reconcile it with Num. viii. 24.) The whole number of Levites from a month old was twenty-two thousand, out of which take eight thousand five hundred and eighty, between thirty and fifty years old, and there remains thirteen thousand four hundred and twenty, of which we may fairly suppose there might be about a thousand fifty years old, and consequently superannuated, and as many as had been born within a year before were born in the wilderness,[d] and therefore should not come into this account. We will suppose then that about twelve thousand might remain for future service upon Mr. K.'s hypothesis. In twenty years' time the whole

---

[c] Numb. iv. [d] See Exod. xvi. 1. Numb. i. 1.

eight thousand five hundred and eighty would be superannuated one after another, going off from the service yearly, one year with another, four hundred and twenty-nine in number, and new ones coming in to supply their places. Allow then out of the first remainder eight thousand five hundred and eighty more, and there remains three thousand four hundred and twenty. Now in ten years' time further, about half the former number would be gone off, as superannuated, besides accidents and casualties, and the whole last remainder would hardly be enough to supply the deficiency; and so after all were come in, there would be a strange blank in the succession for the nine following years, about four hundred at least going off yearly, and none coming in to supply their places; which to me seems a very unfortunate business, and to bear hard upon the Levites that came last. There might, it is true, be some left notwithstanding at the forty years' end, if not perishing by casualties, or worn out with labours, but not near the number of eight thousand five hundred and eighty, which GOD chose at first as requisite for the service; and I know not how we can otherwise make any probable guess what number might be needful, but from GOD'S own appointment of such a certain number at the first. Upon the whole, I think, Mr. Laurence's observation is highly just and reasonable with respect to the Levites; and as to the Priests, a probable conjecture, which as it is hard to prove, so it is harder to disprove: and so I leave it. I shall take no notice of Mr. K.'s observation from Scripture relating to this point, and importing that the first Clergy of the Church were Christians, because nobody, I believe, doubts of it; and as to the inference he would draw from it, it has been obviated above. A word or two must come in here about the Reformed Church abroad, and then we have done with this head.

I had said in my letter with relation to them, that we need not be very solicitous for them in the present dispute; because to defend them upon principles which themselves many of them disown, was what they would not *thank us for*. This I thought answer sufficient to an objection, which has not much weight in it, but that it seems to tax with severity and want of charity. And what could be more to the purpose than to observe, that we are as kind to them in that respect as themselves desire: and that they cannot and will not complain of it? To defend them upon principles which they will not own, but reject in disdain, is only bantering them, and exposing ourselves. Besides that allowing their Baptisms and disallowing their Orders seems only to be playing fast and loose, and giving in one hand to take away with the other. The Church of England, he says, does so: if she does, I am sorry for it, and wish either to see the practice changed or defended. I am sorry that what was condemned as an inconsistency in the Luciferians of old should be thought the current doctrine of our Church now. As to rejecting the pretended ordinations of mere Presbyters, the practice is consistent with the doctrine of our Church, and conformable to our twenty-third canon.[e] But I yet want to know how receiving the pretended Baptisms of laics is either conformable to canons or consistent with them. But that shall be considered in another place. Mr. K. in behalf of the Reformed proceeds thus: "All my request is, that seeing by command of our ecclesiastical superiors we have often prayed for them by the title of Reformed

[226]

---

[e] See Stat. 13 Eliz. c. xii. Act of Uniform. Car. II.

Churches, we would allow them as good a right to that appellation as, in defect of other ministrations, a valid Christian Baptism can confer upon them;" that is as good as none. For if we allow them to be Christians by virtue of their Baptism, yet according to the unanimous doctrine of the ancients, *ecclesia non est, quæ non habet sacerdotes;* they will have no band of unity, no cement to unite them as a church, but will be a disjointed number of independent Christians; no Church in a strict sense, though we may allow them that title in a large and popular sense, which I suppose is sufficient, whatever our opinion be, for giving them that appellation in our prayers; especially when commanded by public authority, which ought to be submitted to, though it were meant in the strict sense, (as it certainly is not,) unless we have full conviction that the appellation is false, which few perhaps have in so disputed a case. But it is now time to subjoin something with relation to the judgment and practice of the Church of England in our present debate.

IV.

I shall be brief upon this last, concluding that by this time you are heartily tired. Upon a careful view of what has been said on both sides relating to the judgment and practice of our Church, I take the case to be thus.

1. The Church of England has nowhere expressly and *in terms* determined the controversy either way.

2. Her practice as well as the stream of her Divines has all along been against us.

3. Yet she has laid down such principles and positions in her public acts, as will, if pursued in all their

consequences, bring us to the conclusion we are proving.

And this is all, I presume, that Mr. Laurence means in reckoning the Church of England on his side of the question: not that our first Reformers, or other great Divines since, actually thought as he does; but that in pursuance of the principles laid down in the Articles, Canons, and Rubrics, they must have thought so, had they attended to all the consequences deducible from them. And indeed if the case be thus; if the doctrine of the invalidity of Lay-baptism can be shown by necessary consequence to be implied in what the public voice of our Church has asserted, and we subscribe to; it must be said that the Church of England is for us; and every subscriber that attends to such consequences, and believes them certain, does implicitly or virtually subscribe them also. And this is what I am persuaded Mr. Laurence has proved sufficiently in the pamphlet entitled, Dissenters' Baptisms Null and Void by the Articles, &c. It must therefore be observed, that those gentlemen take a wrong method of answering Mr. L. who object to him the judgment of many of our eminent Divines since the Reformation: all that is wide of the point. He may think that many of our Divines, and even some compilers of our public forms, had not sufficiently traced all the consequences of their own assertions, or might have drawn conclusions inconsistent with them. And therefore the ready and the only way to confute him is, to show that the consequences which he draws from the premises laid down in our public forms are ill drawn, or are no just consequences from them. Till this be done, the public voice of the Church, as it stands in our Articles, Rubrics, and Canons, will be thought to be on his side of the question; and he that consents to them must consent to him too; because there is no rejecting a necessary consequence once seen, without rejecting the principle itself from whence it flows. We need not therefore talk of the Whitgifts, the Hookers, the Bilsons, the Bancrofts, or others. The Church's public acts are open and common, and he is the truest Church of England man that best understands the principles there laid down, and argues the closest from them: all the rest are but assertions, fancies, or practices of particular men, and are not binding rules to us. And this is all that need be said to the present point; and I shall here only subjoin some few remarks on some passages of Mr. K. under this head. "He seems very angry, that some who call themselves the most zealous assertors of the rights of the Church, should embrace this Puritanical notion, (of Lay-baptism being null,) and cast dirt upon the memory of those excellent men, (Whitgift, Hooker, &c.,) and hardly allow any who come not in their measures, &c." It were easy to retort in that way, and to run out into satire and declamation. But to speak to the point; it is no reflection upon the memory of any men to suppose them fallible; nor any fault in us to set aside their authority, when we can confute their reasons. The gentlemen whom Mr. K. so unkindly censures are, if I know anything of men, persons of as great simplicity, candour, and integrity as any men living; true lovers of religion in its primitive beauty and purity, and sincere promoters of it in their writings, and what is more, in their lives. If it be their misfortune to mistake in the point before us, which does not appear, yet their pious intentions and well meant zeal for the honour of GOD and the souls of their brethren plead strongly in their excuse; and it must be owned that their reasons, if not absolutely convincing, are yet weighty and considerable enough to sway honest and wise men. Their love as well for the order as for the persons of the Clergy is in a manner their distinguishing character; and it is therefore pity that the least spark of indignation from any Clergyman especially should fall upon them, particularly at a time when there is occasion enough to spend our zeal another way; when we are running into Deism with a precipitate course, and Arianism by shaking the prime fundamentals is paving the way to it. But to return.

Mr. L., it seems, "with a very authoritative air takes upon him to instruct and admonish the Clergy, and to interpret the Articles, Canons, &c." To which I shall only say, that innocence makes a man sometimes bold, and a religious zeal will break out into tender and pathetical expostulations. As to his interpreting the Articles, Canons, &c., I find nothing objected to it by Mr. K. but that it makes "the Church inconsistent with herself," an undertaking, he thinks, "not very suitable to the character of so zealous a proselyte, &c." But what does Mr. K. call the Church? Has Mr. L. anywhere pretended to show that the Church contradicts herself in her public forms? No, but practice has run contrary, and some Churchmen, or most Churchmen, have done so too. It may be so: yet the Church is consistent with herself; for the public voice of the Church is the Church, and while she lays down premises, consequences make themselves. However, all such kind of arguments signify little. Is the practice defensible, or is it not? If it be, show it upon principles, and argue not from practice only, the weakest reason in the world. If it be not, the obvious conclusion is, that it ought to be changed. I cannot but think it a wrong way to plead practice and custom for the validity of Lay-baptism, when we want a law to found it upon. What law of GOD, nay, what law of our own Church, authorizes any laic to baptize, that we may have some shadow of authority to pronounce it valid? But the Church, you will say, that is, Churchmen, have so practised, therefore the Church approves it. I deny the consequence. Churchmen have sprinkled in Baptism now a hundred years, or it may be more, without ever inquiring whether the child be weak, and the Rubric in that case is grown obsolete; does it follow from thence that sprinkling without necessity is according to the sense and judgment of the Church of England? The like may be said of the Clerk's placing bread and wine on the communion table, and perhaps of reading the Communion Service in the desk; all practised by public allowance, and yet nowhere warranted by the public acts or voice of the Church. Mr. K. observes, that the Church of England "never made any canon or law for the punishment of a Lay-baptist, who shall presume to do that office in extreme necessity." But what think you of these words in the preface to the Ordination Book? "None shall be suffered to execute any of the functions (of a Bishop, Priest, or Deacon), except he hath had formerly episcopal consecration or ordination." Is not this part of her laws, and Baptism one of her functions? And whence is it that none of our midwives, or any beside Clergymen, pretend to baptize in cases of extreme necessity, but that they think it against law? I deny not however that Lay-baptisms have been constantly received as valid among us. Were it not for that, there would be less occasion for this dispute, designed, if possible, to put a stop to an inveterate practice that has so little to be said for it. Mr. K., I think, is a little too severe upon Mr. Laurence, when he calls his Baptism "a second Baptism, irregular, clandestine, unauthorized, antiepiscopal." It is impossible it should be *a second Baptism*, because he was baptized hypothetically only; and therefore if the first Baptism was good, the last was none. It was not *irregular*, because, as he tells us himself, the minister that baptized him had his proper Diocesan's general license to baptize adult persons, without giving any particular notice first to the Bishop. It was not *clandestine*, being in the public face of a great congregation on a holyday in the time of evening prayer. Lastly, it could not be *antiepiscopal*, being by an episcopal minister, and with the Bishop's license. I hope Mr. K. will think more kindly, and express himself more tenderly of an innocent well-deserving gentleman another time.

Mr. K. having before mentioned the custom of our Church in confirming all without distinction, whether episcopally baptized, or only by lay hands, ends with this dilemma, that we must (upon our principles) either assert that for an important article of doctrine, which the Church of England denies, or accuse her of communicating and ordaining men, whom she knew to be unbaptized. As to the first part of the dilemma, we do not assert anything for an important truth, but what the Church, that is, the public voice of the Church, asserts likewise, though not directly, yet consequentially. As to the second part: it does not follow, that because Bishops confirm all without distinction, that therefore they know any of them to be unbaptized, but only that they do not know to the contrary. I grant, however, that the practice argues so far, that they have in general looked upon it as an indifferent thing, as to the validity of Baptism, whether it be by a Priest or a laic. And how far their judgment ought to weigh with us has been considered above; ᶠ"non quia aliquando erratum est, ideo semper errandum est."

Thus, I hope, we have got fairly off from the dilemma; or if not, let me propose another, and leave it with Mr. K. to show that we are pretty even. It is very certain that the Church of England forbids Baptism Lay, in all ordinary cases, directly, and in extraordinary, implicitly; having made no provision for cases of necessity; which yet she ought to have done, and very probably would have done, had she thought Lay-baptism valid, since the salvation of many infants may be nearly concerned in it.

"I do not therefore see but that those gentlemen who affirm Lay-baptism to be valid lie under a necessity either of owning that they assert that for an important article of true doctrine, which the Church of England denies, or of accusing their Mother the Church of England" of a very culpable omission in making no provision for a case that may often happen, and is of everlasting moment. "I shall be heartily glad to see these gentlemen get handsomely clear from this dilemma:" and in the interim, I presume, we shall have time enough to consider how to deal with the other.

From what has been said, it appears pretty plainly, that there is no law either of GOD or man, either of the primitive Church or our own, whereon to found the validity of Dissenters' Baptism. As to making any-

---

ᶠ Cypr. ad Jub.

thing valid *ex post facto* by a subsequent confirmation, which was not valid before; it is too romantic a notion to need confuting, having no countenance from Scripture, antiquity, or reason, or the principles of our Church, or our Office of Confirmation, which supposes persons baptized, validly baptized before. Seeing therefore the thing looks so suspicious and doubtful, and withal very dangerous, it concerns us to take the safest way, and to act as all wise casuists would advise us in doubtful cases. Mr. Bennet, who had well considered this subject, speaks like a wise and good man.[g] "At present," says he, "I am not able to prove the validity of sacraments administered by lay persons in any case whatsoever; nor on the other hand am I willing to pronounce them utterly invalid. But this I own, that if it had been my misfortune to have been baptized by such a person as was not authorized by GOD to perform that office; I would be conditionally rebaptized, after the same manner which our Church prescribes in dubious cases. For I do not think that it would otherwise be possible for me to enjoy peace of conscience for one single moment."

And now to use Mr. K.'s own words; "He is desired (if it be possible) to find out some way to cure the just suspicions, and remove the endless scruples, which his hypothesis will naturally suggest to the minds of thinking men concerning the validity of their Baptism, and the reality of their being within the covenant of grace, and in a state of salvation."

In the close he subjoins a summary view of the principles which he espouses, relating to the present subject, in twenty-six particulars. The first five are

---

[g] Rights of Clergy, p. 352.

very good; the rest are mostly, in my opinion, either not true, or not accurately expressed. I shall take notice of but one or two.

His twenty-first is, "that the minister is not of the essence" (of Baptism). His twenty-second, "Consequently the Church being, as has been declared, the supreme judge of this matter, if she shall think fit to order those who have been baptized by laymen to be baptized again, I am not the man that shall gainsay it." He must certainly have been under some confusion of thought when he wrote this; for I verily believe he does not mean it. Would any man else argue thus? The minister is not essential, therefore Baptism is valid whether by a Priest or laic; "therefore the Church may choose whether she will receive it or no," when the irresistible consequence from these premises is, that the Church cannot choose but must receive it, since it is valid on either supposition. I suppose he means, that since it does not certainly appear, either that the Minister is essential or not essential, in so doubtful a case, let the Church determine whether the disputed Baptisms shall be valid or not. If the Minister be supposed not essential, there is no room left for the Church to order a rebaptization. What Churchmen, nay what heretics, (except the Marcionists,) ever allowed rebaptization in the strict and proper sense, or did not utterly disclaim it? However, if your friend will be so generous as to admit of two Baptisms in some cases, I hope we may be excused hereafter if we contend for one. Could Lay-baptism be shown to be truly Baptism, I should be the last man that should plead for rebaptization; nay, if all the churches in Europe should order it, I should *gainsay* it, and protest against it as an innovation.

But since it does not appear that such pretended Baptisms are truly Baptisms, but that there is all the reason in the world to think they are not, I must beg leave still to insist upon it, that all such as have been so pretendedly baptized ought to have the true and only Baptism, episcopal Baptism, and so become not pretended but true and real members of the Church of CHRIST.

Thus, Sir, you have my thoughts at length upon a subject difficult enough for wise and good men to differ upon, and yet perhaps clear enough to a careful and diligent inquirer. You had had this long ago, had not my other business and many avocations hindered; and I might no doubt have been more exact in many things, had I more leisure, or could I bear the trouble of transcribing. But since these papers are designed only for private use, I am content to let them pass. You may please to communicate them at leisure to your learned friend, whom I have a great respect and value for. He has shown in espousing the cause of Lay-baptism, that he is very able both to defend and adorn a better; and if he has failed in it, it may be considered that the great Mr. Bingham, not to mention others, has sunk in the attempt before, and neither his fine parts nor voluminous reading could support him against an adversary, who in learning certainly, not to say in abilities, is far inferior to him. I have endeavoured everywhere to treat Mr. K. with that civility and respect due to his character and personal merit. But if anything has dropped from me unawares that seems different from it, I desire you to blot it out with your pen, it being what I should certainly do myself, as soon as apprized of it.

While I differ from him in this, I shall be ever, I

hope, ready to join with him in a fervent zeal for GOD and religion, and vigorously opposing the growing heterodoxies and prevailing corruptions of the present times.

May the Giver of all truth direct us in our searches after it, and both incline us to embrace it, and enable us to pursue it.

I am, dear Sir,

your most affectionate

humble Servant.

APPENDIX A.

It is often said by persons, who speak without much consideration, and sometimes also by those who might be expected to weigh their words,

(i.) That the Church has long ago decided this question of Lay-baptism; and

(ii.) That to raise any doubt as to the validity of Lay-baptism is a "novelty," and only the crotchet of a few insignificant persons.

This is a ready way to impose upon popular ignorance, and to escape from further trouble: but the following brief catena, which might easily be enlarged, will serve to show how entirely false are both the above assertions. As to the first,

(i.) There were three African Councils held in the third century, which ruled unauthorized Baptism to be invalid.

S. Cyprian commenting on one of these decisions says it was "no new thing," but "long ago decreed by our predecessors." (Vide S. Cyprian's Epistles, 70, 71, and 72.)

Whether these decisions were right or wrong, it is plain that up to this time the Church Universal had not decreed in an opposite sense; for if so these provincial synods would not have discussed the question at all.

(ii.) Saint Augustine's elaborate treatise, "De Baptismo," in which he debates the question as to what Baptisms are valid, and in what sense they are so, would never have been written, if the matter had been already decided by the Church.

(iii.) Passing to modern times, Bishop Jeremy Taylor in arguing that Lay-baptism is invalid, takes it as an acknowledged thing that the Church had made no decision on the matter; he says, that in "the first ages" there was "a variety of opinion," and he thinks that the opinion that Lay-baptism was invalid ought to be "considered anew upon the old stock," (i.e. the old standing principles,) now when a contrary opinion had become very common. (Vide "The Divine Institution of the Office Ministerial," iv. 1, 5.)

(iv.) The Lower House of the Convocation of Canterbury A.D. 1712, rejected a motion giving countenance to Lay-baptism on the primary ground that "the validity of such Baptism is a point which the Catholic Church, and the Church of England in particular, hath hitherto avoided to determine by any synodical declaration." (Vide Lathbury, "History of Convocation" ad loc.)

These four considerations are, without going further, sufficient to dispose of the first of the abovenamed mis-statements.

As to the second, it may suffice to refer to the following notable Divines all along the line of the Church of England since the Reformation.

(i.) *Archbishop Ussher* says, "Baptism is a part of the public ministry of the Church, and CHRIST has given warrant and authority to none to baptize, but those whom He has called to preach the Gospel, 'Go, preach and baptize,' (S. Matt. xxviii. 19.) Those only may stand in the Name of GOD Himself, and ministerially set to the seal of the covenant; and it is monstrous presumption for women, or any other private persons, (who are not called,) to meddle with such high mysteries, nor can there be any case of necessity to urge." ("Body of Divinity," 3rd ed. p. 412, quoted by Elwin, "The Minister of Baptism," p. 219.)

(ii.) *Bishop Sanderson* "rejected Baptism by women, saying they would do well to 'go and teach all nations' before they 'baptize' them. He speaks of the permission allowed them to baptize as 'the singular absurdity of the Church of Rome.'" (Ib. p. 219.)

(iii.) *Bishop Jeremy Taylor* in his "Clerus Domini" argues at length against any belief in the validity of Lay-baptism as being contrary both to Scripture and reason, a common opinion, unsupported by any sufficient authority of the Church. If laymen have power and authority to bestow the gifts of the HOLY SPIRIT in Baptism, "it needs," says Bishop Taylor, "no other proof than the plain production of the commission;" but no such commission can be produced.

With reference to the plea of "necessity," Taylor reminds us that Baptism is not the only sacrament "generally necessary to salvation," and that if a layman is justified in presuming to baptize "in case of necessity," lest one, who dies unbaptized, should perish for lack of Baptism; then the same argument will justify a layman in assuming to consecrate and administer the holy Eucharist under a like supposed necessity.

With regard to the argument that it is "safer" to have a child baptized by anybody rather than that it should not be baptized at all, Bishop Taylor says, that "it cannot but be a jealousy and a suspicion of GOD, a not daring to trust Him, and an unreasonable proceeding besides, that we should rather venture to dispense with Divine institution, than think that GOD will; or that we should pretend more care for children than GOD hath, when we will break an institution, and the rule of an ordinary ministry of GOD'S appointing, rather than cast them upon GOD; as if GOD loved the ceremony better than He loved the child: for this must be so, if the child perish for want of it." ("Cler. Dom." iv. 12, quoted in "Lay-baptism, an inquiry," by F. N. Oxenham, 2nd ed., p. 54.)

(iv.) *Bishop Mant*, in his Commentary on the Prayer Book, in a note on "The Office of Private Baptism," says, "I know there are some allegations out of antiquity, which seem to allow laymen to baptize in cases of great necessity; but there are others of the Fathers who disallow that practice, and certainly it is a great presumption for an ordinary person to invade the ministerial office without any warrant. That this is the opinion of our Church is plain from her declaration in the 23rd Article."

Again, he says, "If however it be asked whether Baptism, when performed by an unordained person, be in the sense of our Church 'valid' and 'effectual,' we may answer that according to the best judgment we can form from her public acts and offices, it is not." (Bishop Mant on the C. P. B. vol. i. p. 665.) Vide also *Comber* and *Wheatly*, who in their respective notes on the Office for Private Baptism use similar language.

(v.) *Bishop Wordsworth* (*of Lincoln*) in writing to the Rev.

E. C. Baldwin, one of his clergy, says, " The Church has never *condemned* Lay-baptism : but I have no hesitation in saying that if I had received Baptism from one whose commission to baptize was uncertain, I should wish to be baptized with the hypothetical form by a duly ordained minister." (Vide " A Matter of Life and Death," by E. C. Baldwin, pp. 38, 39.)

This testimony of the learned and devout Bishop Wordsworth is specially valuable as showing that his uncertainty as to the validity of Lay-baptism led him unhesitatingly to that practical conclusion, which those, who in the present day have raised anew this controversy, have ever and urgently in mind, viz. that all those who have received only Lay-baptism ought to be conditionally baptized " by a duly ordained minister."

(vi.) *Dean Hook* in the article on " Lay-baptism" in his " Church Dictionary" argues that there is no ground for believing in the validity of such Baptism ; he says " We have no proof that CHRIST ever promised to sanction Lay-baptism, or that He conferred the power of Baptism on any but the clergy, or that the Apostles ever imparted it to any other but clergy." In a later edition of " Hook's Church Dictionary" (1887) the article on Lay-baptism has been " re-written" by Lord Grimthorpe in a sense directly opposed to that of Dean Hook's own article!

(vii.) *Dr. Pusey*, writing of the Conditional Baptism of persons already lay-baptized, which he says is " the practice" of the Church both in England and Scotland, says, " The practice now adopted [this was written in 1842] by the Scotch Church, and in our own, with regard to persons baptized by such as are not only in schism, but never received any commission to baptize, (a case to which there is no parallel in the early Church,) unites the advantages of the Latin and Greek practice ; of the Latin, in that it avoids the risk of real rebaptizing, which the ancients regarded as a profanation of the sacred Names ; of the Greek, in that it does what in us lies to provide that none of the blessings and grace of Baptism be lost, through our omission, and is an act of piety towards GOD, desiring that whatever may have hitherto been lacking, be supplied." (Note on trans. of *Tertullian*. " Library of the Fathers," vol. i. p. 297.)

(viii.) *Bishop Van Mildert.* This brief Catena shall be concluded by a reference to the "great name" of the last of the Prince Bishops of Durham, because in giving his opinion that "Scripture, Antiquity and Reason" supply "proofs" that Lay-baptism is invalid Bishop Van Mildert is commenting on the Letters of Dr. Waterland. Referring to the first of those Letters, the Bishop says, "It contains a brief summary of the main arguments on which the invalidity of Lay-baptism is grounded, and it shows in a very concise but distinct and luminous manner the proofs to that effect from Scripture, Antiquity, and Reason." (Introductory Review to "Works" of Dr. Waterland, by Bishop Van Mildert, 1823.)

APPENDIX B.

SOME BOOKS ON LAY-BAPTISM.

1. "The Minister of Baptism." By the Rev. Warwick Elwin, M.A.
    (London: John Murray, 1889.)

2. "A Matter of Life and Death." By the Rev. E. C. Baldwin, M.A.
    (London: Longhurst, 1879.)

3. "Charges," 1886—1888. By the Bishop of Argyll and the Isles.
    (Edinburgh: S. Giles' Printing Company.)

4. "Lay-baptism." By the Rev. F. Nutcombe Oxenham, M.A.
    (London: J. Masters & Co., 1888.)

www.ingramcontent.com/pod-product-compliance
Lightning Source LLC
Chambersburg PA
CBHW050842230426
43667CB00012B/2106